On the Right of Exclusion

On the Right of Exclusion: Law, Ethics and Immigration Policy addresses Western immigration policies regarding so-called 'normal migrants', i.e. migrants without a legal right to admission. The book argues that if authorities cannot substantially justify the exclusion of a normal migrant, the latter should be admitted. By contrast, today authorities still believe they may deny normal migrants admission to the territory without giving them proper justification. Bas Schotel challenges this state of affairs and calls for a reversal of the default position in admission laws. The justification should, he argues, involve a serious accounting for the interests and reasons applicable to the normal migrant seeking admission. Furthermore, the first burden of justification should lie with the authorities. To build this case, the book makes three types of argument: legal, ethical and institutional. The legal argument shows that there are no grounds in either sovereignty or the structure of law for current admission practices. Whilst this legal argument accounts for a duty to justify exclusion, the ethical argument shows why the authorities should carry the first burden of justification. Finally, the institutional argument explores how this new position might be implemented. An original, yet practical, undermining of the logic that underlies current immigration laws, *On the Right of Exclusion: Law, Ethics and Immigration Policy* will be essential reading for those with intellectual, political and policy interests in this area.

Bas Schotel is Assistant Professor of Legal Theory at the University of Amsterdam. The book is based on a PhD thesis sponsored by the Vrije Universiteit Brussel.

On the Right of Exclusion

Law, Ethics and Immigration Policy

Bas Schotel

Routledge
Taylor & Francis Group
a GlassHouse book

First published 2012
by Routledge
2 Park Square, Milton Park, Abingdon, Oxon OX14 4RN

Simultaneously published in the USA and Canada
by Routledge
711 Third Avenue, New York, NY 10017

A GlassHouse Book

Routledge is an imprint of the Taylor & Francis Group, an informa business

British Library Cataloguing in Publication Data
A catalogue record for this book is available from the British Library

Library of Congress Cataloging in Publication Data

A catalog record for this book has been requested

ISBN: 978–0–415–57537–9 (hbk)
ISBN: 978–0–203–80292–2 (ebk)

Typeset in Times New Roman
by RefineCatch Limited, Bungay, Suffolk

Contents

Acknowledgements

This book could not have been written without the support of the Research Council of the Vrije Universiteit Brussel. This institution financed my Ph.D. thesis which forms the basis of the book. I am very grateful for the intellectual courage the VUB displayed in supporting this project. Of course, this would not have been possible without my sponsor, Serge Gutwirth, who made it all happen. First, he endorsed my project within the VUB. Second, he acted as a brilliant thesis supervisor, combining critical review, comforting words and humor. After every discussion he left me with the awkward feeling that he already understood better than me, what I was trying to say! Veit Bader was just as important to the success of the project. Officially co-supervisor, he acted as a full supervisor, subjecting all my drafts to a rigorous critical review – I always left his office with an additional stack of books and references. His erudition, pragmatism and commitment has been really inspiring. Arguably, the greatest worry (and thus motivation) any researcher has are fundamental doubts about the soundness of his or her own research project. My two supervisors seemed to have found the right balance between giving me confidence and helping me to avoid complacency.

At different stages of my project I received invaluable input from the members of the thesis jury: Marie-Claire Foblets, René Foqué, Paul De Hert, Mireille Hildebrandt and Jef Van Bellingen. I should especially thank Mireille for always making time to engage with my arguments and pushing me to think them through (in absurdum?). Also special thanks to Jef Van Bellingen for our discussions on Schmitt and for having written the brilliant – but unpublished (!) – thesis, *De Rechtsfilosofie van Carl Schmitt*, which turned out to be instrumental to my understanding of this complex author. I also received important comments from Rainer Bauboeck, Jean-Paul Van Bendegem, Giunnia Gatta, Hans Lindahl, Bert Van Roermund, anonymous referees for Routledge and various conference participants organized by the Vereniging voor Wijsbegeerte en Recht, European University Institute (Florence) and IMISCOE. On a day-to-day to basis, Jeroen Delvoie was a critical touchstone. I still think that the numerous academic coffees and beers we enjoyed had a beneficial effect on the project.

It is one thing to write a thesis and defend it publicly. It is quite another to have it published by an international publisher. A few people helped me frame my book proposal, suggested contacts or simply told me – in advance – never to give up if I was turned down. I should explicitly mention Jo Carens, Phillip Cole, Dora Kostakopoulou, Kees Groenendijk and Thomas Spijkerboer. Special thanks go to Peter Fitzpatrick for encouragement and for introducing my work to Routledge. I was also fortunate to call on the expertise of Marike Schipper when writing my book proposal. The final stage reworked my thesis to a more accessible and shorter book. This was probably the most difficult task of the entire project as it involved killing babies and, worse, discovering many additional weaknesses. My director at the University of Amsterdam, Peter Rijpkema has been of enormous help in ensuring time was allocated to finish the book. The process was monitored by the people at Routledge. I am especially grateful to Colin Perrin and Melanie Fortmann-Brown who seem to understand the delicate balance between patience and pressure.

There is a whole world outside academia, which makes life worthwhile. I should start by thanking Lara who was the first to support me in my initial thinking on the subject. It was her experience as an immigration lawyer that triggered it all. Equally important were the friends who always had a place for me to stay – if not an entire house – when I was writing my thesis. In Brussels: Alexis and Sybille; Yvan, Gilles, Raphael and Betta; Axel, Christine and Theo; Cathy, Francois, Louise, Odille and Victor. In London and Paris: Robbert and Phillippe. Bart beat everyone by organizing a garden party *inside* his house just to celebrate my doctorate! Also I am grateful for all the memorable extra-curricular moments with the *anciens* of the VRG in Brussels and the illustrious H27 in Amsterdam. I should also thank Joeri for defying popular wisdom by being both a good neighbor and a close friend.

The essence of unconditional love and support is that one can take it for granted – because it is *unconditional*. But this is precisely why I do not take it for granted, and I thank Pa, Ma and Lutein for being my family.

As to Nicole, zonder jou was het ook gelukt, maar was ik eenvoudigweg niet zo verliefd en gelukkig.

Introduction

This book is about immigration policy. It concentrates on what I call normal migrants, i.e. migrants who do not have a legal right to admission. Normal migrants *may* be admitted when beneficial to the receiving country. Yet there is no legal duty to admit them, contrary to migrants with a right to admission (e.g. refugees, family members of a permanent resident). This book starts with the simple observation that today authorities believe they can deny normal migrants admission to a country without giving them proper justification for their exclusion. The central objective of this book is to challenge this current practice and call for a change in admission laws and policies. First, when authorities are denying normal migrants admission they must justify the exclusion *vis-à-vis* the excluded migrant. Second, if the authorities fail to give proper justification to the normal migrant they cannot refuse his admission. Third, in principle it is up to the authorities to come up with the relevant facts and reasons to substantiate their denial of admission. In other words, the authorities carry the first burden of proof. The admission logic is to be reversed. Finally, the adequacy of the justification is to be measured against the yardstick of the proportionality principle, especially the necessity test. The authorities must have shown that the exclusion is necessary to obtain the objectives of the immigration policy and that exclusion was the only and the least burdensome measure available. Ultimately, it should be up to the courts to check whether the exclusion satisfies the necessity test.

Over the years many invaluable critical accounts of immigration policy have appeared, calling for changes and improvements. Though often very intelligent, they did not seem to have any significant impact on concrete policy. What can this book possibly add to the growing body of scholarship? More importantly, why would we expect it to have any impact on policy? I believe that the book may bring three new elements to the table, which might make it more difficult for officials to ignore calls for change. First, virtually every account of immigration policy focuses on the effects or outcomes produced by immigration policy. Accordingly the policies provoke a particular state of affairs or a situation that may be economically inefficient, unethical, inhumane or detrimental to our political community. Conversely, this book concentrates not so much on the outcome of immigration policies but rather on the way the authorities adopt and administer immigration policy. The key insight is that when authorities deny normal migrants admission to a territory they do so without giving them proper justification. In other words, immigration policy is a matter of exclusion without justification. The novelty is not understanding immigration policy in terms of exclusion; the point is the absence of proper justification.

Second, the book contends that this problem (i.e. exclusion without justification) is fundamentally a *legal* problem. At first glance, it seems preposterous to claim that taking a legal perspective on immigration policy brings anything new to the table. Immigration policy is obviously a matter of law as the policies are laid down in and executed by legal instruments. Furthermore, immigration law has become an area of law in its own right[1] with highly specialized experts and practitioners. Some of these experts have been keen to point out the shortcomings of immigration policies. One of the major deficits of current policy is the lack of effective legal remedies. This means that when normal migrants are denied admission there is virtually no effective way to challenge the denial before an independent court. This issue is closely related to the absence of justification as we will see later. So what is the 'legal' novelty of the book? Though some experts of immigration law are rightly very critical about our immigration policies, they do not contend that there is a problem with the legal *foundations* of current immigration policies. The legal shortcomings may be serious, yet they do not pose a fundamental legal problem. Apparently, the shortcomings just need a small fix, preferably as soon as possible, but the *legality* or the *legal nature* of immigration policies is not really at risk. Consequently, there is no need to look at the legal structure and foundations of immigration policies. The practical effect is that officials who are making and executing immigration policies are put in a comforting position. Immigration policies may be criticized from the perspective of economics, demographics and morality, yet there is nothing *fundamentally* wrong from a legal perspective. There are, of course, some legal shortcomings but no policy is – legally – perfect. Without overestimating the normative and motivational force of the law, it is difficult to deny how important it is for officials to feel backed up by the law. The novelty of my argument lies in the contention that legal shortcomings are not peripheral but are at the core of immigration policies. Immigration policy contains a fundamental legal flaw, which may affect the legality and legal nature of immigration policies. To substantiate this claim we will have to look into an area which has been left virtually untouched by experts of immigration law, public law and legal theory: the legal 'logic' and theory of immigration policy. If this inquiry into the legal foundations of immigration policy is successful, it will bring something genuinely new to the debate. It will make fixing the legal problems really urgent. More importantly it brings the problem to where it really belongs, i.e. the officials. The legal shortcomings are

1 It is difficult to ignore the irony of 'in its *own right*' when it comes to immigration 'law'.

not a mere imperfection of immigration policy. The situation may be much worse for the officials – as long as the legal problems remain, officials cannot assume they are backed up by the law.

Finally, in spite of all its complexity and richness, the current debate too often leaves out the main character: the normal migrant. The different accounts of immigration policy take very diverging views; these may benefit or be detrimental to the position of normal migrants. Still they have one thing in common. They do not make room for the normal migrant's point of view. To put it differently, the debate is between experts (e.g. officials, scholars, NGO's, lawyers, etc.) but does not give a voice to one of its most important stakeholders. Yet various disciplines have pointed out the importance of ensuring the direct involvement of stakeholders, especially laymen (see for example participatory technology assessment; insights from philosophy and sociology of science; alternative dispute resolution; associative democracy). To be clear, I shall not make any representations of the normal migrant's point of view. I will certainly not try to speak on behalf of normal migrants. Rather, the point of the book is to find ways to give the floor to the normal migrant 'directly'. If successful the arguments in this book will show how to give the normal migrant a voice within the institutional framework. Admittedly, this voice will capture only thin fragments of the normal migrant's view because the voice must speak the language of the law. Positive law recognizes only particular arguments, interests and idioms. The normal migrant will be unable to voice many important mental, physical, material, and cultural aspects of his life, because they simply do not fit the legal categories: they are legally irrelevant (e.g. happiness, love). But with all its limitation, this 'legal' voice may turn out to be the only one that the officials will listen to.

In a way the book makes three kinds of claims: legal, ethical and institutional. The first argues that current immigration policies regarding normal migrants are untenable from the legal perspective. The ethical claim contends that there are overriding reasons from (liberal) political theory to change the policies. The institutional claim suggests that a change is institutionally feasible. Chapter 1 starts by framing immigration policy regarding normal migrants in terms of exclusion without justification. It shows how the law sanctions this practice by the 'rule of inherent sovereign power': states have the power inherent in sovereignty to admit or exclude aliens 'as they deem fit'. The greater part of the book then concentrates on rebutting this rule of inherent sovereign power from the legal perspective. Chapter 2 demonstrates that the rule simply does not fit or follow from the normal powers associated with sovereignty. So apparently the rule has an exceptional – legal – status of its own. The strongest[2] argument in this respect is the exclusion

2 I single out the strongest version of theses that account for the alleged special status of the rule of inherent sovereign power and immigration law. Weaker versions already acknowledge that some normative constraints apply to exclusion. As a result they admit that exclusion is not beyond justification.

thesis, which posits that exclusion is prior to and constitutive to any political and legal order. The ultimate and inevitable implication is that exclusion is fundamentally beyond justification – hence, the rule of inherent sovereign power. Chapter 3 draws on elements of Carl Schmitt's legal and political theory, as well as on recent mobilizations of his theory by Giorgio Agamben and Hans Lindahl. Conversely, Chapter 4 seeks to refute the exclusion thesis. It points out the empirical, logical and conceptual flaws in the assumptions underlying the exclusion thesis. It rejects the centrality of exclusion for *founding* an order. Also, it refuses to adopt an exaggerated understanding of legal order as unity and oneness. By contrast it explores a more plausible and practice-based understanding of legal order as multiple connections. Chapter 5 presents another legal argument against the rule of inherent sovereign power. It relies on the general fact that legal authorities claim that their laws should be obeyed. Immigration law is not an exception. However, due to their lack of justification, immigration policies may be so defective that authorities cannot even claim obedience from normal migrants. As they treat normal migrants as *objects* of law (as opposed to subjects – individual agents), immigration laws may cease to count as law with regard to normal migrants.

Chapter 6 concentrates on another aspect of the book's call for a change: the reversal of the burden of justification. While the legal arguments (see Chapters 1–5) show that authorities must justify the exclusion of normal migrants, the law cannot tell us who is first to justify: the authorities or the normal migrant. Allocating the first burden of justification is largely an inquiry into what *in the abstract* is the normal or default position. It asks the question whether in advance and in general the reasons for the admission of normal migrants are stronger than the reasons for their exclusion. Here we will draw on what has become an almost special branch of liberal political theory, i.e. the ethics of migration.

The final part of the book is informed by the notion that 'ought' implies 'can'. Legal and ethical arguments may suggest that authorities *ought* to justify exclusion and carry the burden of proof. Yet authorities must also have the *capacity* to actually perform the justification. The success of my call for a change depends on its feasibility. To this end Chapter 7 explores how this duty to justify can be institutionally embedded. It concentrates on giving a legal voice to the normal migrant through introducing the proportionality test, especially the necessity criterion, in migration policy. This test is an essential feature of public law, but is ignored when it comes to normal migration policy. Using a draft directive proposed by a group of immigration law experts I will show why the necessity test is a promising institutional vehicle for changing immigration policy from within.

Having briefly spelt out what line of argument to expect, it may be helpful to clarify what *not* to expect. This book is not a ticket to a policy of open borders. My account defies the 'traditional' divide between 'strict' versus 'relaxed' admission policies. If the authorities come up with adequate justifications *vis-à-vis* the normal migrant, and on paper there are good grounds for exclusion, then there is no obstacle to his exclusion.

Yet the question is of course whether those good reasons obtain in the context of concrete cases. A lot exclusions today and in the past cannot be properly justified. Consequently, the admission rate under a new immigration policy (where exclusion must be justified) may be significantly higher than under the current regime. However, this is not the same as endorsing an open border policy.

Neither do I argue in favor of a *legal right* to admission or a *fundamental or human right* to free movement. I contend that the authorities (the state) have a legal duty to justify the exclusion. Failure to do so results in the absence of a legal power to prevent the normal migrant from entering the territory. So due to a lack of justification, the normal migrant may end up entering and staying in the territory. Still, the basis for the admission of the normal migrant need not be a human or fundamental right to free movement or admission. To many this is simply wordplay or nerdish legal sophism. What's the difference? Why are we anxiously keeping the fundamental and human rights discourse at bay? People typically consider human and fundamental rights as the quintessential vehicle for emancipation and justice. So framing my case in terms of human rights would be an astute tactic. Yet for several reasons, which will be elaborated in Chapter 7, I do not pursue the human rights route. I believe that the human rights approach will not be productive and politically feasible in the short and medium term. Also, adding another star to the human rights firmament may contribute to inflating the notion of human rights. More importantly, human rights typically turn an issue into an international concern. Now, at its face immigration is by definition an international phenomenon requiring an international response. By contrast, I believe that too much focus on an internationally coordinated response distracts us from what we already ought and can do in a national and regional context.

It is difficult to ignore moral intuition when reflecting on immigration policy. My own thoughts on migration policy were initially driven by moral intuition – probably to do with liberty and distributive justice. The exclusionary nature of immigration policy goes against a deep sense of individual liberty: every man who does not seek to do harm should be able to move freely. Moreover, while clearly arbitrary, one's place of birth is highly significant for one's prosperity. Exclusionary immigration policies prevent people from escaping the poverty of their place of birth and reinforce the unequal distribution of wealth in the world. I believe many people thinking about immigration policy will share these thoughts. In fact, many scholars writing on the ethics of migration or normative theory of migration start from the same place.[3] I will draw on these writings. I will use

3 One of the leading political theorists suggested quite rightly (and not without a touch of drama) that the current exclusion of aliens or rather the denial of free movement is our modern version of bondage; 'Liberals objected to the way feudalism restricted freedom, including freedom of individuals to move from one place to the other. But modern practices of citizenship and state control over borders tie people to the land of their birth almost as effectively. If the feudal practices were wrong, what justifies the modern ones?' Joseph H. Carens, 'Migration and morality: A liberal egalitarian perspective' in Brian Barry and Robert E. Goodin (eds), *Free Movement. Ethical Issues in the Transnational Migration of People and Money* (London: Harvester Wheatsheaf, 1992), at 26–7.

insights from the ethics of migration to make a very specific point, namely to shift the burden of proof to the authorities. Yet my argument is ultimately not a moral appeal, but a legal claim.

The public debate (including debates in the pub) about migration policy is informed not only by moral intuition but also by common sense. While an exclusionary immigration policy can be criticized from a moral point of view, common sense points to its inevitability. A viable political community ultimately requires demarcation and exclusion. This reflects a 'deeper logic' that there cannot be an inside without an outside. Moreover, this common-sense view is closely connected to the idea of scarcity. There are obviously not enough resources – in particular welfare benefits – for everyone. By definition, it is impossible not to have an exclusionary immigration policy. Conversely, another – rather pragmatic – strand of common sense urges for more open borders to cope with labor shortages and to compensate for the ageing population. At first glance, these common-sense views have a strong concrete reality and fact-driven appeal. Hence, the appropriate venue from which to address these views are empirically-oriented migration studies (e.g. economics, sociology, public finance, demography); this is clearly beyond the scope of this book. However, empirical migration studies indicate that the data hardly supports the common sense views. This suggests that rather than being concrete and fact driven, common-sense views are more ideological and normative in nature. This book will deal with them accordingly.

As a final clarification I should say something about a new element that entered into the equation of immigration policy: death. It is one thing to consider liberty and the equal distribution of wealth from a moral perspective. It is quite different when some of the main players wash up dead on sunny beaches. Like the human rights discourse, the drama of the dehydrated, undernourished or simply dead bodies of migrants lying on our shores or stuck in containers, should strengthen any case for changing immigration policy. Similarly, the ubiquitous practice of 'controlling' illegal immigrants through fully fledged detention/prison schemes should alert even the most naïve observer to the fact that something may be fundamentally wrong with our immigration policy. These tragedies may be the inevitable symptoms of a deeply flawed practice.[4] Yet I will not play this card. Far from trivializing these horrors or treating them as mere incidents, I do believe they capture only a small portion of the total number of normal migrants. In fact, the large majority of normal migrants seek entry via the conventional access points (e.g. airports, roads, sea ports). Though emotionally very powerful, the argument from human tragedy will not advance the larger problem, which I am trying to address.

In short, this book need not be understood as another liberal or progressive call for a better treatment of migrants seeking admission. 'Progressive' readers hoping for a highly moralistic or revolutionary account will be disappointed. Similarly,

4 See in this respect the pertinent analysis of Thomas Spijkerboer, 'The Human Costs of Border Control', *European Journal of Migration and Law* 9 (2007), 127–39.

conservative readers should not expect a strange thesis that they can easily discard as merely utopian. By contrast, I hope to show in the following pages that there is nothing utopian, radical or even strange about my critique of current immigration policy. In effect, the stranger in our legal order is not so much the normal migrant seeking admission, but exclusion without justification. The quintessential social institutions and normative systems of Western society, i.e. law and political morality, do not constitute an obstacle to the proposed change in immigration policy. On the contrary, law and political theory call for such arrangements. Probably, the book may be understood as an illustration of the broader claim that accounting for the interests of others is not a matter of *idealism* or *heroism*, but something ordinary people do as a matter of their ordinary practices, in the case at hand the practice of law.

Chapter 1

A legal problem

Exclusion without justification

The main concern of this book is that admission policies regarding normal migrants constitute a practice of exclusion without justification. Furthermore, the authorities believe that this practice is sanctioned by law. But are the policies really so exclusionary? Are not authorities constantly providing reasons for their immigration policies? These are legitimate questions and they call for explanations and empirical material. Also, if we want to proceed with our inquiry we should have a precise understanding of *how* the law sanctions this practice of exclusion without justification. In short, before challenging the current state of affairs we should produce the facts showing that there is something to be concerned about in the first place. Accordingly, this chapter provides the empirical material that constitutes the basis of our central concern. First, it explains what we mean by exclusion and justification. Second, probably superfluously, it substantiates the observation that admission policies can be understood in terms of exclusion. Third, this chapter should show that authorities no longer justify the exclusion. This is a more complicated task as it boils down to showing the absence of something. Finally, we will lay bare the mechanics that legally justify this lack of justification under current normal migration policies. Before addressing these items, we should remark on the type, scope and levels of policy we will be discussing. We must identify the playing field for our discussion.

Policies, authorities and migrants

The central contention of the book is that immigration policies constitute a form of exclusion without justification. Conversely, I claim that this practice is untenable from a legal perspective and that the authorities have a duty to justify. But what do we actually mean by policies? And who are the authorities? And why just concentrate on the so-called 'normal' migrants?

Immigration regimes differ hugely from country to country depending on the level of granularity.[1] In the EU, admission regimes are still governed by each

1 On the issue of divergence and convergence of national policies, see for example François Crépeau and Idil Atak, 'Les politiques migratoires au Canada et en Europe: des convergences', in Jean-Yves Carlier (ed.), *L'étranger face au droit. XXes Journées d'etudes juridiques Jean Dabin* (Brussels: Bruylant, 2010), 319–49.

Member State individually. Under the Lisbon Treaty the EU has undertaken to frame a common policy on immigration but it remains very likely that, even under an EU framework, many decisions about the admission of normal migrants will remain a competence of individual Member States.[2] Things get even more complicated if we add the self-professed non-European immigration countries with advanced quota systems, particularly the United States, Canada and Australia. It is crucial both for science and practice to account for these differences and complexities. Our investigation concentrates on the structure (basic 'logic' or anatomy) of admission policies. For our purposes it comes up with a rather schematic representation of the admission policies. As this scheme is generic it will capture the structure of most admission regimes, including the non-European countries; however this account is mainly oriented towards admission regimes in the EU.[3]

2 Cf. Art. 79(5) The Treaty on the Functioning of the European Union (consolidated version) (hereafter: TFEU), which recalls that the Member States retain the right to determine the admission volumes for labor migration.

3 For my analysis I relied on, inter alia, the following overviews. For international migration law: Alexander Aleinikoff and Vincent Chetail (eds), *Migration and International Legal Norms* (The Hague: TCM Asser Press, 2003); C. Tiburcio, *The Human Rights of Aliens under International and Comparative Law*, International Studies in Human Rights (The Hague: Kluwer Law International, 2001); Richard Plender (ed.), *Basic Documents on Migration Law*, 2nd edn (The Hague: Kluwer Law International, 1997); Richard Plender, *International Migration Law* (Dordrecht/Boston/The Hague: Martinus Nijhoff Publishers, 1988); Guy S. Goodwin-Gill, *International Law and the Movement of Persons* (Oxford: Clarendon Press, 1978). For the Europeanization of immigration law I relied on, inter alia, Steve Peers and Nicolas Rogers (eds), *EU Immigration and Asylum Law. Text and Commentary* (Leyden/Boston: Martinus Nijhoff Publishers, 2006) (primarily Section I Framework of EC Immigration and Asylum Law and Section II Visas and Border Controls); F. Pastore, 'Visas, Borders, Immigration: Formation, Structure, and Current Evolution of the EU Entry Control System', in Neil Walker (ed.), *Europe's Area of Freedom, Security and Justice* (Oxford: Oxford University Press, 2004), 89–142; Evelien Brouwer, 'Effective Remedies for Third-country nationals in EU Law: Justice Accessible to All?', 7 *European Journal of Migration and Law*, (2005), 219–36; Richard Cholewenski, 'The Need for Effective Individual Legal Protection in Immigration Matters', 7 *European Journal of Migration and Law* (2005), 237–62; Ryszard Cholewenski, 'No Right of Entry: The Legal Regime on Crossing the EU External Border' in Kees Groenendijk, Elspeth Guild and Paul Minderhoud (eds), *In Search of Europe's Borders* (The Hague/London/New York: Kluwer Law International, 2003), 105–30; Dora Kostakopoulou, 'The Area of Freedom, Security and Justice and the Ethics of Migration' (Paper presented at the Conference on the Normative Foundations of European Immigration Policy, Tilburgh University, 10–11 May (2007)); Dora Kostakopoulou, 'The "Protective Union": Change and Continuity in Migration Law and Policy in post-Amsterdam Europe', 38 *Journal of Common Market Studies* (2007), 497–518. For an overview of domestic immigration regimes I relied on, inter alia, Christine Adam and Alexandre Devillard (eds), *Comparative Study of the Laws in the 27 EU Member States for Legal Immigration Including an Assessment of the Conditions and Formalities Imposed by Each Member State for Newcomers* (Geneva: IOM, 2008); Imelda Higgins and Kay Hailbronner (eds), *Migration and Asylum Law and Policy in the European Union* (Cambridge: Cambridge University Press, 2004); ECOTEC Research and Consulting Limited (on behalf of European Commission (DG Justice and Home Affairs)), *Admission of Third-country nationals for Paid Employment or Self-Employment Activity* (2001); S. Angenendt (ed.), *Asylum and Migration Policies in the European Union* (Berlin: Research Institute of the German Society for Foreign Affairs, 1999); G. Brochman and T. Hammar, *Mechanisms of Immigration Control. A Comparative Analysis of European Regulation Policies* (Oxford: Berg, 1999).

One typically distinguishes between policies of entry, stay and citizenship. This book concentrates on admission, which in a way comprises both entry and stay. It looks at the structure of the policies that govern the treatment of migrants who seek entry to the territory for purposes of a (mid-) long-term stay. Our inquiry does not bear on questions about entitlements and duties associated with residence. These are matters captured by a discourse on citizenship and integration. The citizenship question is about what we do with respect to those who are *already inside* the territory. Ours is a question about how do we treat those who are on the *outside* but seek admission. The two policy areas are connected.[4] Still, the regimes are different from an analytical, legal, political and ethical perspective.

For the purposes of our discussion it is helpful to distinguish between the different stages of immigration policies in function of their level of individualization. The stages correspond roughly with the classic distinction between the branches of government. Accordingly, the first stage of immigration policy is very general. Here the legislative branch of government enacts an immigration law (either at a national or supra-national level, e.g. a EU directive). This law sets the general criteria and conditions for admission and exclusion. If applicable it will indicate the possibility and basic constraints for quota. It typically contains provisions that grant powers to competent ministeries, departments, secretaries and/or governmental agencies to develop more detailed and applied implementation frameworks. The second level, where the executive branch elaborates a more specific regulation, is targeted at more particular categories of migrants (e.g. where the general law may only distinguish between EU and third-country nationals, the regulations may distinguish between categories of third countries). The immigration policy becomes really individual when the normal migrant has to obtain one or all of the three 'tickets' to admission: long-stay visa, residence permit and working permit. Admission and long stay are typically dependent on working permits, which are granted if there are no sufficient EU residents available for the job for which the migrant is (to be) contracted. The exclusion of the individual normal migrant takes place when his application for a permit is rejected. The policy is at its most individual when the immigrant brings his exclusion case for review before an independent court. And the court's rejection of the appeal constitutes the most individuated exclusionary instance of admission policies.

Of course, in practice, the picture is more complex. Within each stage one can distinguish several sub-stages. Also, the three stages suggest a clear separation between the three branches of government: legislative, executive and judicial

4 Schematically there are two ways of obtaining permanent residence or a permit for indefinite stay. Either one obtains the permission directly from outside the receiving country. Or one obtains it through phases while already temporarily present in the receiving country. Under the latter, when granting the temporary permits authorities already take into account the adequacy of long stay as the temporary permit is a stepping stone for a long stay permit. The book concentrates on migrants outside the territory.

power. In reality, the executive power more often dominates stage one.[5] Furthermore, the three stages give the impression of a linear chronology, whereas the interaction between the stages is often reiterative. Yet for our purposes and the sake of clarity this threefold scheme should do. The reason for distinguishing the different levels of generality and individualization is that it helps us grasp the nature of the justification for the policy one may expect from the authorities. It will also facilitate identifying those who are directly and intentionally affected by an immigration policy.[6]

So far, we understood immigration policy as *legal norms* directed at officials (e.g. consular instructions) and migrants (e.g. immigration laws prohibiting entry without proper permission). Obviously, these directives only become effective through concrete material measures. One can think of organizational measures such as setting up the visa application processes and remote control by carrier personnel, or more tangible measures such as the construction of border fences and border crossing points. And probably the most physical instance of admission policies is the moment when a border official uses physical force to prevent an individual normal migrant from entering the territory. For purposes of this book we understand immigration policy as comprising both the legal directives and factual measures.[7]

The book concentrates on what it calls 'normal' migrants, i.e. migrants that do not have a legal right to admission. Normal migrants *may* be admitted when

5 In the US this is the subject of longstanding controversy in public law: whether immigration is a matter of exclusive presidential competence or whether Congress has the ultimate say. Carolyn Patty Blum *et al.*, *Brief of Law Professors as Amici Curiae Supporting Affirmance. US Supreme Court Janet Reno v Kim Ho Ma*, 1 (2000), at fn. 3 at 8. A tendency to shift from the merits of migration law to a battle for competence among different institutions is also imminent in EU migration law. See the struggle among the Commission and the Council as to whether or not the Council can reserve the right to exercise implementing powers itself with regard to the Schengen *acquis*, in particular the Common Manual (now Schengen Borders Code) and the Common Consular Instructions (now Visa Code). The Court ruled that in the case in point the Council had respected the principle of proportionality and subsidiarity, and dismissed the Commission's petition. The content of the powers were not at issue. Case C-257/01, ECJ, 18 January 2005: *Commission of the European Communities v Council of the European Union*. See also Pastore who prior to the ruling of the ECJ predicted that it 'will undoubtedly have a forceful impact on the actual development of the European migration control in years to come', F. Pastore, 'Visas, Borders, Immigration: Formation, Structure, and Current Evolution of the EU Entry Control System' in Neil Walker (ed.), *Europe's Area of Freedom, Security and Justice* (Oxford: Oxford University Press, 2004), at 102. It is not unlikely that the battle for competence becomes a central theme especially in the field of EU policy on normal migrants, as the Lisbon Treaty still leaves significant room for Member States to shape normal migration policy in terms of actual admissions and enforcement.

6 See the recent discussions in political theory between Abizadeh and Miller on whether or not immigration policy is a matter of state coercion affecting the migrant, see Chapter 6.

7 In effect, under the new 'migration management' paradigm migration policy is characterized more by the factual measures than the legal norms directed at migrants. See Bas Schotel, 'EU's Management of Migration Flows and the Rule of Law: From Legal Norm Subject to Migration Flow', *Journal of Ethnic and Migration Studies* (forthcoming 2011).

beneficial to the receiving country. Yet there is no legal duty to admit them, contrary to migrants with a right to admission (e.g. a refugee,[8] family member of permanent resident, nationals of a party to a bi-lateral (labor) migration treaty). The migrants are labeled as 'normal' to underscore the idea that they cannot benefit from the *special* arrangements. They represent the normal situation or starting point in the law. You are a normal migrant if you cannot invoke a special preferred status. Furthermore, the notion 'normal' refers to quantity. As we will see hereafter, normal migrants constitute the largest group of migrants seeking admission. Finally, in a more provocative fashion, the term 'normal' creates a stark contrast with the exceptional discretionary powers the authorities have at their disposal; the admission of *normal* migrants is addressed through *exceptional* powers.

The notion 'normal migrant' should allow us to distinguish clearly from the migrants with a preferred status, especially refugees. The point is that there is longstanding consensus about refugees deserving special protection. Although in practice many states fail to live up to their legal obligations in this respect, nobody contests the normative legal principle of the protection we owe to refugees. In the field of family reunification states are moving in the same direction. There is a basic right to family life, which can give rise to a right to admission for some family members. The principle is more or less well established, but the practice is still lagging. Well-intentioned voices suggest that we should abolish the distinction between types of migrants. After all, are not economic migrants in fact *economic refugees*? I believe that we should keep the distinction between normal migrants and those with a right to admission, especially refugees. Putting refugees and normal migrants on an equal footing will probably undermine the already weak protection offered to refugees. It will inflate and devalue what it means to be a refugee. As a result it will weaken the normative case for the 'genuine' refugees. Furthermore, a refugee's right to admission is normally not susceptible to a balancing exercise involving national economic interests and expediency. This has to do with the rationale behind granting refugees special status. A refugee is fleeing from a life-threatening situation. This is not the case for a normal migrant. Of course, this does not mean that his reasons for seeking admission are frivolous or without value. It simply means that we have already established the special status of refugees and there is no prima facie reason – let alone elaborated ones – to conflate it with normal migrants. There is still enough room to argue in favor of improving the legal position of normal migrants seeking admission. That is

8 Strictly speaking, a refugee does not have a right to admission as such, but rather a right to protection which includes the right to non-refoulement. See Hugues Dumont, 'La politique Européenne d'immigration. Synthèse des travaux en atelier', in Jean-Yves Carlier (ed.), *L'étranger face au droit. XX*[es] *Journées d'etudes juridiques Jean Dabin* (Brussels: Bruylant, 2010), at 376. Still, if authorities were serious about fulfilling their legal duty and honor this right to asylum, the latter should, in most cases, entail a right to admission.

precisely the point of this book. But we should not do this at the expense of the legal position of refugees.

I have provided little or no characterization of normal migrants in terms of their motives and profile. They largely coincide with economic migrants and should not be qualified as refugees. There is not much more we can say about them in general, as we have so little general stable data on their profiles, motives, intentions and actual behavior. The book leaves this white spot intentionally open. It refrains from substituting our lack of information with speculation on the true motives, intentions etc. of normal migrants. One such assumption is that the migrant seeking admission has the wish and intention to obtain membership and ultimately citizenship of the receiving country (hence, the emphatic and speculative connection between admission policy and citizenship policy). Legitimate reasons for being exclusive about *citizenship* turn into reasons for being exclusive about *admission*. But what if the normal migrant is not seeking citizenship or membership (or at least not in the thick sense)?[9] To avoid these pitfalls we will say little about the normal migrants and stick to what is at least expressed by the normal migrant: he seeks admission to the territory and he seeks employment in the territory.

Just a final word on terminology. The book uses primarily the term 'migrant', as it has become the dominant term in public policy and academia. However, the term 'alien' would be more exact and productive.[10] 'Alien' is a specific *legal* category, which still refers to a legal *subject*.[11] By contrast the migrant is a much more socio-economic notion which is easily captured by pure policy (in terms of factual measures), as opposed to laws. In effect, one painlessly moves from 'migrant' to 'flows of migrants'. And from 'flows of migrants' one easily arrives at 'migration flows'. We end up with the 'management of migration flows'. This concept turns the alien into an *object* of policy, rather than a *subject* of law. Less problematic but still clumsy, 'migrant' refers to a person who has migrated, is in the process of migrating, or is about to migrate. The problem with normal migrants seeking admission is that most will never reach either of these stages – they remain aliens and never become a migrant. Though we must go along with the dominant language of public policy and academia, many of our analyses rely on

9 Migration is also becoming increasingly circular and temporary, depending on the socio-economic, cultural and regulatory conditions in source and receiving states.

10 EU immigration law uses the term third country national. Though much more exact than 'migrant' it puts too much exclusive focus on EU law (as opposed to national legal systems). Also, its aesthetic qualities are relatively poor (consider its abbreviation 'TCN') which can become problematic if used on almost every page of an entire book.

11 We might have called the normal migrant an 'alien of jus commune' referring to the normal legal regime governing aliens who do not have a preferred or privileged status. Cf. 'le statut de droit commun des étrangers' John Gilissen, 'Le statut des étrangers', in *L'Étranger; Recueils de la Société Jean Bodin pour l'Histoire Comparative des Institutions*, IX, Vol. 1, 2nd edn (Paris: Dessain et Tolra, 1984) [1958], 21.

'hard core' instruments of positive law. Consequently, it is impossible not to switch occasionally to the term 'alien'.

Exclusion

The notion of exclusion should be taken quite literally: denying someone access to something, shutting someone out from a place.[12] So the primary meaning is denying people access to a place. Accordingly, immigration policies denying admission to normal migrants may be understood as a form of exclusion as they deny migrants access to a particular place, i.e. the territory of the target state. As a result of this denial of access to the territory, the normal migrant will not have access to a whole set of other items situated in the territory: goods, lifestyle, practiced language, opportunity, environmental conditions, etc. It seems that the scope of the exclusion is almost inexhaustible. But by stretching its scope we run the risk of inflating the notion of exclusion. The key is to understand exclusion as an *intentional act* of denying someone access to something. The mere fact of not being present somewhere and not being able to access something does not constitute exclusion in itself. What matters is the intention to exclude the person from particular places and items. So absence does not equal exclusion. In this respect, exclusion is a normative act. The excluded person is *not permitted* (ought not) to access a particular item. Still, it remains difficult to fix the scope of the items from which a normal migrant is excluded when denied admission. Probably the safest response is to frame immigration policies in terms of exclusion from goods. But what goods are we talking about? Unsurprisingly, the exclusion does not so much concern the so-called economic goods that are valued in money and are tradable, i.e. which can be bought and sold by private parties. Denial of admission does not prevent a normal migrant from taking a property interest in assets situated in the territory of the target state.[13] Full enjoyment of these property rights may require presence in the territory of the target state where the goods are situated, but if physical use is impossible, there is the option of selling the assets. Even if the goods are not sold and the owner cannot use them due to his physical absence, the goods are still his exclusive property. This means that the nationals residing on the territory cannot use the goods without the permission of the owner. Thus the denial of admission cannot be understood as an exclusion from private assets. More likely items from which the migrant is to be excluded are *public* goods. But here also we must distinguish between the types of goods. It seems we only want to exclude normal migrants from particular public goods. For example authorities are hardly exclusive about traditional public goods such as roads and spaces, or highly valued items of cultural heritage. On the contrary, most states strive for a *high* and *permanent* utilization rate of these assets by foreigners (cf. presence of

12 *The Shorter Oxford English Dictionary* (Oxford: Oxford University Press, 1973).

13 Typically liberal states even allow foreigners to acquire real estate.

foreign investments, foreign transportation companies and of course tourism). Individual foreigners – at least when it comes to tourists – do not permanently use these assets. Yet aggregation of the incidental and temporary use by individual foreigners makes for a permanent use of these standard public goods by foreigners. In effect, the public goods about which (liberal) states are really jealous are the items we typically associate with the debate on immigration in general: social-welfare arrangements, the labor market, security and a particular social and political way of living. The question, of course, is to what extent these items – apart from social-welfare benefits – are best understood in terms of goods. By regulating (normatively and materially) the labor market, public order and socio-political life, the authorities have a kind of hold on these items. But rather than goods the items appear to us as practices. As a result it is quite difficult to isolate these goods as they are so much a part of simply living in the territory of the state. This is clear for the labor market and the economy in general. It is difficult to fully exclude persons from the labor market and the economy as of the moment they are in the territory, as the widespread phenomenon of illegal employment demonstrates. It is especially evident for security as its benefits are not limited to nationals but extend to foreigners, including those staying illegally.[14] The same goes for many aspects of social life.[15] Even political life is easily accessible[16] apart from formal participation such as voting and standing for office. In a sense, as of the moment one enters the territory there is a real opportunity to take part in these practices – hence, the importance of keeping the normal migrant out of the territory. This means that the exclusion must be understood not so much as an exclusion from goods in terms of assets, but rather particular *practices* associated with living in the territory. In a way, these practices are never fully tied to a particular state territory. So, a labor market is usually regional, sometimes even global depending on the industry. Even very local political life has many regional and global aspects to it. This means that even if the target state succeeds in excluding the normal migrant from its territory, the latter may still participate in these practices if neighboring or otherwise connected countries admit him. Nevertheless, territoriality matters a lot to the target state. Though social life may cross borders, the quintessential social institution that supports it partially stops at the borders, i.e. the law. Probably the primary way of understanding borders is in terms demarcating jurisdiction. This means that the legal powers of the state do not go beyond its borders.[17] Only rarely do national laws have extra-territorial pretensions and effect. Paradoxically, precisely by not extending jurisdiction beyond their borders

14 The costs associated with ensuring (perceived) security are typically higher for foreigners, especially for those with an irregular legal status.

15 Obviously there are many social and cultural barriers that obstruct a foreigner's participation in every group and level of social life. But this is also the case for nationals.

16 By obtaining information on political issues, discussing politics, publish opinions, organize rallies, etc.

17 States may still affect indirectly the law in other jurisdictions through supra- and international law.

unless necessary, states are able to shut migrants out from the particular social life of their territory. If the migrant could subject himself to the jurisdiction of the target state outside the territory a whole set of legal arrangements would apply to him. This mechanism is dramatically illustrated in the field of refugee law. Here authorities try to keep immigrants at bay – literally. As the immigrants remain on the high seas they are not within the jurisdiction of the target state and as a result the authorities believe they need not receive the asylum application. This is even more the case for the normal migrant. His legal position radically improves simply by entering the territory – legally or illegally. The areas of life from which the normal migrant is supposed to be excluded (the labor market, security, social and political life) are supported by legal arrangements. Most aspects of these arrangements have a direct or indirect positive effect on the legal position of the migrant who is present in the territory (legally or illegally). These protective schemes include labor safety regulations, laws of contract and torts, protection of family life. Even his access to justice will improve. Not only does the migrant have a better chance of obtaining legal assistance, including pro bono if he cannot afford it, but also the judicial review of a decision of *expulsion from* the territory is likely to be more substantial than the judicial review – if any – of a *denial of access to* the territory. This suggests that it is crucial for target states to let the normal migrant's exclusion from the territory go hand in hand with his exclusion from their legal order. To summarize we may say that the exclusion involves denying normal migrants access to the following items in the target state: territory, welfare-arrangements, labor market, security, social and political life, and the legal order.

Obviously, not all demands for admission are honored. So there are normal migrants who are not admitted. This denial of admission means that those normal migrants are excluded from the items mentioned above. In short, current admission policies constitute a practice of exclusion. However, the fact of exclusion itself does not make it necessarily problematic. For example, if the exclusion of normal migrants only takes place sporadically then it surely does not deserve our attention in terms of a general point of concern. So, size (or rather scale) does matter. There is probably an intuitive threshold for taking the issue 'seriously'. But I do not think it is necessary to establish this threshold, because anecdotal evidence already suggests that the number of normal migrants excluded per year by Western states is far from negligible. Though it remains a matter of rough (and perhaps too modest)[18] estimation it is probably safe to say that EU Member States exclude more than 2 million normal migrants per year.[19] Another way to picture this is to look at the actual number of economic migrants admitted. From this perspective, even self-professed immigration countries like the US only admit a small percentage of normal migrants. The bulk of resident permits are based on some form of family reunification.[20] So, irrespective of the number of normal

18 See Annex 1 – 'A modest estimate?'

19 See Annex 1.

20 See Annex 2.

migrants that are admitted, it is reasonable to take the exclusion of normal migrants as the starting point for our analysis.

Justification

While it is easy to see the exclusionary nature of immigration policy, the absence of proper justification is not so evident. I have in mind a particular form of proper justification. There is proper justification *vis-à-vis* the excluded migrant if the authorities take into account the interests of the excluded migrant and provide acceptable reasons for the exclusion. This should involve at least two things. First, the reasons for the exclusion must be backed up by sufficient relevant facts derived from stakeholders and scientific research. Authorities must render explicit instability of data and scientific inconclusiveness or disagreement. In short, generic and abstract reasons for exclusion do not constitute proper justification. Second, the authorities must show that in light of these relevant facts they have conducted the difficult exercise of balancing the migrant's (legitimate) interest in immigration against the interests of the receiving country. This does not mean that they must give preference to the migrant's interests, but if they do not, they should be able to explain why they decided to exclude.

Obviously, this notion of proper justification is not without its problems. It may place too much pressure on the authorities: Will they ever be able to sufficiently substantiate the reasons for exclusion taking into account the incredible complexity of migration? The exclusion of a normal migrant is never properly justified, or if it is, it is only via a long and cumbersome procedure. Alternatively, when authorities do not take the notion of proper justification seriously, it may be obtained too easily. Who is to say that the reasons for exclusion are not sufficiently substantiated? What prevents the authorities from simply stating that the migrant's interest in migration has been accounted for, but that the national interest prevailed? These serious objections should not worry us for now, because we only want to explain that authorities are excluding normal migrants without giving them this particular kind of 'proper justification'. Later on we will elaborate on the role of justification in the law. Yet I can already say that the notion of justification poses similar problems in other areas of the law. Sometimes it is really unclear when the justification is sufficient. But in many more cases legal practice has developed a consensus on when the justification is sufficient. These cases are often highly complex.

Searching for justification

Having spelt out what I mean by 'proper justification', I should now substantiate my claim that authorities fail to give proper justification when excluding normal migrants. It is always difficult – from a methodological perspective – to establish the absence of something. How can we make sure we have looked in the right places? Have we dug deep enough? It is impossible to cover all bases, yet we can try to single out the stages in the immigration policy where one would expect the proper justification to take place. To put it differently: if the authorities were to give proper justification for the exclusion of normal migrants when or where would this take place? Here we will reiterate our schematic representation of the different instances of immigration policy: enactment of the policy and elaboration of regulations, individual exclusion decisions and judicial confirmation of the exclusion decision. We recall that if authorities do give any justification, it will be different at different stages. In fact, the level of concreteness, contextualization and individualization increases moving from the enactment of the policy down to judicial review. It is impossible to provide a concrete and individualized justification when designing and enacting immigration policy. By contrast, when a normal migrant challenges his particular exclusion through the courts, there is obviously – in theory – plenty of opportunity to provide a contextualized, concrete and individualized justification.

At first glance recent developments suggest that EU immigration policy is becoming more inclusive towards migrants in terms of actual admission and legal protection. The entering into of force of the Lisbon Treaty in December 2009, gives the impression that a new era of EU immigration policy has come. Under the Treaty, the EU undertakes to frame a common[21] policy on immigration that is *fair* towards third-country nationals.[22] Moreover, the Treaty turns the Charter of Fundamental Rights of the European Union into a legally binding document.[23] Pursuant to the Charter competent authorities are now obliged to give reasons for their actions affecting both citizens and non-citizens.[24] This has enormous potential to improve the legal position of migrants seeking admission. Furthermore, the EU is gradually extending the possibility of easy admission and incorporation to an increasing number of categories of third-country nationals. Most impressive is of course the enlargement of the EU itself – transforming millions of third-country

21 The lack of harmonization and the patchwork nature of EU immigration policy have been criticized by many. Arguably, the Lisbon Treaty created an opportunity for the EU to harmonize its immigration policy as it need not act unanimously (ex Arts 62 and 67 TEC), but can legislate through qualified majority (Art. 79(2) Treaty on the Functioning of the EU (hereafter: TFEU) and Art. 16(3)–(4) Treaty on EU (hereafter: TEU)). However, some experts pointed out that due to political/electoral dynamics and the tendency among Member States to make opportunistic reservations and exceptions, harmonization will still be extremely difficult to attain. Philippe De Bruycker, 'L'émergence d'une politique Européenne d'immigration' in Jean-Yves Carlier (ed.), *L'étranger face au droit. XXes Journées d'etudes juridiques Jean Dabin* (Brussels: Bruylant, 2010), at 352. From a more evaluative or normative perspective one may even wonder whether harmonization is desirable. Today, there is still so little experience with and information about sound immigration policies, which account for the legitimate interests of both nationals and migrants. Against that background, migrants and nationals may be better off with unstable and diverging policies leading to strategic behavior (forum shopping, anticipating regularization schemes) than with a comprehensive and harmonized EU policy.

22 Article 67 TFEU.

23 Article 6(1) TEU.

24 Article 41(2)(c) Charter.

nationals into EU citizens. But equally spectacular has been the so-called 'Blue Card Directive', facilitating the admission of highly skilled migrants.[25] This promising picture nicely fits the draft directive providing the right to effective judicial review in all types of migration cases, as proposed by a committee of immigration law experts.[26] More generally, it seems that the EU has been responsive to calls from the field for a more realistic perspective on migration.[27] Under the Lisbon Treaty migrants are no longer the undesired individuals whose admission and exclusion must be strictly regulated and enforced. Instead migration is a potentially beneficial and much-needed phenomenon, which can and should be managed.[28] It seems we have come a long way from the discriminatory and outright racist migration laws of recent Western history:

> They [third-country nationals] are no longer 'aliens' subject exclusively to national immigration rules and to the discretion of the national authorities. On the contrary, those authorities in the application of this new EC immigration law will have to comply with the proportionality principle and the minimum procedural guarantees as laid down in the jurisprudence of the Court [ECJ] and in the EU Charter of Fundamental Rights.[29]

In effect, these observations suggest that the EU is in the process of making Europe's Area of Freedom, Security and Justice more just for an increasing number of migrants. This is certainly the case for some categories of migrants, yet it does not apply to normal migrants seeking admission. For example, further reading of the TFEU indicates that the EU's commitment to a common immigration policy, which is *fair* towards third-country nationals only extends to

25 Council Directive 2009/50/EC, 25 May 2009, on the conditions of entry and residence of third-country nationals for the purposes of highly qualified employment, *OJ*, 18 June 2009, L155/17 (hereafter: Blue Card Directive).

26 Meijers committee (P. Boeles *et al.*, 'Draft Directive on Minimum Guarantees for Individual Freedom, Security and Justice in Relation to Decisions Regarding Movement of Persons', *European Journal of Migration and Law*, 7 (2005), 301–6). See below, Chapter 7.

27 Cf. EU Commission's announcement of 'a major change in the external dimension of the European migration policy over recent years, namely the shift from a primarily security-centered approach focused on reducing migratory pressures, to a more transparent and balanced approach guided by a better understanding of all aspects relevant to migration, improving the accompanying measures to manage migratory flows, making migration and mobility positive forces for development, and giving greater consideration to decent work aspects in policies to better manage economic migration'. Communication of the Commission, 'Strengthening the global approach to migration: increasing coordination, coherence and synergies', 8 October 2008, COM(2008) 611/3, at 3. See also Bas Schotel, 'EU's Management of Migration Flows and the Rule of Law'.

28 Article 79 TFEU.

29 Kees Groenendijk, 'Citizens and Third-country Nationals: Differential Treatment or Discrimination' in Jean-Yves Carlier and Elspeth Guild (eds), *L'avenir de la libre circulation des personnes dans l'EU. Analyse de la directive 2004/38 du 29 avril 2004 relative au droit des citoyens de circuler et de séjourner librement* (Brussels: Bruylant, 2006), at 98–9.

third-country nationals residing legally in the EU.[30] It does not include normal migrants. Neither does the Charter really improve the legal position of normal migrants. Authorities now have a legal duty to give reasons when denying normal migrants admission. But this does not mean that these reasons have to be substantiated, let alone sound. Reference to the legal ground and some superficial evidence may already count as giving reasons. More importantly, the obligation to give reasons does not mean that the administration must take into account the interests and reasons applicable to the normal migrant. By contrast, if the proportionality principle were to apply, then the interests of normal migrants would have to be accounted for. At first glance, this is precisely what the Charter does:

> Subject to the *principle of proportionality*, limitations [on the exercise of the rights and freedoms recognised by the Charter] may be made *only if* they are *necessary* and *genuinely* meet objectives of general interest recognised by the Union or the need to protect the rights and freedoms of others.[31]

This proportionality principle has a broad application and makes no distinction between citizens and third-country nationals. However, a closer look shows that the Charter remains fully in line with the standing ECJ and ECtHR case law on the proportionality principle: it only applies to 'the rights and freedoms recognized by the Charter'. But what right or freedom under the Charter and more generally EU law does a normal migrant have that may be compromised by a decision-denying admission (e.g. visa refusal)? The characteristic of the normal migrant is that he is neither eligible for a right to asylum, family reunification or any other preferred status, nor does he enjoy the freedom of movement reserved for EU citizens and legal residents.[32]

The Blue Card Directive, though potentially favorable to some highly skilled normal migrants, does not change the *legal position* of those *seeking admission*. For example, the directive is still structured as a scheme of permission/refusal and not rights. It provides a harmonization of entry conditions for the purposes of coordinating and promoting highly skilled labor migration. However, the fulfillment of the entry conditions does not grant a right to entry.[33] Furthermore, the directive still allows Member States to put a full stop to the admission of highly

30 Article 79 TFEU.

31 Article 52(1) Charter (emphases added).

32 This was precisely the value of the draft directive proposed by the experts of immigration law. See n. 27 and Chapter 7. It extends the scope of the proportionality test to all decisions in migration matters even if the migrant cannot invoke a fundamental right or liberty.

33 'The proposal does not create a right of admission. These provisions lay down the mandatory and possible grounds for refusal . . .' Proposal for a Council Directive on the conditions of entry and residence of third-country nationals for the purposes of highly qualified employment, Brussels, 23.10.2007, COM(2007) 637 final 2007/0228 (CNS), 'Explanatory Memorandum', at 10.

skilled migrants, as each Member State reserves the right to determine its own volume of admissions.[34]

It is more difficult to gauge the effect on normal migrants of the so-called 'sanctions directive', which is supposed to penalize the employers of illegal migrants, but not the illegal employees.[35] It should certainly improve the position of those already – illegally – inside the EU. Yet it leaves unaltered the legal position of those *seeking admission*. At best it attenuates the normative force of the admission laws prohibiting unauthorized access and stay in the EU. The directive provides protection precisely to those who violated the immigration laws.[36]

Finally, the coming into force of the Lisbon Treaty legally sanctioned a new paradigm in immigration policy: efficient management of migration flows.[37] Various well-intentioned policy proposals have endorsed the idea of migration as something beneficial that should be managed rather than treated as a threat to be combated.[38] Prominent scholars of immigration law have welcomed the management paradigm.[39] However, the notion of migration management drives the 'law' out of EU immigration policy. The problem is not that migration management cannot *promote the interests* protected by human rights (e.g. social justice). Rather, the mechanics of migration management resist or reject the structure of law. In effect, 'management' and 'flows of migration' are radically non-legal notions. Migration management may lack two basic legal categories: legal directives claiming obedience (norms) and individual norm subjects (norm subjects/addressees). The migrant is no longer a norm addressee who must obey a legal norm. Instead, he has become an *object*, an element of a quasi-natural phenomenon, i.e. migration flow. A migration flow cannot obey; it can only be managed. Scholars have made critical observations about the dominance of efficiency, disciplinary and controlling dynamics and lagging legal protection under current

34 Article 6 Blue Card Directive.

35 Directive 2009/52/EC of the European Parliament and of the Council, 18 June 2009, providing for minimum standards on sanctions and measures against employers of illegally staying third-country nationals, *JO*, 30 June 2009, L 168/24.

36 This is another example of the anomie in immigration law. Similarly, Michael Bommes recently pointed out that on the one hand, there is a set of rules that seeks to keep out the alien, while on the other, there is an official and unofficial normative and social structure that is actually pulling the alien to the inside and keeping him in. He wondered whether this tension or mismatch could be understood as a kind of Durkheimian anomie. Views expressed during the session 'Normative Begründungen und politische Rationalitäten: Zur Rechtfertigung und Kritik der Abwehr unkontrollierter Zuwanderung' at the V. Jahrestagung Illegalität 'Irreguläre Migration – zwischen Grenzüberschreitung und Ausgrenzung' by the Katholische Akademie Berlin on 4 March 2009.

37 Article 79 TFEU. Cf. Schotel, 'EU's Management of Migration Flows, and the Rule of Law'.

38 E.g. Theo Veenkamp, Tom Bentley, and Alessandra Buofino, *People Flow. Managing Migration in a New European Commonwealth* (London: Demos, 2003).

39 E.g. Alexander T. Aleinikoff, 'International Legal Norms and Migration: A Report' in Alexander T. Aleinikoff and Vincent Chetail (eds), *Migration and International Legal Norms* (The Hague: TCM Asser Press), 2003, at 1.

immigration policies.[40] Yet what remains underexposed is the role of the elimination of norms and norm addressees. The problem is that legal protection only kicks in insofar as there are relevant legal norm subjects.[41]

In short, though promising at first glance, the recent developments in EU immigration policy do not improve the legal position of normal migrants seeking admission.[42] In effect, a closer look at the different levels of immigration policy confirms the picture of 'exclusion without justification'.

The first opportunity for authorities to justify the exclusion of normal migrants appears when they conceive and enact immigration policies and regulations. This stage of the policy is necessarily general and cannot deal with the interests of particular normal migrants. At this stage we should look for the considerations behind the policy. What did the authorities take into consideration when designing and enacting the policy? If immigration policy constitutes a form of exclusion then the considerations behind the policy constitute the reasons or justification for the exclusion. We actually want to see how the considerations behind immigration policy score against the two criteria of proper justification. First, we try to establish to what extent the considerations behind immigration policy are factually and scientifically substantiated. To put it differently: when authorities design and enact immigration policy, do they rely on facts and insights from research, or just intuition and common sense? Second, we want to find out whether among the many considerations behind immigration policy, the normal migrant's interest in immigration has been taken into account. Though still quite diverse in their particular technicalities, all contemporary immigration policies in Europe are motivated by some or all of the following considerations:

- national[43] security;
- public health;
- national economy;

40 Cf. Jef Huysmans, *The Politics of Insecurity. Fear, Migration and Asylum in the EU* (London/New York: Routledge, 2006).

41 Hence, the paradoxical irony of the criminalization of migration law. It may enhance the migrant's legal protection against state action because it at least explicitly identifies norms and norm addressees. For the criminalization of migration law, see Elspeth Guild and Paul Minderhoud (eds), *Immigration and Criminal Law in the European Union: The Legal Measures and Social Consequences of Criminal Law in Member States on Trafficking and Smuggling Human Beings* (Leyden/Boston: Martinus Nijhoff Publishers, 2006).

42 Probably the only material improvement brought by the Lisbon Treaty is the abolition of *ex* Art. 68 TEC. The first paragraph of this Article prevented lower national courts from asking prejudicial (interpretation of EU law) questions to the ECJ in migration matters. Only courts of last instance were allowed to ask prejudicial questions. This procedure clearly did not correspond with the urgency of cases in which the migrants are held at the border and denied access ('refoulement'). The abolition of the second paragraph is equally important (denying the ECJ jurisdiction when public order is involved) but the measures pertain to *internal* border controls, whereas we focus on the external border and migration policies.

43 One may add 'European' when the policy is issued by the EU.

- social and cultural cohesion;
- balanced national demographics; and
- rewarding favored nations and penalizing unfriendly states.[44]

To what extent do the authorities substantiate these considerations? Any serious substantiation involves at least two things: (1) it demonstrates a connection between the particular concerns and normal migrants, and (2) it shows that exclusion of normal migrants addresses these concerns. In short, the authorities should say something about the *effects* of normal migrants and the particular policy. This account must be informed by well-established facts and some sort of scientific analysis. One would expect to find this in the explanatory reports to the relevant immigration and alien acts. Yet reports contain hardly any substantiation of the effects of immigration and immigration policy. They rather reiterate the considerations and make very generic statements about the economy, security, social cohesion, and immigration stocks and flows. It suggests that the considerations for having the particular immigration policies are so self-evident they need no further substantiation. In reality these things are far from obvious. For example, it is rather obvious that the connection between security and social cohesion and immigration and immigration policy are far from self-evident.[45] But even the concern for national economy – though more plausible on paper – is not patently obvious. There is of course a methodological obstacle because one must first determine what counts as a relevant economic criterion (e.g. GDP, inflation, the real estate market, the stock market, interest rates, etc.). Also, things get really complicated when we are identifying relevant stakeholders and the time frame used to measure the effects of immigration and immigration policy. Furthermore, the nature of the available data and analyses is either too specific or too generic for policy purposes. Migration policy in the EU has the additional problem of lacking comprehensive, reliable and standardized data on immigration. Moreover, the poor level of granularity makes it very difficult to establish relevant correlations (let alone cause and effect) with economic phenomena. Most striking is the lack of data and analyses on the effect of migration and policy in the field of irregular migration. The persuasion and dedication with which authorities undertake to combat illegal migration stand in sharp contrast with the extremely limited

44 Authorities often use more relaxed (e.g. waivers) or strict visa/admission requirements to express the quality of the relationship with a foreign country.

45 For sure in the event a particular immigrant poses a clear and present security threat, exclusion is certainly justified. But it does not follow that security should be a central consideration and concern for immigration policy. Only if it is established that immigrants in general pose a security threat – for example significantly more than nationals – is it justified to make it a central concern for immigration policy. For virtually all policy areas one can imagine scenarios or find actual incidents related to security; however this does (not yet) entice us to make security a central concern in all policy areas. Also, security is understood in terms of *national* security as opposed to local public order. It is far from clear how immigrants can have an impact on a 'national' level.

knowledge available about irregular migration and the effects of the policies 'combating' it. The authorities do not even have criteria for what are accepted and desired levels of irregular migration. This turns irregular immigration policy into a highly symbolic and chimerical exercise. It directly affects normal migration policy, as irregular migration is the corollary of regular migration. When denied admission many normal migrants turn into 'potential' irregular migrants. The actual effectiveness of excluding normal migrants depends on the effectiveness of irregular migration policy. This fuels speculation about whether normal migration policy is ultimately a matter of symbolism rather than actual effect. Not only data on irregular and regular migration, but also standard economic data and analyses can be problematic. Most EU Member States only issue work permits and thus admission to the extent that the normal migrant finds employment in a sector in which unemployment of EU residents is not beyond a certain level. Yet the policymakers did not produce any serious data and analyses to indicate that preventing the migrants from taking up the jobs really decreases unemployment (growth) rates among EU residents in that particular sector. However, in some countries, the authorities seem to be making serious efforts to actually produce more specific data and analyses. For example the UK government has developed a practice of producing policy impact assessments.[46] It seems to incorporate insights from studies on migration and economics and has created a special forum: the 'Migration Impacts Forum'. In support of its Points Based System (PBS) as well as its proposed reform of the legal and regulatory framework at large, the UK does produce some data and analyses. The PBS should strengthen the UK economy by admitting immigrants needed for the national economy, primarily those who are highly skilled, and excluding those not needed, primarily those who have low skills. Some studies indicate that the admitted workers contribute to the economy and do not have a negative impact on employment and wages of nationals. In other words, they justify the admission. But admission is only one part of the equation. They do not substantiate the exclusion of the other normal migrants that do not fit the profile. If indeed the central reason for their exclusion is the strength of the national economy, then this reason must be substantiated. Yet the authorities do not provide data and analyses showing that the so-called unqualified migrants who are admitted become unemployed, push nationals from the job market and/or cause a drop in wages of low-skilled nationals. I am not necessarily denying the legitimacy of these concerns. I am simply saying that without any serious substantiation, these concerns cannot count as *proper justification* for the exclusion of normal migrants.

Let me recapitulate. At first glance the authorities seem to justify the exclusion as they more or less clearly state the reasons for their policy, namely the policy

46 See for example: UK Home Office/UK Border Agency, *Final Impact Assessment of Draft Immigration Bill*, 12 November 2009, available at http://www.ukba.homeoffice.gov.uk/managing-borders/simplifying, last consulted June 2010; House of Lords Select Committee on Economic Affairs, *The Economic Impact of Immigration*, Volume I: Report, April 2008.

considerations. However, under our terms, proper justification requires not only the statement of reasons, but also their substantiation by data and analyses. The effect of immigration and immigration policy on the items of concern must be established. Even in the domain most suitable for some sort of fact-based substantiation, i.e. economics, authorities fail to produce data and analyses. At best they substantiate why some categories of normal migrants must be admitted. They do not substantiate why the others must be excluded.

Apart from substantiating the reasons for exclusion, *proper justification* should also involve a balancing of the normal migrant's interest in migration. Here it becomes very clear that authorities are failing when they conceive and enact immigration policies and regulations. The policies are issued from an outright unilateral perspective. This is obvious from the list of stated purposes behind immigration polices mentioned above and is again reflected in the working permit scheme protecting EU workers, briefly discussed above. The scheme entails that the interests of a remotely identified and basically statistically constructed group of unemployed EU workers in principle prevail over the interests of a normal migrant seeking admission to work in a particular sector of the economy. Now, the problem is not that the interests of nationals often prevail over the interests of normal migrants (as there may be good reasons for doing this). But what makes the immigration laws unilateral is that there is no mechanism that balances the national interest against those of the normal migrant. If any balancing is taking place, it is between the different state interests (e.g. national economy versus security), or between the interests of the authorities and EU nationals/residents (employers).

Our discussion of recent EU developments draws a similar picture. From now on immigration policies should be fair towards migrants, but only to those residing legally in the territory, not to those who are seeking admission. At best the interests of source countries are considered, not individual normal migrants seeking admission (the 'brain-drain' argument).[47] The Blue Card Directive emphasizes that it does not create a right to admission, even if admissions criteria are satisfied.[48] In effect, the unilateral nature of immigration laws and the disregard for the normal migrant's interest in admission is reflected in the general legal fact that aliens (and thus normal migrants) do not have a right to a visa. Under international, EU and domestic law states are free to deny aliens a visa without the need to justify the denial.[49] A typical way to phrase the relationship between the issuing of a visa and the fulfillment of the visa requirements is as follows: 'The alien who meets the

47 Blue Card Directive, at recitals 22 and 24.

48 See supra n. 34.

49 Tiburcio, *Human Rights of Aliens* (2001) at 218. During the revision of the Common Manual into the Schengen Border Code the rapporteur proposed an amendment effectively introducing a right to a visa, but his proposal was not upheld. Cholewenski, 'The Need for Effective Individual Legal Protection in Immigration Matters', 7 *European Journal of Migration and Law* (2005), at 248 and fn. 66.

following requirements *may* be granted a visa'.[50] In other words, when the alien meets the criteria there is *no obligation to grant the visa*, but when the alien does not meet the criteria the state has a *duty to deny the visa*. It may be argued that my characterization of the visa system as permissive is incorrect, because it tacitly relies on the distinction between privileges and rights. This distinction is supposed to be outdated, because 'the concept of legitimate expectations generally prevails over the semantic distinction [between rights and privileges]'.[51] I believe it suffices to say that to the extent the concept of legitimate expectations applies to immigration matters, scholars of international law consider it to apply to a situation where the alien has already received some form of official permission to enter or to stay. It is clear that under current positive law this concept of legitimate expectations does not apply to the issuance of the visa itself; the concept may only apply after a visa has been granted. More importantly, even if such a right to visa or entry were to be introduced, the states are still free to impose whatever conditions (unless racist) to the effect of leaving such a right without any substance.

At the level of policy implementation, especially individual admission denials, and the judicial review of the denials things are not much better. On paper officials have plenty of opportunity to provide proper justification when rejecting a visa application, precisely because it is an individual case. It allows them to select the relevant data and analyses to substantiate the reasons for exclusion. Also they are in an ideal position to gather information about the interests of the individual migrant and then balance those interests. In practice this is the exact opposite. In most EU countries the competent authorities do not even have to provide a reason for a visa denial.[52] The entering into force of the EU Charter of Fundamental Rights should change this practice. But even if the authorities give a reason, it is simply a matter of referring to one of the reasons for refusal provided in the regulations without any need for further substantiation. They certainly do not balance those considerations against the interest of the normal migrant. It seems that the last resort for the excluded migrant to get his exclusion properly justified is judicial review. In theory this is the quintessential legal protection and an ideal platform for examining the reasons for exclusion, not least because the courts are independent from the immigration authorities. But again the reality is completely different. The number of judicial reviews of visa denials is extremely limited, as countries tend to limit the right of appeal especially when it comes to work-related permits.[53] Furthermore, the fact that an appeal has been lodged, does not suspend

50 Compare Art. 5 Schengen Convention. Hailbronner also concludes from the term 'may' that aliens cannot derive rights from Art. 5 Schengen Convention. Hailbronner, *Asylum Law and Policy of the European Union* (The Hague/London/Boston: Kluwer Law International (2000), at 152.

51 J.A.R. Nafziger, 'Review of Visa Denials by Consular Officers', 66 *Washington Law Review* (1991), at 49–50, with reference to US Supreme Court rulings.

52 Christine Adam and Alexandre Devillard (eds), *Comparative study of the Laws in the 27 EU Member States for Legal Immigration Including an Assessment of the Conditions and Formalities Imposed by each Member State for Newcomers* (Geneva: IOM, 2008), at 33–4.

53 Adam and Devillard, at 44.

the removal process – a normal migrant can still be removed from a country even if he has lodged an appeal against the denial of his visa.[54] Typically, normal migrants must apply for a visa in their country of origin or residence (or the closest country if no consular mission is present in their country). As a result most visa denials are issued abroad. From a practical point of view, it is extremely difficult to lodge an appeal against a visa denial from outside the target country.[55] But even when a visa denial makes it to court, the review does not make things much better. Often during the proceeding before the court the immigration authorities simply substitute the actual grounds for rejection with others that seem more solid and pertinent.[56] More importantly, judges refrain from any substantial review. They do not look into the merits. But the merits verify and substantiate the reasons for exclusion and the adequacy of the balancing of interests. So when courts confirm a visa denial they neither substantiate their decision with data and analyses nor take into account the normal migrant's interest in migration. This is of course reflected precisely by the fact that the proportionality test is not applied in cases of normal migrants (because they cannot invoke a right protected by the Treaty or the constitutional traditions of the Member States). In short, the court's confirmation of a visa denial also constitutes exclusion without justification.

How the law justifies exclusion without justification

The previous paragraphs showed that we can understand current immigration policy regarding normal migrants as exclusion without justification. This practice of exclusion without justification constitutes the first part of our central concern. The second part has to do with how this practice is justified. Our problem is that the exclusion without justification is not so much perceived as an imperfection in the system, an irregularity from the official code of conduct. On the contrary, it is the official way of dealing with normal migrants as this practice is considered to be legally valid and sanctioned by law. So how does the law justify the exclusion without justification? The central vehicle is what we may call the rule of inherent sovereign power: states have the power inherent in sovereignty to admit and exclude aliens (migrants) as they see fit, subject to their obligations under international law. The remainder of this chapter examines how this rule is captured in the different sources of law: international treaty and soft law; international, supra-national and domestic case law; and legal doctrine. We will have to adapt

54 Ibid.

55 For a discussion of the almost impossible extra-territorial nature of the visa application and review procedures, see Staples, 'Adjudicating the External Schengen Border' in Kees Groenendijk, Elspeth Guild and Paul Minderhoud (eds), *In Search of Europe's Borders* (The Hague/London/New York: Kluwer Law International, 2003), at 225–8.

56 The immigration authorities can do this because they do not have to provide reasons, while they can invoke a wide range of grounds for rejecting a visa. Adam and Devillard, at 34.

our terminology to this legal investigation and use the term 'alien' instead of (normal) migrant for the purposes of this particular discussion.

Treaties dealing with the subject of admission of migrants as such are rather scarce. In fact the current body of treaties is a testament to the conventional view that state discretion in migration matters is the default position. To date there have not been particular occasions or motives for states to restate this default position into specific treaties. Only when special international arrangements regarding particular types of movement (e.g. business, asylum) are put in place, do states sometimes find it useful to explicitly recall the fact that these particular arrangements do not create any general requirement for the state to admit aliens. Similarly, sources of so-called 'soft law' rarely address the existence or the absence of a qualified right to free movement or admission. In fact the few sources that mention admission all confirm the principle of state discretion in migration matters. So according to Article 1 of the Inter-American Convention on Territorial Asylum (1954): 'Every state has the right, in the exercise of its sovereignty, to admit into its territory such persons as it deems advisable, without, through the exercise of this right, giving rise to complaint by any other state.'[57] A few other instruments contain similar provisions (e.g. Convention on the Status of Aliens, Havana (1928);[58] General Agreement on Trade in Services (1994);[59] United Nations General Assembly, Declaration on the Human Rights of Individuals Who are not Nationals of the Country in Which They Live (1985);[60] Human Rights Committee,

57 OAS Official Records OEA/Ser. XII Treaty Series No. 19, in Plender (ed.), *Basic Documents on Migration Law*.

58 'States have the right to establish by means of laws the conditions under which foreigners may enter and reside in their territory.' Convention on the Status of Aliens, 20 Feb 20, 1928, Art. 1, 22 *Am. J. Int'l L.* Supp. 136, 137 (1928).

59

> Annex on movement of natural persons supplying services under the agreement. [. . .] 4. The Agreement shall not prevent a Member from applying measures to regulate the entry of natural persons into, or their temporary stay in, its territory, including those measures necessary to protect the integrity of, and to ensure the orderly movement of natural persons across its borders, provided that such measures are not applied in such a manner as to nullify or impair the benefits accruing to any Member under the terms of a specific commitment.

33 *ILM* 1168 (1994) cited in Plender (ed.), *Basic Documents on Migration Law* (1997), at 888–91. With respect to measures that may nullify or impair the commitments under the Agreement, Richard Plender commented that requiring a visa from some persons and not others does not constitute such measures. Ibid. at 891.

60

> *Nothing in this Declaration shall be interpreted as legitimizing any alien's illegal entry into and presence in a state, nor shall any provision be interpreted as restricting the right of any state to promulgate laws and regulations concerning the entry of aliens* and the terms and conditions of their stay or establish differences between nationals and aliens. However, such laws and regulations shall not be incompatible with the international legal obligations of that state, including those in the field of human rights. (emphasis added)

Declaration on the Human Rights of Individuals who are not Nationals of the Country in Which They Live, UNGA Res. 40/114, Art. 2(1), 13 Dec. 1985 cited in David A. Martin, 'The Authority and Responsibility of States' in Aleinikoff and Chetail (eds), *Migration and International Legal Norms* (2003), at 32.

General Comment No. 27 (1999).[61] The state's power to exclude is not absolute as it is subject to obligations of international law. But these obligations do not make much difference when the alien is a normal migrant. The so-called material international obligations only concern the special migrants with a right to admission (e.g. refugees, family reunification). As to the procedural obligations (e.g. due process) we have already seen that in practice they lack any quantitative and qualitative substance.

While treaties and soft-law instruments hardly take up the issue of general admission of aliens, international, supra-national and domestic courts have confirmed the principle of state discretion in immigration matters on numerous occasions (from the end of the nineteenth to the beginning of the twenty-first century). The wording of the rulings reflects the alleged self-evidence of the rule of inherent sovereign power.

> When an alien comes to the frontier, seeking admission, either as a settler or on a visit, the State has an *unfettered* right to refuse admission.
>
> International Court of Justice (1955) (emphasis added)[62]

> As a matter of well-established international law and subject to its treaty obligations, a state has the right to control the entry of non-nationals into its territory.
>
> European Court of Human Rights (1985–2003)[63]

> [E]very sovereign nation has the power, *inherent in sovereignty*, and *essential* to its self-preservation, to forbid the entrance of foreigners.
>
> US Supreme Court (1889–2001) (emphases added)[64]

61 General Comment 27. Paragraph 4. The question whether *an alien is 'lawfully' within the territory of a state is a matter governed by domestic law,* which may subject the entry of an alien to the territory of a state to restrictions, provided they are in compliance with the state's international obligations. (emphasis added)

Cited in B.S. Chimi, 'Development and Migration', in Aleinikoff and Chetail (eds), *Migration and International Legal Norms* (2003), at 256.

62 The *Nothebohm* Case (*Liech v Guat.*), 1955 ICJ 4 (Apr 6).

63 *Abdulaziz, Cabales and Balkandi v United Kingdom*, ECtHR (28 May 1985), para. 67; *Guel v Switzerland*, EctHR (19 Feb. 1996), para. 38; *Ahmut v the Netherlands*, ECtHR (26 Oct. 1996), para. 67; *Dalia v France*, ECtHR (19 Feb. 1998), para. 52; *Boultif v Switzerland*, ECtHR (2 Aug. 2001), para. 46; *Al-Nashif v Bulgaria*, ECtHR (20 Sept. 2002), para. 114; *Slivenko v Latvia*, ECtHR (9 Oct. 2003), para. 115. All decisions are available at http://www.echr.coe.int/Eng/Judgments. htm (last accessed May 2005).

64 Quote from *Nishimura Ekiu v U.S.*, 142 U.S. 651 (1892). See also *Chae Chan Ping v U.S.* (The Chinese Exclusion Case), 130 U.S. 581 (1889); *Fong Yue v U.S.*, 149 U.S. 698, 711 (1893); *Kleindienst v Mandel*, 408 U.S. 753 (1972). Discussed in J.A.R. Nafziger, 'The General Admission of Aliens under International Law' 77 *AJIL.* (1983), 804–47. See also *Zadvydas v Davis* 121 S.Ct. 2491 (2001).

> One of the rights possessed by the supreme power in every State is the right to refuse to permit an alien to enter that State [. . .] and to expel or deport from the State, *at pleasure, even a friendly alien* . . . [quote from Lord Atkinson in Attorney-General for *Canada v Cain* [1906] AC 542, at p. 546].
>
> Supreme Court of Canada (1991–1992) (emphases added)[65]

It is probably this very strong wording by the courts that informs the widespread consensus among legal scholars that states have the right inherent in sovereignty to exclude aliens as they deem fit, subject to international obligations (e.g. Doehring (1985); Jennings and Watts Harlow (*Oppenheim's Law*) (1992); Pérez-Vera (1996); Plender (1997); Brownlie (1998); Tiburcio (2001); Aleinikoff (2003); Martin (2003); Chetail (2003); Bhabha (2003); Chimi (2003); Fisher and Schoenholtz (2003); Shaw (2003); Pastore (2004)).[66] As another illustration of the apparent self-evidence of this rule, the legal experts do not provide any serious explanation, let alone justification for this rule. They simply report its validity as an uncontested matter of fact. The rare attempts in the past to challenge this

65 Quotation from majority opinion by Justice La Forest in *Kindler v Canada* (Minister of Justice), 2 S.C.R. 779 (1991) available at http://www.canlii.org/ca/cas/scc/1991/1991scc70.html (last accessed on 2 August 2005). See also *Canada (Minister of Employment and Immigration) v Chiarelli*, 1 S.C.R. 711 (1992) available at http://www.canlii.org/ca/cas /scc/1992/1992scc25.html (last accessed 2 August 2005). There are tendencies in Canadian case law and immigration practices that suggest an attenuation of the *a priori* aspect of the state's power to exclude aliens. See recent rulings of the Federal Court of Appeal of Canada: '. . . although the statutory scheme under which immigration control is administered does not leave admission decisions to the untrammeled discretion of the Minister or her officials.' *Chiau v Canada (Minister of Citizenship and Immigration)*, 2 F.C. 297 (2001), *ratio decidendi* nr. 38, available at http://www.canlii.org/ca/cas/fca/2000/2000fca10482.html (last accessed 2 August 2005) and *Zazai v Canada (Minister of Citizenship and Immigration)*, 2 F.C. 78 (2005), *ratio decidendi* nr. 41 available at http://www.canlii.org/ca/cas/fct/2004/2004fc1356.html (last accessed 2 August 2005). However, the restrictions on the Minister's discretion have probably more to do with the supremacy of the legislative branch to set the standards and policies for immigration. Compare the 'plenary power' doctrine in the US, *supra* n. 6.

66 Karl Doehring, 'Aliens, Admission', in Rudolph Berhardt (ed.), *Encyclopedia of Public International Law* (Amsterdam/New York/Oxford: North Holland, 1985), 8; Robert Jennings and Arthur Watts, *Oppenheim's International Law* (Harlow: Longman Group UK, 1992), at 897; E. Perez-Vera, *Citoyenneté de l'Union européenne, nationalité et conditions des étrangers*, in Académie de Droit International, Recueil des Cours, (The Hague/Boston/London: Martinus Nijhoff Publishers, 1996), at 261; Ian Brownlie, *Principles of Public International Law*, (Oxford: Clarendon Press, 1998); Tiburcio, *Human Rights of Aliens*, at 234; Aleinikoff, 'International Legal Norms and Migration: A Report'; Martin, 'The Authority and Responsibility of States', at 31–2; Vincent Chetail, 'Freedom of Movement and Transnational Migrations: A Human Rights Perspective' in Aleinikoff and Chetail (eds), *Migration and International Legal Norms* (2003), at 47; Jacqueline Bhabha, 'Children, Migration and International Norms' in Aleinikoff and Chetail (eds), *Migration and International Legal Norms* (2003), at 204; Chimi, 'Development and Migration', at 256; David Fisher *et al.*, 'Migration and Security in International Law' in Aleinikoff and Chetail (eds), *Migration and International Legal Norms* (2003), at 87; Pastore, 'Visas, Borders, Immigration'.

consensus seem to have failed. For example two excellent studies by Nafziger did not provoke the much-needed debate about the *legal* nature of the rule of inherent sovereign power.[67] Nafziger argued that under positive international law there is a qualified duty to admit aliens. A qualified duty means that a state does not have the duty to admit all aliens seeking to enter its territory, but that they should admit them 'when they pose no danger to the public safety, security, general welfare, or essential institution of a recipient state'.[68] He made the following points to support his view of a qualified duty to admit aliens.

1 The most recent case law (in particular the US Supreme Court rulings) endorsing the discretionary powers of the state to exclude aliens is doubly flawed.[69] The case law is based on late nineteenth and early twentieth century racial prejudices, which would not stand the test today. The case law is based on an incorrect interpretation of the writings of Vittoria, Grotius, Vattel, Wolff and Pufendorf who contrary to the Court's interpretation favored the idea of a qualified duty to admit aliens;
2 Under international customary law states have at the least a qualified duty to admit aliens;[70]
3 The concept of sovereignty cannot justify a discrete right to exclude aliens.[71]

I believe that Nafziger is right with this last point. The concept of sovereignty does not warrant an absolute right to exclusion and some of his arguments that support this point shall be reiterated in Chapter 2. But these arguments – though extremely important – only set the stage for a qualified duty to admission; they are not sufficient. As to points (1) and (2), they simply do not obtain. The materials Nafziger produces to support his point (2) either refer to aliens with a special status (e.g. refugees, family members of residents, diplomatic and military staff) or do not constitute a source of customary law (e.g. Draft regulations).[72] So,

67 Nafziger (1983); J.A.R. Nafziger, 'A Commentary on American Legal Scholarship Concerning the Admission of Aliens', 17 *University of Michigan Journal of Law Reform* (1984), 165–81.
68 Nafziger (1983), at 805.
69 Ibid., at 823–9.
70 Ibid., at 829–41.
71 Ibid., at 816–22.
72 I believe that my position corresponds with the generally accepted view of the formal sources of international law.

> . . . when it comes to sources of international law, *Draft Codes* of the International Law Commission *merely represent a subsidiary means for the determination of rules of law*. They may reflect legal considerations largely shared by the international community, and they may expertly identify rules of international law, but *they do not constitute state practice* relevant to the determination of a rule of customary international law (emphases added).

ICTY, Trial Chamber, *Vasiljevic*, 29 November 2002, para. 200. This quotation was brought to my attention by Ward Ferdinandusse, *Direct Application of International Criminal Law in National Courts*, Ph.D. thesis (Amsterdam, 2005), in fn. 23 at 17.

Nafziger did not show that under customary law as such there is a direct qualified duty to admit aliens. Point (1) is also problematic because the classical publicists actually did not support a duty to admit aliens. The passages Nafziger cites refer to a special category, namely 'exiles'. The classical publicists did not extend this duty to 'normal' aliens. At best they found it barbaric not to let a friendly alien enter (more like a guest right), but they clearly did not think of it as a duty, let alone a legal duty.[73] As to the racist motives of the past, today the rulings seem to have a standing of their own.[74]

A brief analysis of the legal instruments confirmed the apparent legal validity of current practices. In effect, according to international law, states have a right inherent in sovereignty to exclude aliens without justification subject to the obligations of international law; there is no *qualified* legal duty to admit normal migrants. It may seem strange that only a handful of regional treaties and a couple of – more or less explicit – judicial rulings can establish the legal validity of current practices. How can a few legal instruments sanction such widespread practice? More importantly, it is quite unusual for the law to provide for powers and rights without any competing or counterbalancing arrangements. In other words, it is one thing to have the inherent sovereign powers rule. It is another to accept that this rule has full effect on its own. It is more likely that the inherent sovereign power rule has become so effective due to the absence of competing or counterbalancing legal vehicles. In effect, two standard – interrelated – legal safeguards against unfettered state action are missing when it comes to normal migrants: individual legal liberty and purpose-constrained state powers.

Legal liberty means that an individual may do as he likes, provided that it is not forbidden by law and does not unlawfully harm the liberty/interests of others (the harm principle).[75] This means that *in principle* an individual does not need a special subjective right or legal permit to do as he likes. In the context of

73 See further our brief discussion of the classic publicists and Kant in Chapter 6.

74 '. . . whatever the initial correctness of the nineteenth century readings, their affirmation of sweeping state authority to control migration became so deeply rooted in state practice and popular understanding, at a critical historical moment when exploration, conquest, and settlement were reaching the limits of frontiers, *as to displace any earlier framework and to provide the appropriate starting point for modern legal analysis*' (emphasis added). Martin, 'The Authority and Responsibility of States', at 31 in fn. 1.

75 It must be noted that the concept of legal liberty is not value neutral. First, legal liberty is the quintessential vehicle to promote the value of human autonomy. It does not mean that legal liberty cannot promote other values, such as artistic expression or scientific knowledge, but those values may also be promoted by other vehicles. Second, the harm principle is based on the dichotomy between lawful and unlawful acts. This dichotomy determines where the harm will lie. Or to be more precise: what harm is to be tolerated without giving rise to injunction or compensation. The actual distinction between lawful and unlawful acts is a matter to be decided by the legal authority (legislator and/or courts). The legal authority will often rely on the conventional view of what is and what is not acceptable. This view is, of course, totally vested in the particular values of a particular community (or groups within the community), e.g. the reasonable prudent *pater familias*.

immigration, legal liberty would have meant that a migrant – like a citizen – has the freedom to do as he likes provided that he does not unlawfully harm others; this freedom includes, in principle, freely accessing the territory of a receiving state. In this scenario the state can still exclude aliens, as it suffices that it makes laws whereby a particular exercise of a person's liberty must be curtailed because it poses an unacceptable risk to the legitimate interests of others. But it is clear that these laws will always have to be justified in terms of the curtailment of liberty. In addition, since these laws constitute the exception to the rule of individual liberty their construction should be restrictive, i.e. in the case of doubt the laws should be interpreted in favor of the migrant's liberty. In other words, legal liberty would create a situation whereby the migrant's interests in free movement are not only accounted for, but where his liberty is the rule and exclusion the exception.

Yet, under international law states do not have a legal obligation to recognize the principle of individual liberty. This may seem odd to some, because quintessential treaties on human rights (e.g. ICCP, ECHR) all contain explicit reference to the right to liberty. There are also special provisions of freedom of speech, freedom of movement within the territory, privacy, due process etc. However, further analysis shows us that these 'liberties' do not constitute a general concept of legal liberty. The reference to liberty is understood in the very specific sense of freedom from illegal detention and the like. The other liberties are founded on a substantive concept of human dignity and not autonomy. The liberties serve the purpose of promoting human dignity. It is clear that the concept of human dignity is something quite different from the concept of autonomy.[76] Now, some scholars of legal and political theory have taken up the challenge to interpret these liberties as a confirmation and expression of the concept of legal liberty against the background of promoting diversity and pluralism.[77] It is too early to decide if their enterprise has been a success. In domestic fundamental rights law, the liberty principle seems to have a much stronger position. Liberal democracies increasingly recognize that their legal and political system is founded on the concept of liberty. However, the concept of legal liberty does not extend to normal migrants.

76 In critical cases – cf. family life, sexual life, abortion, euthanasia – the two concepts may be incompatible. One way to express this difference between human dignity and autonomy is to understand the former as liberty *from* something (e.g. torture) and the latter as liberty *to* something (e.g. creating a business). In the context of immigration, legal liberty would be best understood as the alien's liberty *to* move into the territory of another state (rather than the alien's right to be free *from* the policing measures). The distinction has some practical relevance. If a state simply puts up fences and establishes limited border crossing opportunities then it becomes difficult to invoke the curtailment of a liberty *from*. This is precisely the issue of *de facto* exclusion, the factual measures under immigration policies.

77 See, inter alia, Serge Gutwirth, *Privacy and the Information Age* (Lanham/Oxford: Rowman & Littlefield, 2002), at 41–2, with reference to François Rigaux, *La protection de la vie privée et des autres biens de la personnalité* (1990) and Paul De Hert, *The Idea of Liberty in Western Legal Systems. The Unchallenged Rise of Social Control Explained*, Ph.D. thesis (2001).

Where does this all leave the normal migrant? The law does not organize the *rights of* the alien but only the *rights over* the alien. This is precisely the problem with the absence of the second safeguard: purpose-constrained state powers. A corollary of legal liberty is the notion that the powers of the state are constrained by the purposes for which these powers are granted. To ensure that liberty remains effectively the default position the state's possibility to interfere with the actions of an individual must stay limited. By the same token, it is accepted that the state has the legal power to issue 'prohibitions by law' and take (administrative) measures that render it impossible for individuals to do as they like. A seemingly powerful countermeasure is to grant the individual rights which he can invoke against a particular 'prohibition by law' or administrative measure. Yet, this solution is insufficient because it may entail that individual liberty is only warranted insofar as the individual can invoke a right. In other words, a system of rights can shift the default position from liberty to a license regime.

In fact what is needed is a means to attenuate the state's *creativity* and *initiative* to penetrate the realm of individual liberty. What if we can constrain the state not only from the outside (my rights versus the state), but also from within? The obvious candidate is to deny the state the condition of freedom or liberty. So unlike an individual human being the state lacks the condition of personal liberty.[78] It means that, in principle, the individual can do as he likes while the state cannot. In fact, the state cannot do as it likes because the state does not have any likings of itself other than its purposes.[79]

The connection between individual legal liberty and purpose-constrained state powers is very productive for nationals and residents as they benefit from individual legal liberty, as noted above. Yet for the normal migrant this connection becomes highly problematic: the alien cannot invoke individual legal liberty or subjective rights. As a result, the alien cannot benefit from the constraints on state power from purpose. This explains why two standard tests for judicial review of state actions – necessity and proportionality *sensu stricto* – do not apply to the exclusion of normal migrants. In other words, when it comes to normal migrant the state is not constrained by its purposes: the state is free.

78 See in general for the mechanics of purpose-constrained powers (in private law) W. Van Gerven, *Beginselen van Belgisch Privaatrecht I. Algemeen Deel* (Antwerpen: Standaard Wetenschappelijke Uitgeverij, 1969), at 173–5; and for its application to the state Walter Van Gerven, *Hoe Blauw is het Bloed van de Prins* (Antwerpen: Kluwer Rechtswetenschappen, 1984), at 9. See also Lothar Hirschberg, *Der Grundsatz der Verhältnismäßigkeit* (Göttingen: Verlag Otto Schwartz & Co., 1981), at 169. He makes the same point but starts from the opposite direction. While it makes sense to understand the powers and actions of the state as constrained by purpose, transferring the same notion to individual human beings becomes problematic; how are we to determine the appropriate, intended and actual purpose of individual action? See for a clear account of the role of *legal* liberties as a constitutive element of the (democratic) Rechtsstaat, Gutwirth, *Privacy and the Information Age*.

79 In the next chapter, I will try to show that even in the absence of individual legal liberty (or rather in the absence of legal liberty as the starting point) there are good reasons to adopt the view that state powers are purpose constrained.

This problematic situation is aggravated by the fact that the (non?-)legal status of the normal migrant is as much a matter of domestic as international law. It is ironically to the credit of domestic law that it at least *tries* or *pretends* to consider the normal migrant as a norm subject, since it determines what he ought to do (e.g. do not enter without permission). Domestic law may not establish any legal *rights* of the normal migrant, but at least it sets the legal *obligations* of the normal migrant.[80] By contrast, international law only establishes rights or power *over* the alien. In effect, in international law, the notion of purpose-constrained state powers is replaced by a problematic principle (or even rule) of state liberty. The principle of state liberty is probably best captured by the aphorism 'ce qui n'est pas interdit, est permis'. It is supposedly[81] confirmed as a rule of international law by the Permanent Court of International Justice in its ruling in the *Lotus* case (1927).

> Far from laying down a general prohibition to the effect that States may not extend the application of their laws and the jurisdiction of their courts to persons, property and acts outside their territory, it [international law] leaves them in this respect a wide measure of discretion ['liberté' in the French text] which is only limited in certain cases by prohibitive rules; as to other cases, every State remains free to adopt the principles which it regards as best and most suitable.[82]

Though primarily a rule of international law organizing the external sovereignty between states, it is clear how this principle can enhance the rule of inherent sovereign powers, and thus the power to exclude aliens without justification. The principle of state liberty allows states to issue rules applicable to persons outside their territory. In other words, the state liberty principle of international law grants states power *over* aliens, without establishing any rights *of* aliens. The only constraints on this power come from prohibitions from international law. At this point the rule of inherent sovereign power kicks in. It says that when it comes to the admission or exclusion of aliens states have an unfettered right, subject to the state's international legal obligations. And since there are no international legal obligations with regard to the normal migrant, it surrenders him to the 'free will' of states.

Up to now we have presented an analysis that understands immigration policies with regard to normal migrants as a practice of exclusion without justification. Moreover, the analysis is a legal one as it explains how this practice is legally

80 In Chapter 5 it is argued that this attempt to treat the normal migrant as a norm subject fails radically to the effect that immigration laws may fail to qualify as law *vis-à-vis* the excluded normal migrants.

81 Chapter 2 mobilizes the critical observation from scholars of international law against the principle of state liberty and the role of the *Lotus* case.

82 The Case of the S.S. 'Lotus' (*Fr. v Turk.*), PCIJ (7 Sep. 1927), (ser. A) no. 10, at 19.

sanctioned by the rule of inherent sovereign power. But the title of this chapter claims more; it is not just a legal topic, it is a legal *problem*. Why? The original concern has to do with basic moral intuitions. Exclusion has a major, often adverse, impact on the lives of a very large number of people (in the case at hand normal migrants). Furthermore, the act of exclusion is not an accidental or 'natural' phenomenon: it is an intentional act by officials. This by itself should already trigger profound reflections from moral philosophy, many of which will be addressed in Chapter 6. However, the problem here is not whether or not the exclusion is justified in the sense of being just, but rather the fact that the authorities simply do not justify the exclusion. The claim is that this poses not just a moral problem but a legal one. The legal intuition is that there is something wrong – from a legal perspective – if authorities can have it their way without any form of proper justification. The difficulty lies in the fact that the law itself makes this possible. So how can this practice of exclusion without justification be a *legal* problem, if it is sanctioned by a legal rule, i.e. the rule of inherent sovereign power? The way out is to argue that this rule is untenable from a legal perspective. I deliberately opt for the notion 'untenable' as it expresses an idea that the rule holds a position within the legal system and practice that cannot be maintained. It leaves room for different doctrinal views on legal change and legal validity. One may claim (*de lege lata*) that the rule already fails to count as law and so lacks legal force, which immediately affects the legal position of authorities and immigrants. Alternatively one may contend that there are overriding legal reasons to change the law (*de lege ferenda*). In any event, the arguments for both types are the same: the most basic legal arrangements, structure and practices of the law do not support this rule of inherent sovereign power. This precisely frames the central aim of the following chapters: debunking the rule of inherent sovereign power from the perspective of the law.

Chapter 2

Exclusion and standard prerogatives of sovereignty

The objective of the following chapters is to challenge the inherent sovereign power rule from the legal perspective. In this particular chapter we will try to come up with arguments directly derived from positive law. So, we will try to stay as close as possible to the standard sources and reasoning used by practicing lawyers. By the same token, if the inherent sovereign power rule is a rule directly related to the notion of sovereignty, we are faced with an insurmountable obstacle. For of all legal and political notions sovereignty is perhaps the most controversial: sovereignty is either redundant or incoherent.[1] The argument for redundancy claims that sovereignty is outdated. The argument for incoherence asserts that sovereignty is confused, if not contradictory.[2]

This chapter will largely circumvent the controversy. First, it neither challenges nor justifies the notion of sovereignty. It argues that the notion of sovereignty cannot account for the power to exclude without justification. To make this claim one need not challenge or justify the notion of sovereignty. We may simply deny that a particular notion (*in casu* sovereignty) does comprise a certain property (*in casu* the power to exclude without justification). This claim does not presuppose a full account of the notion itself. In addition, for the purpose of explaining a notion it often is of little help to state the properties that are not comprised in the notion. Second, the controversy is largely an academic one, which concerns primarily political scientists, political theorists and legal philosophers. Most legal practitioners are rarely bothered by the conceptual problems provoked by sovereignty, or in any event, sovereignty is not specifically more problematic than other legal concepts. The reason is that the issue of sovereignty rarely makes it to court and if it does, it is often a very technical and legalistic matter (e.g. border disputes, economic zones, etc.). In such cases the concept of sovereignty is not so much at stake, but rather the distribution of the advantages associated with sovereignty. Third, and most importantly, the structure of sovereignty has little to do with the relationship between state and a normal migrant seeking admission. So in a way

1 Bert Van Roermund, 'Sovereignty: Unpopular and Popular' in Neil Walker (ed.), *Sovereignty in Transition* (Oxford/Portland: Hart Publishing, 2003), at 33–41.

2 Ibid., at 34.

the problem is not sovereignty. What is at stake is the belief that sovereignty can account for a state's power to exclude migrants without justification.

Let us consider the following minimalist definition of sovereignty, which probably corresponds with most textbooks on international law.[3] Sovereignty is the ultimate or supreme[4] power or authority to regulate. This authority governs two types of relationships: internal and external. First, sovereignty claims obedience from the subjects within the sphere where the sovereignty is claimed (internal relationship). Second, by virtue of its sovereignty a sovereign entity (*in casu* a state) claims respect from other sovereign states to the effect that other states do not interfere with its sovereign rule within the sphere of its sovereignty (external relationship).[5] This basic description immediately explains why the conceptual problems associated with sovereignty itself (as opposed to the inherent sovereign power rule) are hardly relevant in legal practice. Conflicts about sovereignty are always about the two (or more) competing rule makers, internally or externally. At the external level the conflict is typically about one state trying to take over – *de jure* or *de facto* – the rule-making power of another state. The contemporary European version is the penetration of the supra-national European order (EU and ECHR) into the domestic legal order of the Member States. Internal conflicts

3 For an overview of the different attempts to define the notion of sovereignty, see Stéphane Beaulac, *The Power of Language in the Making of International Law. The Word Sovereignty in Bodin and Vattel and the Myth of Westphalia* (Leyden/Boston: Martinus Nijhoff Publishers, 2004), at 1–2. Beaulac provides an extensive quotation from Richard Bilder's 'Perspectives on Sovereignty in the Current Context: An American Viewpoint', 20 *Canada-United States LJ* (1994), at 9.

4 The notion of 'supreme' is of course highly problematic if taken in its literal and theological sense (rather than practical). But this is not the place to address this issue. See Siegfried Van Duffel, 'Sovereignty as a Religious Concept', 90 *The Monist* 126 (2007).

5 This notion of sovereignty counters the objections from redundancy. It puts rule making at the center of the meaning of sovereignty, rather than coercion and 'commands backed by force'. Also it leaves room for alternative sources of law. Studies conducted by so-called legal pluralists successfully challenge the idea that the state has the monopoly of law making. See the case studies of the lex mercatoria, regulations issued by multinational enterprises, mega-insolvencies, labor law and human rights as discussed in the contributions of Bercusson, Bianchi, Flood and Skordaki, Mertens, Robé and Teubner in G. Teubner (ed.), *Global Law without a State* (Ashgate/Dartmouth: Hants/Burlington, 1997). In my view legal pluralism does not challenge the conception of state sovereignty itself. For the most plausible conception of state sovereignty (which also corresponds with Jean Bodin's concept of sovereignty) is *not about the monopoly* of law making, but about being the *ultimate or supreme law-maker*. The state as the supreme law-maker can and does leave ample room for other law-making entities (local or global) to create legal orders. Legal pluralism convincingly describes these cases. But the state may step in and *replace* (not merely constrain or facilitate) the legal order created by other law-making entities with its own state-made legal order. A case in point is the replacement of canonic law with state-made law in the area of family law and the labor status of the clergy. Other cases are failed regimes of self-regulation by the industry. Here too, states stepped in and put in place new legal standards (e.g. recent comprehensive financial reporting laws, securities laws). Finally, this minimalist notion of sovereignty is not necessarily linked to the phenomenon of the nation-state or liberal democracy.

about sovereignty are less fundamental and frequent since the demise of the secular authority of ecclesiastical institutions. Yet federal states still have their fair share of issues on jurisdiction. And even within unitary states, different branches of government often seek to expand their rule-making power at the expense of each other. Sporadically, the same goes for the decentralized levels of government (municipal, provincial, regional, national, etc.). In these cases what is at stake is not so much the notion of the ultimate rule-making power, but rather *who* is to hold this power (with regard to what subject matter and persons). As a result, the practical and conceptual problems (redundancy and incoherence) associated with sovereignty do not really pose a problem for our discussion.

In fact, these observations anticipate our arguments to the effect that sovereignty cannot account for the inherent sovereign power rule. Why is that? The reason is quite simple. Sovereignty is about competing claims for rule-making power. It governs the relationship between actual and potential claimants of the rule-making power. The normal migrant does not contest the receiving state's rule-making power. Migrants do not seek to take over the receiving state's power to make rules (*de jure* or *de facto*). Neither do migrants seek admission to establish a new legal order. To put it differently, sovereignty is simply not the kind of vehicle that can capture the relationship between the receiving state and the normal migrant seeking admission. In this chapter we will elaborate on this issue and discuss some typical legal arrangements that intuitively seem to support the rule of inherent sovereign power. The most obvious candidate is the set of prerogatives associated with territorial sovereignty: territorial integrity, *jus excludendi alios* and the state's title over its territory. At first glance these prerogatives seem to cater to the rule of inherent sovereign power. Yet closer examination will show that these arrangements simply cannot capture the relationship between the state and the normal migrant seeking admission.

Conversely, the notion of state liberty as discussed in the Chapter 1 is clearly an enabler for the exclusion of migrants without justification. If states are indeed free to do as they like – subject to their international obligations – then surely they may exclude migrants without justification. As a result, rather than showing that the inherent sovereign power rule does not follow from state liberty, we will challenge state liberty in itself. And even if we cannot fully refute the notion of state liberty, we will try to show that if liberty for the state were to have any meaning, it must be constrained. This last argument appears rather philosophical and far removed from our standard positive law reasoning. Still, I hope it will become clear, that this last argument is in its nature not different from any other legal argument attempting to shape, understand and underpin one of law's greatest inventions: a legal entity's (i.e. a non-human being) capacity to perform material and legal acts.

Territorial integrity and *jus excludendi alios*

There is a view that if a state were to have an obligation to admit subjects from another state, the latter may actually intrude upon the domestic affairs of the former.[6] Similarly, when an increasing number of foreign nationals have a right to stay in the territory, this territory may cease to remain part of the state's territory, which affects territorial integrity. In both scenarios immigration poses a threat to the right of non-intrusion and territorial integrity respectively. Therefore, these two central features of sovereignty justify the state's right to exclude migrants without justification. This line of reasoning is deeply flawed. Migrants cannot challenge the territorial integrity of a state, because individual migrants cannot make jurisdictional claims (only entities of public (international) law can do this). The mere presence in and even physical occupation of territory by migrants does not constitute a threat to the territorial integrity of a state, because the territorial integrity and the jurisdiction associated with it are essentially about claims to legal authority. Migrants can make private property claims with regard to state territory, but even when their claims are successful, the territory in which the property right is vested remains part of the state territory. As we will see later, the relationship between a state and its territory is not one of property. It follows that a state's right to territorial integrity can never justify the exclusion of migrants without good reason, because the right to territorial integrity is solely directed to other states, not migrants.

A similar argument applies to the right to non-intrusion into internal affairs. Migrants cannot pose a threat to the domestic jurisdiction of a state, as they cannot and do not claim any domestic jurisdiction. This argument might only be valid if the migrants are considered to be representatives of their source state. Under international law, only particular categories of physical persons may be in a position to represent and legally commit a state. In most, if not all cases, candidate immigrants do not fall in this category.[7]

As to the so-called *jus excludendi alios* it is not evident that apart from other states, 'alios' also include individuals (migrants). And in light of our discussion of the right to territorial integrity and non-intrusion it should be clear why the *jus excludendi alios* is not directed at migrants. Actually all three prerogatives of sovereignty discussed above are designed to maintain the state's sovereignty and are therefore exclusively directed to other states.[8] In other words, territorial integrity, right to non-intrusion and *jus excludendi alios*

6 Nafziger, 'The General Admission of Aliens under International Law', 77 *AJIL* (1983) at 804. Nafziger only reports this view, but he does not agree with it.

7 What to do with stateless migrants? They can never be considered to be in a position to challenge the state's sovereignty in favor of their source state. In any event, to the extent that immigrants are intruding the policies of the receiving state it often does not favor the official interests of the source state (e.g. activism of Cubans in the USA against the Cuban Government; Turkish nationals of Kurdish ethnicity residing in Germany against the Turkish state).

8 When I say that individuals cannot challenge the jurisdiction of the state, I mean that they cannot challenge the legal authority of the state. The capabilities to effectively dominate the domestic affairs within its territory may be affected by migrants, as well as other material phenomena (catastrophes, wars, multinationals, etc.). This does not affect the concept of sovereignty, which is essentially about (legal) authority. For an excellent explanation – including a simple but powerful matrix – of the

can never account for the relationship between a state and a migrant. It follows that these prerogatives cannot justify the state's power to exclude migrants without justification.

Self-preservation is another state 'prerogative' which is necessary for the continuity of a state.[9] The idea of self-preservation relies heavily on an anthropomorphic conception of the state: the state, like a human being, seeks and has the right to preserve itself. Although the concept is outdated, it is still deeply rooted in the language of international law.[10] In addition, in the second half of the twentieth century another anthropomorphic conception popped up in international law: the self-preservation and self-determination of peoples.[11] Contrary to the state, which is as a matter of definition an institutional and administrative construction, the concept of people seems prima facie much closer to the concept of a human being. Yet, the moment one leaves the concept of an individual human being and enters the realm of collectivities, the concepts that applied to individual human beings cease to have the same meaning when applied to collectivities.[12] Of course, one can make sense of the concept of self-preservation, people and state, without falling into the anthropomorphic fallacy. Probably the most persuasive attenuation of the self-preservation argument is not the refutation of its anthropomorphic character, but the fact that the notion of self-preservation is inherently contextual. It is not always evident that the self-preservation of a people is at stake.[13] It follows that the state should argue and justify why preservation is at stake in a particular case. Consequently the state's right to self-preservation cannot account for the acclaimed right to exclude migrants without justification.

distinction between state authority and capabilities, see Jack Donnelly, 'State Sovereignty and Human Rights', *Human Rights & Human Welfare*, Working Paper No. 21, (2004).], at 4, available at http://www.du.edu/korbel/hrhw/workingpapers/2004/21-donnelly-2004.pdf.

9 The US Supreme Court rulings explicitly state that the power to exclude aliens is essential to the preservation of the sovereign nation, see Chapter 1.

10 See, for example, Cassese's textbook on international law, where he quotes US Secretary of State Robert Lansing in 1921: 'National safety is as dominant in the *life* of a nation as *self-preservation is in the life of an individual*' (both emphases added). Antonio Cassese, *International Law* (Oxford: Oxford University Press, 2001), at 89.

11 See e.g. Fatsah Ouguergouz, *The African Charter on Human and People's Rights. A Comprehensive Agenda for Human Dignity and Sustainable Democracy in Africa* (The Hague/London/New York: Martinus Nijhoff Publishers, 2003).

12 It does not mean that we cannot apply the term liberty or self-preservation to the concept of a people. It simply means that this liberty is to be distinguished from the concept of individual liberty. Similarly the concept of self-preservation when applied to a people should be understood to be categorically differently from the self-preservation of a human being. In other words, my objection to the concept of the people's right to self-preservation is one about the circumstances in which one can use/apply to the concept meaningfully.

13 Nafziger also argues that self-preservation cannot justify the discretionary power to exclude aliens. As a matter of plain empirical fact, the demise or extinction of a state or nation is simply not at hand in the context of immigration. Nafziger (1983), at 817–18.

Property theory

Some have argued that, like a private property owner, the state may prevent persons who do not belong to it from trespassing on its property.[14] In other words, the state's alleged power to exclude without justification relies on a type of property ownership of its territory. This argument presumes two things: first the relationship between the state and its territory is one of property; second, this property (-like) right provides a right to exclude individuals without justification. Modern scholars of international law have shown that the first presumption is wrong: the relationship between a state and its territory cannot be understood in terms of property.[15] This means that the second presumption also becomes obsolete. Yet, since the property argument has some intuitive force, I will briefly address the two underlying presumptions. The first relates to the question about the legal nature of (state) territory.[16] There are roughly three competing theories that account for this legal nature:[17] object or patrimonial theory; Eigenschaftstheorie and competence theory.

According to the 'object theory' a state has a property-like right to its territory. This right is one of international law. It has two typical features in common with property rights under private law: the power to exclude others (*in casu* other states); and the right to freely dispose of the territory.[18] The state exercises its right over the territory like a landowner exercises its right over his private property (but this is *not* the same as a real right under private law[19]).[20] Though the object theory

14 P. Heilborn, *Das System des Voelkerrechts* (1892), at 22, referred to by Richard Plender, *International Migration Law* (Dordrecht/Boston/The Hague: Martinus Nijhoff Publishers, 1988), at 72 and endnote 87. François Rigaux, 'L'immigration: droit international et droits fondamentaux' in *Les Droits de l'homme au Seuil du Troisième Millénair. Mélanges en Hommage à Pierre Lambert* (Brussels: Bruylant, 2000), at 700, who does not support this view but simply reports it. See also Chapter 6 for a discussion of the classic international law theorists.

15 Charles Rousseau, *Droit International Public. Les sujets de droit*, vol. 2 (Paris: Editions Sirey, 1974), at 51; Malcom N. Shaw, *Title to Territory in Africa. International Legal Issues* (Oxford: Clarendon Press, 1986), 15, who actually, in his mixed view, leaves room for property-like features to account for cession of territory, leases etc.; R.Y. Jennings, *The Acquisition of Territory in International Law* (Manchester: Manchester University Press, 1963), at 3.

16 In this respect, I relied heavily on Schoenborn's description of the development of the different territorial conceptions from antiquity to the times of modern constitutional states. W. Schoenborn, 'La Nature Juridique du Territoir', in *Académie de Droit International. Recueil des Cours*, vol. 30, (Paris: Librairie Hachette, 1929).

17 I left out other theories for I believe them to be less serious (or appealing) contenders or versions of one of the three doctrines (e.g. Lebensraum theory, territory as on object of sovereign real rights, territorial as a limit of competence, mixed theory). See Rousseau, *Droit International Public. Les sujets de droit*, at 48–50, 52–4; Shaw, *Title to Territory*, at 15. As to the mixed view see *supra* n. 15.

18 Schoenborn, 'La Nature Juridique du Territoir', at 104.

19 Schoenborn shows how from the times of the late feudal states up to the end of the absolutist states, distinct concepts such as 'Obereigentum' or 'eminent domain', imperium and dominium resulted in a real right conception of territory. Though this clearly influenced the Object theory, the latter must be distinguished from private property in terms of the powers associated with it. Ibid., at 92–102.

20 Shaw *Title to Territory*, at 13–14.

may at first sight account for legal acts under international law (such as the cession and lease of parts of state territory) it has some serious weaknesses. First, it is based on a confusion of the notions of property and sovereignty. Property is established in the sole interest of the owner, while sovereignty is granted to allow the state to fulfill its functions and realize certain goals. Furthermore, property (in its more traditional sense) is primarily about material acts (collection of fruits, use, transformation or destruction of the asset) and legal acts (transfer, assignment) are rather secondary. On the contrary, sovereignty is essentially about legal acts (legislative functions, administrative and judicial), while the material acts (e.g. use of violence, coercion) are only carried out on the basis of prior legal acts and are conditioned and justified by those legal acts.[21] Third, the object theory cannot really account for the situation of multiple states on the same territory, such as federal states. Moreover, there is some domestic case law that contradicts the property conception.[22] How does the object theory account for a situation where the state, or even a foreign state, takes a private property interest in parts of state territory?[23] Finally, the object theory has serious difficulties in accounting for mutations in state territory. The object theory allows the state to detach itself from the territory. This is highly problematic, because a state without territory ceases to be a state – a fundamental principle of modern international law. The object theory cannot account for this principle.[24]

The Eigenschaftstheorie developed as a response to (especially the last) objections to the object theory. Under this theory the territory is an integral part of the personality of the state. It follows that an attack on the territory of the state is not an attack on, or a violation of, the property of the state, but it directly affects the personality of the state.[25] The main problem with the Eigenschaftstheorie is that, under modern international law, a mutation in (a part of the) territory does not affect the personality of the state. A similar objection is that this theory cannot account for transfer of parts of the territory.[26] The theory that is believed to accommodate the objections raised against the object theory and Eigenschaftstheorie is the competence theory. The starting point is the state competence, i.e. the power to command. The territory is the local sphere where the state exercises its competence. The theory distinguishes three types of state competence:[27]

21 Rousseau, *Droit International Public. Les sujets de droit*, at 49, with reference to Basdevant's 'Règles générales', *RCADI* (1936), IV, 615–16.

22 Ibid., at 49, with reference to French case law of administrative courts in 1935, where the territorial sea were not considered to belong to the public domain (i.e. the property holding of the states under Civil and Administrative law), while the territorial sea is a part of the territory and falls under the sovereignty of the (French) state.

23 Schoenborn, 'La Nature Juridique du Territoir', at 112.

24 Ibid., at 113.

25 Ibid., at 114–15; Shaw, *Title to Territory*, at 14.

26 Schoenborn, 'La Nature Juridique du Territoir', at 116.

27 The following is a summary of Schoenborn's discussion of the Competence theory, ibid., at 117–19.

- Substantive competence (*ratione materiae*): it covers the competence regarding all possible areas where the state invokes its sovereign rights: military, judiciary, finance;
- Competence over persons (*ratione personae*). By virtue of its personal sovereignty the state may decide which persons are to acquire the quality of citizen and who should be admitted to the national community;
- Local competence (*ratione loci*): or territorial sovereignty. The territorial sovereignty enables the state to, inter alia, annex or cede territory.

The concept of territorial sovereignty is crucial, but the territory itself – (the physical object) is only secondary. There is actually – in legal terms – no real relationship between a person (the state) and a thing (territory). In fact there is only one side: the state having certain legal qualities and capacities. In other words, the territory is nothing more than a reflection of a particular legal quality of the state. One of the advantages of the Competence theory is that it corresponds with the techniques of public law, whereby state prerogatives are understood as simple competences granted to officials to fulfill certain functions of general interest.[28] Moreover, it accounts for a situation where the state, or even a foreign state, takes a private property interest in parts of state territory. Private property and territorial sovereignty have become fully compatible.[29] Finally, the theory can address both territorial mutations and the phenomenon of multiple states in the same territory.[30] The Competence theory has become the dominant view among modern scholars of international law.

This short discussion on the legal doctrines concerning the legal nature of state territory showed that the state's claim on its territory – pursuant to the concept of territorial sovereignty – is not one of property, but of primarily jurisdictional competence. Even if the state had a property-like claim on the territory, the powers associated with this form of holding cannot be the same as private, or even public, property. I want to challenge the second presumption of the property argument, which asserts that the property (-like) right provides a right to exclude individuals without justification. First, the proponents of the object theory – though referring to the concept of property, are actually speaking of a property of international law ('*propriété du droit des gens*'). The *jus excludendi* that also applies to this right is distinct from that in private law. In private law the right to exclude others is aimed at other owners or persons, while the 'alios' under the object theory refers to other states. Nowhere is it mentioned that, apart from other states, 'alios' also includes individuals (migrants).[31]

28 Rousseau, *Droit International Public. Les sujets de droit*, at 51.

29 Schoenborn, 'La Nature Juridique du Territoir', at 119.

30 Rousseau, *Droit International Public. Les sujets de droit*, at 52; Schoenborn, 'La Nature Juridique du Territoir', at 119.

31 I do not believe that an *a fortiori* argument like '*qui peut le plus, qui peut le moins*' will work here, as this would imply that the power to exclude a state is necessarily higher or stronger than the power to exclude persons that are non-states. But this is not the case. The difference between the two powers is not a matter of degree; the difference is categorical. The power to exclude other states is particular because it allows the state to deny another state to exercise jurisdiction over its territory. It is clear that a simple property right over the territory will not do to reject the claims of

Second, while there is a moral foundation for the 'comprehensiveness' of the powers associated with private property (or the 'sticks in the bundle of rights'), the same moral foundation cannot apply to the state's 'property' right to its territory. The concept of private property has a particular status in liberal theory. According to some scholars of liberal theory (and especially the libertarian strand) the ultimate foundation for private property is liberty and autonomy. Others find the ultimate moral foundation for private property in the concept of human dignity. From a moral perspective, the two foundations – human dignity and liberty – are very different. However, they share at least one property – they are essentially linked to individual human beings. Both are values that essentially apply to individual physical human beings.[32] Private property both justifies and protects these values. Since these values are believed to be essential to humanity (or at the least 'Western humanity'), the scope of the rights/powers associated with private property is rather comprehensive. To a large extent the right to exclude under private property has an absolute discretionary character. So the question is whether the state's international property right to its territory can benefit from a similar absolute discretionary right to exclude. I believe that here the analogy fails. In the context of the state there is no such thing as liberty or dignity of state comparable to human liberty or dignity. The meaning of individual liberty or human dignity that justifies the right to exclude under private property, cannot justify the state's power to exclude without justification. For the state as a matter of meaningful language cannot have individual liberty or human dignity. Therefore the ultimate justification for the exclusionary powers associated with private property simply cannot work for the state's 'property' right.

Third, if one still believes that the state's territorial 'property' right grants the state a power to exclude without justification, which is identical to the exclusionary powers under private property, it is equally justified to believe that the typical constraints on private property should apply.[33] Two legal constraints are particularly challenging for current state practices. First, in theory depending on the factual circumstances, it is conceivable to consider the state's ownership of its territory to be monopolistic and dominant. This may mean that the current possibilities and conditions for accessing and using the state's territory by migrants is actually the result of an abuse of a dominant position by the state. So, one should try to find the benchmark for the fair market conditions for accessing state

another state, because property rights do not give any jurisdiction. By the same token, it is odd to invoke the right to exclude other states, if one wants to exclude migrants. The right to exclude other states is about competing claims of jurisdiction, whereas the normal migrant doesn't claim any jurisdiction over the territory of the receiving state. Individual migrants simply cannot claim jurisdiction, as this matter belongs, by definition, to states.

32 There are of course borderline cases like the 'inhumane treatment' of animals, but I believe one can safely assert that the two values are essentially human.

33 The application of these constraints actually constitutes a *reductio in absurdum*: for it shows the incapacity of property and in particular private property concepts to account for exclusion without justification by the state.

territory. What would be the conditions if the state territory were divided between multiple owners? Second, as mentioned earlier, municipal courts have adopted the legal principle of the abuse of rights and in particular, the abuse of property rights. There can be abuse of a property right if the damage to interests of the other is so high compared to the benefits that it is unreasonable to exercise this right.[34] One can easily see the benefits for migrants in this legal institution. Migrants need not challenge the state's right in itself. They just have to challenge the way the state exercises its property right. Moreover – and most importantly – the migrants do not need a *right* to free movement or settlement to challenge the exclusionary powers of the state. For under the judicial principle of the abuse of rights (partially based on tort law), it suffices that the plaintiff has an *interest*. As discussed earlier under positive law, the normal migrant does not have a right to free movement or settlement. Neither does he have a legitimate interest in immigration. But if the problem is framed in terms of property and assets, the normal migrant may try to prove that he has an interest in using some parts of the territory. Things are getting out of hand; applying principles of competition law and abuse of rights to state territory turns the discussion into a legal fantasy. Maybe so. But this just goes to show property is really an implausible vehicle for framing the relationship between state and migrant.

State liberty

Outdated and incoherent

The prerogatives discussed above are, in themselves, not contested but they simply cannot account for the rule of inherent sovereign power. By contrast, state liberty has a dubious legal status but seems to support the rule of inherent sovereign power. The principle of state liberty is captured by the aphorism '*ce qui n'est pas interdit, est permis*'. This was supposedly[35] confirmed as a rule of international law by the Permanent Court of International Justice in its ruling of the *Lotus* case (1927).[36] Though primarily a rule of international law organizing the external sovereignty between states, we have already shown how this vehicle endorsed the inherent sovereign power rule. Yet, the notion of state liberty does not hold. First,

34 G.E. van Maanen, *Eigendomsschijnbewegingen. Juridische, historische en politiek-filosofische opmerkingen over eigendom* (Nijmegen: Ars Aequi Libri, 1987), at 77–8.

35 It should be noted that some scholars of international law argue that the *Lotus* case did not establish the rule of state liberty, but that this principle is just the result of a misinterpretation of the *Lotus* case. See Lowe Vaughan, 'Jurisdiction' in Malcom D. Evans (ed.), *International Law* (Oxford: Oxford University Press, 2003), at 335. I will presume that the state liberty principle is not the outcome of a misinterpretation of the *Lotus* case, but that the *Lotus* case did establish the principle of state liberty. If the liberty principle appears to be really nothing more than a misinterpretation of the *Lotus* case, it would only reinforce my normative claim (see *infra*).

36 See *The Case of the S.S. 'Lotus' (Fr. v Turk.)*, 1927 *PCIJ*. (ser. A) No. 10, at 19 (7 Sep.).

it is an incorrect reflection of actual practice. Second, state liberty is based on two outdated ideas: state positivism and an anthropomorphic conception of the state.[37]

The *Lotus* case may be, in fact, an incorrect reflection of state practices. The ruling finds that when states are contesting the scope of another state's jurisdiction they are trying to find a rule that limits the jurisdiction of another state. But this is not what states do. They do not try to find such a rule, they just invoke that another state does not have the right to do so. The burden of proof lies with the state that tries to extend its powers.[38] This argument coincides with the relativity of the reserved domain. The reserved domain or domestic jurisdiction is a dynamic concept that must be viewed in the historical context of international relations.[39] No matter is *a priori* excluded from the realm of international law, including the exclusion of migrants.[40] The reserved domain at best serves as a prima facie instrument.[41]

State liberty is the unfortunate legacy of two outdated ideas: (state) positivism of the nineteenth century and anthropomorphic conception of the state from the eighteenth century.[42] The first idea takes the state as the prius of international relations. Using this theory, the state is only bound by positive (international) law to the extent that it (the state) consented to it. It is then easy to see how one comes to the idea of state liberty. This position is then reinforced by the anthropomorphic conception of the state. According to this conception the state – similar to a human being – is the holder of fundamental and inalienable rights and freedoms. So like an individual human being the state should have the liberty to do as it likes unless prohibited by an explicit rule. The theory of state positivism is incorrect. Even if the characterization of international law is fundamentally consensual (which is also debatable), it doesn't follow that the sovereign is free to do as it wishes.[43] Neither does it follow that the state is prior to international law. On the contrary while state sovereignty allows the state to determine what the laws are in its territory, the state cannot regulate the rules that define the conditions for state sovereignty.[44] Third, the principle of state liability *vis-à-vis* other states also rejects an

37 For a 'genealogy' of the principle of state liberty see two excellent studies by Professor Kolb. Robert Kolb, *Réflexions de philosophie du droit international. Problèmes fondementaux du droit international public: Théorie et philosophie du droit international, La Collection de droit international* (Brussels: Éditions Bruylant/Éditions de l'Université Libre de Bruxelles, 2003); Robert Kolb, 'La règle résiduelle de liberté en droit public ("Tout ce qui n'est pas interdit est permis"), aspects théoriques', 34 *Revue Belge de Droit International* 100 (2001).

38 Vaughan, 'Jurisdiction', at 335.

39 Nafziger (1983), at 820.

40 Ibid.

41 Kolb, *Philosophie du droit international*, at 338.

42 Ibid., at 105–9; 117–18; 335.

43 Vaughan, 'Jurisdiction', at 335.

44 See Anthony D'Amato, 'The Concept of Human Rights in International Law', 82 *Columbia Law Review* 1110 (1982), at 1113 who refers to H.L.A. Hart. I paraphrased D'Amato's reference to Hart. See also Rousseau, *Droit International Public. Les sujets de droit*, at 60.

absolutist or discretionary conception of state powers.[45] The anthropomorphic concept of the state is, as we have seen earlier, also highly problematic. The reasons why individual human beings should be entitled to liberty cannot be applied *mutatis mutandis* to the state. Interestingly, the idea of state liberty did not take root in domestic public law. Though the state (in particular the government) has some discretionary powers, in the end all its powers are constrained by the purposes for which those powers were granted in the first place. Some scholars had already applied this concept to international law in the era of the *Lotus* case.[46] Finally, even if one were to accept the anthropomorphic conception of state liberty, there is still no way to account for the absolute character of the power to exclude without justification. Even the concept of individual liberty does not grant a human being absolute rights or powers.[47]

45 Rousseau, *Droit International Public. Les sujets de droit*, at 61.

46 See the following powerful account.

> Jadis absolu [les droits des États], ne rencontrant que les limites imposés par des accords volontaires, ils sont maintenant relatifs, n'ayant que la portée indispensable pour répondre au but social qui les a créés; en d'autres termes tandis qu'autrefois on les fondait sur l'individualisme, on les base désormais sur la solidarité. [While the rights of states were previously considered absolute – only constrained by voluntary agreements, today they are relative with only a scope indispensable to cater to the social purpose which created them; in other words, whereas previously [the rights of states] were founded on individualism, they are now grounded on solidarity] (translation BS)

N. Politis, *Les Nouvelles Tendances du Droit International* (1927), at 41 cited in Kolb, *Philosophie du droit international*, at 337 with reference in fn. 393.

47 There is, however, an intuitively attractive argument in favor of state liberty, or at least the state's freedom to treat migrants as they like (subject to international legal obligations), i.e. reverse discrimination. Abandoning the power to exclude without justification would mean that the state must justify the exclusion of a normal migrant *vis-à-vis* the excluded migrant. It means that the state should balance not only among state interests, but also between state interests and the migrant's interest to immigration. In a lot of cases, states do not even justify their acts *vis-à-vis* their own nationals. If states can ignore the interests of their own citizens, *a fortiori* they may certainly ignore the interests of migrants. But with similar intuitive force we may state the exact opposite: it is because the normal migrant is not a member of the particular legal and political community that the state should account for his interests in the particular case of immigration. A member of the community may take part in a larger trade-off and balancing between his interests and the interests of other community members. It follows from this trade-off that the state not only owes special duties to its nationals but may also impose particular burdens on them. Since the normal migrant cannot benefit from the upside of the special treatment reserved for nationals, he should not bear the burden. In other words, there should be cases where the national may be treated worse than a migrant. In fact positive law confirms this view. For example standing case law and legal doctrine of the European Community hold that, in principle, Member States may treat their own nationals more unfairly than nationals of other Member States. See for a general discussion of the case law and legal doctrine on reverse discrimination P.J.G. Kapteyn and P. VerLoren van Themaat, *Introduction to the Law of the European Communities. From Maastricht to Amsterdam* (London/The Hague/Boston: Kluwer Law International, 1998), at 170–1, 581–4; Paul Craig and Graínne De Búrca, *EU Law. Text, Cases, and Materials* (Oxford: Oxford University Press, 2003), at 720; Peter Oliver and Malcom Jarvis, *Free Movement of Goods in the European Community Under Articles 28 to 30 of the EC Treaty* (London: Sweet and Maxwell, 2003), at 146–53.

Identifying the free will of the state

The capacity to act on the basis of *liberty* can be contrasted with agency based on *competence* – to be more precise: *purpose-oriented and constrained* competences. Another way to refute the liberty thesis with regard to the state is to show that state powers are to be understood in terms of purpose-constrained and oriented powers. This argument partially anticipates our discussion on the proportionality principle in Chapter 7. Though this argument is derived more from the structure of law, rather than particular statements of law, it fits the general doctrine of (domestic) public law according to which the state actions are purpose oriented and constrained. The typical justification for the concept of purpose constrained state powers is the protection of the individual liberty of citizens. Yet I believe there is also another reason why state liberty should be replaced by purpose. It has to do with the possibility of actions by the state. From a legal perspective, the state is understood as a legal entity having legal personality, which means that it is holder of rights and obligations. In general, rights and obligations are the legal *effect* caused by particular facts. Legal attribution rules make it possible to connect particular material facts with legal facts or legal acts. Their legal *effects* (rights, obligations, status) are attributed to a particular person (physical person or legal entity). Obviously, only physical persons can produce material facts, because legal entities lack the capacity to perform physical acts. Yet, pursuant to a special attribution rule, the act performed by the physical person who acts as an organ of the legal entity, is considered to be an act performed by the legal entity self. In other words, through its organs, the legal entity has the capacity to perform material acts.

This capacity to perform material acts is *fully absorbed* by the legal entity's capacity to undergo the legal effects of material acts. In fact, the only *material* acts that are considered to be performed by the legal entity self, are those that produce a legal effect attributable to the legal entity. So, the acts attributable to a legal entity are either a legal act (e.g. the entering into of a contract) or a legal fact (e.g. a tort). A purely material act with no legal effect is not attributable to a legal entity. It follows that when it comes to legal entities the notion of *action* is rather irrelevant. To put it differently the legal entity's capacity to act, if any, is an exclusively legal matter. Accordingly, the legal attribution rules are in a sense self-sufficient for making the notion of the action by legal entities intelligible. There is simply no action beyond legal effects. In other words, the notion of the legal entity's capacity for *action* must not be taken at face value, it is rather a capacity to undergo and produce legal effects.

The sovereign state is probably an important exception. I will argue that it makes sense and is conceptually necessary to understand the state as having the capacity for *material* action. The argument goes as follows. Like other legal entities the state is only accessible through its organs. But in the case of the sovereign state the legal attribution rules are not self-sufficient. In a lot of instances the legal attribution rules provide sufficient guidance to determine whether or not a particular action performed by a physical person must be attributed to that person or to the state. In all these cases, there is no point in identifying the material action separately from its legal effects. Yet, from time to time the material act is not about producing legal effects pursuant to the attribution rules, but rather determining what counts as a legal effect in the first place. Contrary to the other legal entities, the state has the control over its own attribution rules. It controls what facts will produce legal effects attributable to the state, because it determines ultimately what counts as law and what does not. There are legal rules that determine the procedure for changing the law, but they can mandate neither the *initiative* to make a change nor its content. In other words, there is an essentially non- or pre-legal aspect to legal change. To put it differently, there is an aspect of legal change that involves a material act that cannot be fully absorbed by its legal effects identifiable by a legal attribution rule. Not only does constituting and amending the constitution involve a so-called pre-legal initiative, but also all law setting and law applying presuppose more or less non-pre-mandated actions (i.e. decisionism).[48]

So what? The question arises to whom we should attribute this material fact, this 'initiative'. Again in the case of other legal entities, e.g. corporations, it does not matter to whom one attributes the material act: what matters is to whom one assigns the legal effects. This attribution takes place on the basis of the legal attribution rules, which ultimately do not depend on the legal entity and its organs. The same mechanism cannot work for the sovereign state. The 'initiative' cannot be fully understood in terms of legal effects; the whole question of whether or not the initiative produces legal effects depends on whether or not it is taken by the state. This follows from the notion that only the sovereign (state) has a power of initiative. Individual human beings must utter the words to change the law, but these become meaningless or weak if they do not claim the authority on behalf of an entity that is sovereign.[49] In other words, there are material acts (i.e. initiatives) that cannot be understood purely in terms of legal effects determinable according to legal attribution rules. Unlike other

48 See Chapter 3.

49 We must distinguish between making a claim in the name of a *normative system* (e.g. morality) to *justify* an action, and a claim in the name of an *entity* to *attribute actions* to that entity. The two are connected. The law, a normative system, contains attribution rules. The same goes for morality. But while the normative systems need not adhere to a particular hierarchy or lexical order of values, claims in the name of an entity are different. It matters in whose (entity) name you act, irrespective of the normative justification of the act. You must make sure that you make the claim in the name of an entity that has at least the potential competence to take the initiative. Moreover, you must make sure that your competitor or opponent is not making a claim in the name of an entity that stands at least in potential higher on the hierarchy of competences. This 'formal' proliferation of invoking (or appealing to) more senior entities will require alleged agents to claim to be acting in the name of a sovereign entity.

legal entities, however, these material acts cannot be attributed to the physical human beings performing them; the initiative must be attributed to the sovereign state.

The problem is how to attribute this material initiative to the state, if sometimes the attribution rules are expressed through the same agents. In other words, the alleged agents claim to act in the name of the sovereign on the basis of attribution rules, which the agent claims to be competent to issue on the basis of rules, which again he claims to be competent to issue, etc., because he acts in the name of the sovereign. This circularity – or rather infinite regress – marks the end of the entity's capacity to act. It becomes impossible to identify the agents of the state and, as a result, impossible for the state to act. Since anybody can claim to act in the name of the state based on the attribution rule, which anyone can posit, it is impossible to distinguish the real ones from the imposters.

The circularity or infinite regress leads to identification between the state and the agent. If the state actions can ultimately only be identified through the statements of those allegedly acting on behalf of the state, then the agent can absorb the state. The agent can issue the following attribution rule: 'All my acts are acts of the state' ('*l'État, c'est moi*'). This rule makes it impossible to distinguish between acts of the state and acts of the agent. It follows that either the agent or the state disappears: the state is absorbed by the agent, or vice versa. In any event, the state has become incapable of acting. If the state is absorbed by the agent, it simply ceases to exist. Alternatively, if the state absorbs the agent, it is incapable of acting. Not only is there a risk of identity between the state and the agents, but also an identity between the state and life. There is nothing to prevent the alleged agent from issuing a rule that all life represents the state.

A way out exists by constructing a point of reference that is not monopolized by the agent but is still a property of the sovereign entity. I believe that the notion of the 'purpose of the sovereign state' is a good candidate. In fact, it is thanks to the notion of purpose that we can make sense of a legal entity in general and the state in particular. Why? If we consider the state to have a purpose, it means that it cannot act in terms of its likings and creative free will. The state has discretion, but it should be in compliance with and oriented towards, its purpose. While this purpose is a property of the state, it does not determine its own purpose. If the state were capable of determining its own purpose it does not have a purpose, it has liberty. Again, such liberty will ultimately lead to the identity between state and agents, or even between state and life. By contrast, if the state has a purpose and it does not determine its own purpose, then an agent has no privileged access to such purpose. For example, an alleged agent cannot claim that according to a particular attribution rule (issued by himself in the name of the state) he is competent to determine in the name of the state its purpose. This is impossible, because the purpose of the state cannot be determined in the name of the state; this would imply that the state is competent to determine its own purpose. The upshot is that the purpose of the state is something which the agent must explain and justify, but to which he has no privileged access. The only way, then, for the agent to show he is not an imposter – acting on his own behalf – is to show that he submits his acts to the constraints of the relevant practice of determining and justifying the purpose of the state. Such practice includes, of course, mobilizing different forms of practical reasoning (e.g. law, morality, prudence). However, as soon as the agent withdraws from this justificatory practice, there is simply no way for the norm subjects to tell whether the agent is mandated or not. In short, if state action is to have any practical meaning, it must be purpose oriented and constrained. If the powers of the state are to be understood as competences granted and restricted to a purpose, the notion of state liberty must be rejected.

Conclusion

This chapter presented the arrangements from positive law that are the most likely to support the rule of inherent sovereign power: territorial integrity, *jus excludendi alios*, state's title to its territory and state liberty. Territorial integrity and the *jus excludendi alios*, probably the most far-reaching prerogatives, could not do the job for the rule of inherent sovereign power – even these far-reaching powers are not absolute but contingent. They are always constrained by necessity. As a result their use can and must be justified, which goes against the essence of the inherent sovereign power rule. In addition, these prerogatives are not intended to protect the state from migrants – as individual human beings but from legal and *de facto* claims by other alleged sovereigns. The state territory as property proved to be a flawed and outdated concept. And even if the state owned the state territory as a private property today's practiced conception of property does not warrant the absolutist discretion associated with the rule of inherent sovereign power. State liberty appeared to be a dubious legal arrangement in itself. Its legal status is far from stable. An analysis of state liberty from the perspective of practical meaning showed that any meaningful version of the notion must exclude the absolute freedom associated with the rule of inherent sovereign power. The reason is that as a matter of practical meaning the state as a legal entity must have constrained powers; if it does not we simply cannot distinguish state acts from acts performed by others. In short, the most obvious and intuitively appropriate vehicles of positive law cannot cater to the rule of inherent sovereign power.

This puts the rule of inherent sovereign power in an awkward position. Typically, legal arrangements – especially those of (international) public law – rarely stand on their own: they are either derived from, or supported by, other legal arrangements. By contrast, the rule of inherent sovereign power clearly goes against the other quintessential prerogatives of state sovereignty. This means that the rule of inherent sovereign power cannot ride piggyback on other legal arrangements and must find a foundation and rationale of its own. What foundation can be so legally persuasive to the effect of granting the state such discrete powers over a person? The objective of the next two chapters is to show that no such foundation is available, and that the rule of inherent sovereign power remains without any point of reference within the legal system. Yet, to make this point we will have to negotiate what is probably the most material obstacle: the exclusion thesis. As we will see due to its intuitive and rhetorical force, the exclusion thesis almost succeeds in providing the legal foundation for the rule of inherent sovereign power.

Chapter 3

The exclusion thesis

Chapter 2 showed that the standard powers associated with sovereignty do not support the rule of inherent sovereign power. Without exception the exercise of sovereign powers are subject to constraints and susceptible to justification. But maybe the exclusion of migrants happens to be the exception par excellence. Perhaps there is something so special about exclusion and migrants that justifies the absence of justification. But what can this be? What is beyond justification? Arguably, only things that are in a way essential, necessary, inevitable or constitutive are beyond justification. By contrast, anything less than the essential or necessary already falls within the realm of justification. To put it differently, the rule of inherent sovereign power holds if and only if it can be shown that exclusion of normal migrants is in some way necessary and essentially beyond justification. Any weaker claim already allows for justification. We can frame this existential argument for the rule of inherent sovereign power in terms of what I call the exclusion thesis. It roughly goes as follows:

- prior to the political and legal order there is no legal and political standard for justification;
- to create a legal order it must be determined what and who is included in the order;
- inclusion is prior to and constitutive of a legal and political order;
- inclusion implies exclusion and exclusion co-determines what is included;
- exclusion is also prior to and constitutive of a legal and political order.

It follows that exclusion is necessary for the creation and continuation of a political order (because it is constitutive). In addition, since the exclusion is prior to the legal order, there is *ultimately*[1] no standard for justifying (or criticizing) the exclusion. What does this mean for the rule of inherent sovereign power and

1 By contrast, there is a justification standard applicable to *subsequent* exclusions, namely the initial exclusion.

(immigration) law? First, it establishes that states are *necessarily free* to decide *at will* who to include and exclude. In effect, the expression of the sovereign will is ultimately an act of inclusion and exclusion. If states were not free to decide who to exclude they would be subjected to a standard, i.e. a standard beyond the sovereign will. Yet standards only exist if there is an order in the first place. This is only possible thanks to an act of exclusion which is in itself beyond justification. Second, the exclusion thesis establishes why exclusion is also necessary for *preservation* of the order. Unwanted immigration can challenge the actual grounds for the exclusion beyond the initial exclusion. But since the state cannot justify this initial exclusion, unwanted immigration is challenging the order itself. The authorities have a duty to fend off immigration (by every means) to restore order.

In the preceding chapters it became clear that scholars of positive law do not elaborate on the rationale behind the rule of inherent sovereign power. They simply report or restate its existence. Nor do they say much about the alleged special nature of exclusion and migration. Consequently, it comes as no surprise that positive legal scholarship is not the primary source for the exclusion thesis. At first glance, it seems we have to leave the realm of the law altogether, if we want to find sources dealing with exclusion and migration. Political theorists have been interested in exclusion and migrants. Over the last decades, an almost specialized branch of liberal political theory has emerged dealing with the ethics of migration policy. Yet this branch of scholarship is not interested in an existential and ontological inquiry into the relationship between exclusion and order. Rather they are looking for sound reasons for restricting or relaxing immigration policy. These arguments will be of value for determining the first burden of justification (see Chapter 6). However, the exclusion thesis deals with the preliminary question as to whether authorities can and must justify exclusion.[2] A recent debate on a perennial challenge for liberal political theory seems more directly related to the tensions revealed by the exclusion thesis. The recurrent paradox of liberal democracy is that politics cannot be both liberal and democratic. To put it in oversimplified terms: politics is either the free will of the people (democracy) or it is respect for fundamental rights and liberties (liberalism). In a recent mapping of the debate Bonnie Honig contrasts deliberative theory (Benhabib: cosmopolitan democracy; Habermas: constitutional democracy) with decisionism (Mouffe) adding her own third

2 Michael Walzer's suggestions about exclusion and admission come closest to being relevant for the exclusion thesis. Cf. 'Admission and exclusion are at the core of communal independence. They suggest the deepest meaning of self-determination. Without them, there could not be communities of character, historically ongoing associations of men and women with some special commitment to one another and some special sense of their common life.' In *Spheres of Justice: A Defence of Pluralism and Equality* (New York: Basic Books, 1983), at 62. Yet even this communitarian account only provides a rudimentary and intuitive picture of the structure and mechanics of exclusion.

agonistic approach.[3] And many notions that resonate with the themes of the exclusion thesis appear in this discussion: demarcation, exclusion, decisionism, constituting the 'we', otherness, etc. In a way these discussions set the stage for an inquiry into the exclusion thesis. Yet they cannot deliver the material, because of the central preoccupation of political theorists. They concentrate on finding a place for genuine 'politics' or 'the political' within liberal democracy. This makes political theory less fertile for exploring the exclusion thesis than expected for several reasons. Apparently, the notions 'politics' and 'the political' are so clear and self-evident to the authors that nobody bothers to explain what he or she understands by it. Yet, their meaning and content remain extremely vague. Even if we get some idea of what it practically comprises,[4] the authors fail to indicate what remains of the law when – in practice – we are involved with genuine 'politics' or 'the political'. Consequently, if one were to suggest that exclusion of normal migrants belongs to the realm of 'politics' or 'the political', we are still left with questions about the role of the law, especially the notion of legal force. So, when decisionists only recognize the polemic function of human rights, one really wonders what is distinctively legal about the law. The same goes for Honig's focus on contestation and the 'slips and slippages of law'.[5] Arguably, Honig's agonistic politics may be distinguished from the hegemonic politics of decisionism as the former focuses on the plural, the precedents and remainders of decisions. When it comes to their role, law and legal rights have the same polemic function as in decisionism. Deliberative theorists are not doing much better. Either they do not speak of law properly, but universal morality (e.g. Benhabib's universal right to membership). Or they speak of law but have in mind a law that already incorporates its founding democratic and universal liberal values, particularly equality and autonomy for all addressees (norm subjects) of law (Habermas).[6] This constitutional version of liberal deliberative theory may explain why – necessarily – liberal democracy will and should evolve as an inclusive project granting more (private and political) equality and liberty to more people. Although there is

3 Bonnie Honig, 'Between Decision and Deliberation: Political Paradox in Democratic Theory', *Rechtsfilosofie en Rechtstheorie* (2008a), 2, 115–36 (reprint from *American Political Science Review* (February 2007), 1–17); 'An Agonist's Reply', *Rechtsfilosofie en Rechtstheorie*, (2008b), 2, 186–99. Honig discusses inter alia Seyla Benhabib, *The Rights of Others: Aliens, Residents, Citizens* (Cambridge: Cambridge University Press, 2004), Juergen Habermas, 'Constitutional Democracy: A Paradoxical Union of Contradictory Principles' (trans. William Regh) *Political Theory* (2001), 766–81; Chantal Mouffe, 'Carl Schmitt and the Paradox of Liberal Democracy' in Chantal Mouffe (ed.), *The Challenge of Carl Schmitt* (New York: Verso, 1999).

4 See for example the political activism and concrete actions discussed by Honig and which I understand as instances of her agonistic politics, Bonnie Honig, 'Proximity and Paradox: Law and Politics in the New Europe', in Hans Lindahl (ed.), *A Right to Inclusion and Exclusion? Normative Fault Lines of the EU's Area of Freedom, Security and Justice* (Oxford: Hart, 2009), at 234 and 237.

5 Honig (2008b), 199.

6 Habermas (2001).

some sympathy for such a project from a substantive political point of view, it avoids the question raised by the exclusion thesis.[7] Why should the law adopt these democratic liberal values in the first place? Liberal democracy may require this, but surely law *qua* law is not necessarily a liberal democratic project? Habermas only explains that we can design laws so that we may include others. He does not explain why the *law* (as opposed to liberal democracy) is necessarily an inclusive project, which requires that exclusion must be justified. Again, the exclusion thesis is about the legal nature of the rule of inherent sovereign power. As such, the concern is not whether the rule of inherent sovereign power facilitates or limits genuine 'politics' in liberal democracies. In fact, it is not even about liberal democracy. On the contrary, by exploring the exclusion thesis we seek to discover why the rule of inherent sovereign power is so resistant within liberal democracies. Perhaps it goes hand-in-hand with the law, irrespective of the political system in place. In other words, it may explain and justify the existence of the rule of inherent sovereign power *notwithstanding* liberal democracy.

The exclusion thesis is based on the coming about and preservation of a legal order. This explains why standard positive legal scholarship and political theory are not fertile ground for exploring the thesis. The former takes *order* for granted. The latter neglects the *legal* aspect. Still, the recent debate in political theory has the merit of directing our attention to elements of Carl Schmitt's legal and political theory as well as recent mobilizations of his theses by Giorgio Agamben and Hans Lindahl. While the three authors clearly fit into the current debate among political theorists on the challenges of liberal democracy, they are much more relevant for the exclusion thesis than their colleagues because of their explicit focus on order, law and exclusion. In fact, in the following pages we will present the three authors as if they present a version or substantiation of the exclusion thesis. To be fair to all, I should make some clarifications and qualifications. First, none speak of 'the exclusion thesis' as such. Neither do they mention or support the rule of inherent sovereign power – Agamben says little about migration, while Schmitt does not address it at all. Second, there is a huge risk of misrepresentation or simply misunderstanding on my behalf. To put it mildly, the works do not make easy reading. While misrepresentation and putting up a straw man are of course very embarrassing,[8] they need not harm our project. What matters is that we present the strongest case for the rule of inherent

7 See also Lindahl who rightly points out that by making these moral requirements inherently juridico-political, Habermas does not address the problem of migration but simply dissolves immigration. Hans Lindahl, 'Breaking Promises to Keep Them: Immigration and the Boundaries of Distributive Justice', in Hans Lindahl (ed.), *A Right to Inclusion and Exclusion? Normative Fault Lines of the EU's Area of Freedom, Security and Justice* (Oxford: Hart, 2009), at 143.

8 I often wonder whether Agamben's project is not a sort of *reductio in absurdum*, a form of reverse psychology. Like he is saying 'This is what happens if you leave the law in the hands of pure metaphysics and policy making.' As if he intentionally draws us an intelligent but inadequate picture of the law, so as to ensure jurists continue to take up their responsibility.

sovereign power, straw man or not. Again any claim weaker than the exclusion thesis already disqualifies the rule of inherent sovereign power. Third, the authors seem to be depicted as the 'bad guys'. Yet their intentions are laudable. Agamben's central concern is how the law is structurally violated *with impunity* by a governmental violence through an omnipresent state of exception. Lindahl seeks to bring the inclusion and exclusion of migrants under the aegis of the law. They are both trying to find a proper place for politics within (liberal) democracy. Even Schmitt's motives may be given a charitable reading as he tries to find ways to avoid and curtail total destructive and absolute war (*Hegung des Krieges*). To a large extent I share these concerns. I also think that the authors have identified important problems and excesses in law and politics. So I recognize the symptoms. But I do not agree with their diagnosis. Let alone the cure.

Jus includendi et excludendi according to Hans Lindahl

Legal order and borders

Lindahl starts where standard political theory left off. Where standard political theory examines to what and whom we have duties of distributive justice, he questions how distributive justice is possible in the first place. The notion 'to each his own' presupposes that there is someone who is in a position to distribute something. The same goes for the law. An inquiry into what one deserves (right, liberty and/or obligation) according to the law, also presumes that there is someone who determines this 'what'. In effect, a political and legal order is about a space that marks the who, what, where and when of justice.[9] This is precisely the function of borders or boundaries. According to Lindahl, immigration policy should be understood as ultimately a matter of positing and enforcing borders by exercising the right to inclusion and exclusion.[10] The legal space necessary for any legal order is created by borders, as they establish a spatial unity of the inside, precisely by distinguishing inside from outside.[11] They determine what and who belongs inside or outside. This 'belonging' is primarily a normative one. Borders

9 Lindahl (2009), at 150.

10 Hans Lindahl, '*Jus Includendi et Excludendi*: Europe and the Borders of Freedom, Security and Justice. A review of Europe's Area of Freedom, Security and Justice edited by Neil Walker 2004', 16 *The King's College Law Journal* (2005):

> '. . . policy coherence [of AFSJ: Area of Freedom Security and Justice] is related to the fact that, however different in content, asylum, immigration control, family reunification, judicial and police co-operation all draw their meaning from, and are ways of addressing, problems related to borders and border crossings.' at 235–6.
>
> '. . . the politics of borders deployed in the framework of AFSJ may well be characterised as the exercise of *jus includendi et excludendi*.' at 239.

11 Lindahl (2005), at 239–40.

create a space of what Lindhal calls legal 'ought-places': 'The law orders individual action *by way of boundaries* that establish where human behavior ought or ought not to occur.'[12] And the boundaries not only tell us *where* the behavior ought or ought not to occur, but also *whose* behavior, *what* kind of action and *when*. The typical instance of this normativity is the crossing of borders: the crossings are either legal or illegal.[13] So a third-country national (who), ought not cross the border (what) of an EU Member State (where) if he has no valid title of entry provided by law (when). Not only do the borders create these 'ought-places', they also make sense of them by establishing a *unity* of the legal space. This makes it possible for the 'ought-places' within the legal space to refer to the *totality* of places. At the same time, they also derive their meaning as an ought-place from the unity.[14] So, the ought-places are joined by the fact of separating them from the outside ('join by separating'). Interestingly, Lindahl argues that even the places separated from the inside are in way joined in a greater whole. When authorities are qualifying a border-crossing as illegal they are actually claiming that the individual ought to be in another place. By recognizing the other ought-place, the two different ought-places (inside and outside) are joined 'in an encompassing whole'.[15]

'De facto' nature of the first borders and the right to exclude

The question is what comes first: the spatial unity, positing the borders or the right to inclusion and exclusion? More importantly, what is the *legal title* underpinning them? Paradoxically, it is precisely the *act of claiming* a particular inside and outside that gives rise to a *right* to inclusion and exclusion.

> [N]ot only does a polity lay claim to such a right [to inclusion and exclusion] when exercising a politics of borders, but, conversely, a collective self-closure that includes and excludes gives rise to a legal-political order – and in this sense to 'right' or 'jus'.[16]
>
> [T]he claim to a *jus includendi et excludendi* and a corresponding politics of borders are, in one way or another, constitutive features of any political community.[17]

But how is this possible? Lindahl mobilizes Carl Schmitt's contention that 'the law is the "unity of order and emplacement" '.[18] The unity and order shape

12 Lindahl (2009), at 144 (emphases added).
13 Lindahl (2005), at 240.
14 Lindahl (2009), at 144.
15 Ibid., at 145.
16 Lindahl (2005), at 240.
17 Ibid., at 239.
18 Ibid., at 241.

the distribution and subsequent exploitation of resources, but before exploitation and distribution is the actual taking of the resources. According to Schmitt 'no human being can give, distribute and apportion without taking'.[19] The primordial taking is the actual taking of land (Landnahme). This founds the law internally (allocation of property) and externally (demarcating the community from other communities).[20] Since the taking of land was prior to the legal order, those who performed it 'had received no legal mandate to this effect from all possibly affected parties . . .'.[21] Lindahl provides a pertinent illustration of the absence of a legal mandate for founding an order as he refers to the founding treaty of the European Communities[22] as well as the landmark cases of the European Court of Justice stating the existence of distinct order of European Community law.[23] This means that any foundation of a particular unity is 'never only *de jure*; it is also always *de facto*'.[24] In short, the legal order and thus the law is the result of a *de facto* (non-legal) taking of land. The right to claim an inside and outside, i.e. the right to include and exclude, is based on a non-legal act of inclusion and exclusion. The right to include and exclude is ultimately a matter of *might*, not right.

Exclusion as legal interpretation: legal, illegal and a-legal

The violence of taking land is not just a one-off, unique, historical event we have to get over.[25] Rather inclusion and exclusion are omnipresent in the law. This has to do with the normal business of law, i.e. law applying and setting. The former consists of determining what the law is in standard cases. In terms of adjudication, standard cases address facts that are very similar to the facts addressed in previous judicial cases (so both the meaning of the legal norm and the legal relevance of the facts are pretty much established). In terms of legislation it concerns enactment of laws that do not set new rules, e.g. prolonging existing legislation that is about to expire. Law setting involves bringing new facts under the realm of the law or applying new legal meaning to facts that previously had a different legal meaning, e.g. landmark cases and new legislation on previously unregulated issues. Lindahl

19 Lindahl (2005), at 241, quotation in Lindahl's text, with reference to Schmitt's 'Nomos-Nahme-Name' and 'Nehmen/Teilen/Weiden' in fn. 8.

20 Ibid., at 241. The external positing of the legal order also means that those outside the legal order are expected to recognize the community's right to inclusion and exclusion. This implies that those outside are also included in a sense. Ibid., at 242. This is, I believe, an important argument against the centrality of the notion of exclusion (*infra*).

21 Lindahl (2005), at 241.

22 Lindahl (2009), at 151.

23 Hans Lindahl, 'The Paradox of Constituent Power. The Ambiguous Self-Constitution of the European Union' 20 *Ratio Juris* (2007), 485–505.

24 Lindahl (2005), at 241.

25 Cf. Honig's discussion of Rousseau's suggestion to get through the founding Honig (2008a), at 120.

(correctly) argues that law setting involves applying the law and vice versa. 'On the one hand, every standard case requires at the least a minimal reformulation of the general legal norm, given the changed context in which this norm must be applied. On the other hand, a landmark case does not produce an entirely novel rule; it reformulates a legal norm, applying it in a new way.'[26] And '. . . every legislative act claims to apply to general values. Without this claim, legislation would forfeit its claim to objectivity'.[27] The process of law setting and application thus involves giving meaning to a prior body of law. This is a matter of legal interpretation. Generally speaking interpretation can be described as determining the meaning of something, or more precisely, 'disclosing something as something'. Central to legal interpretation is that it involves inclusion and exclusion of possible meanings of the law (what the law requires). If no legal norm is singled out as meaning 'something', legal norms may well mean 'anything'; this renders the law useless in normative terms. Legal interpretation involves two categories of inclusion and exclusion that operate coevally. First, there is the interpretation of what is legal and illegal according to a particular legal norm. So when a particular act falls under the application of a legal norm, one must interpret the particular applicable meaning of the norm: is the act legal or illegal? Here one selects a particular meaning (include a 'something') and discards other meanings (exclude 'other' things). Second, disclosing the applicable meaning of a legal norm presupposes that the legal norm, or generally the law, applies to the act or event under consideration. This in turn presupposes that the particular fact is relevant to the law. It follows that legal interpretation must involve revealing certain facts and values as possessing a legally relevant meaning. The legal norm must be interpreted as the criteria for what facts and values are included in the law and what are excluded.[28] This is an interpretation of the distinction between the legal and non-legal (or a-legal). At the same time, this distinction is what founds the law,[29] because without the distinction *any*thing may be law, whereas only *some* things can be law. In other words, legal interpretation involves the interpretation of the founding act of the legal order; thus, by implication, inclusion and exclusion are present at all instances of legal practice.

Exclusion as inevitable omnipresent violence

The structure of legal interpretation shows that inclusion and exclusion go hand in hand. Of course, this coexistence does not mean that inclusion *necessarily implies* exclusion. Yet this is precisely one of the central tenets of Lindahl's account:[30]

26 Hans Lindahl, 'Dialectic and Revolution: Confronting Kelsen and Gadamer on Legal Interpretation' 24 *Cardozo Law Review* (2003), at 780.

27 Lindahl (2003), at 780.

28 Lindahl (2003), at 776.

29 Ibid.

30 'No legal order can establish itself without exclusion'; 'Closure is a necessary condition for disclosure' and 'Disclosure is necessarily a normative closure of the interpreted'. Lindahl (2003), at 777.

> *Closure is indispensable* for normative orientation by the members of a community; in its absence, they would not know how they ought to behave. On the other hand, the operation of normative inclusion *and exclusion* implies that . . . legal interpretation effects a normative reduction of what it reveals.[31]

With reference to Gadamer's notions of familiarity and strangeness, Lindahl reminds us of the fact that the interpretation of what is familiar to the legal order equals the definition of identity or the self of that particular legal order: '[T]he act of positing a legal norm always involves taking up a relation to a broader or narrower range of possibilities as the order's *own* possibilities. Having to take up a relation to possibilities is precisely what characterizes ipseity.'[32] Defining the 'own (possible meanings)' or 'self' of the legal order also means taking up a relation with what is excluded from the legal order, i.e. the 'other' or the non-legal.[33] The definition of the 'own' left out *other* possible meanings. But to qualify or disclose 'other' as 'other' or as 'non-legal' it must be interpreted in a sense; the non-legal is in some sense interpreted for the sake of leaving it out of the legal. The excluded other 'embodies *another possible legal order*, another way of drawing the distinction between law and non-law. . . . More simply, no legal community can call itself a "we" other than in relation to a "they".'[34] In a way the 'outside' is included in order to exclude it. Yet this distinction cannot be based on a normative inside and by the same token the outside is never really removed from the inside. This is reflected in what Lindahl calls the 'experience of legal contingency':

> The values excluded by a legal order do not simply vanish into thin air. . . . [T]hey remain at the fringes of positive law, embodied in forms of behavior that retain the potential of subverting the normative distinctions drawn by law. In short, the operation of inclusion and exclusion condemns legal order to an irredeemable *contingency*. . . . The instability and contingency of a legal order are two sides of the same coin.[35]

The contingent nature of the distinction between law and a-law corresponds with the *de facto* origins of the taking of land discussed earlier. It leaves the insiders and outsiders of the legal order with exactly the same problem: both sides run out of (legal) reasons to substantiate their respective claims. Neither the insiders nor the outsider of the legal order can *justify* why 'their values' are to be protected. The insiders can only defend the existing distinction between law and non-law by reference to a *de facto* act that posits the distinction. Conversely, the claims

31 Lindahl (2003), at 777, emphasis added.
32 Lindahl (2003), at 784, emphasis added.
33 Ibid., at 785.
34 Ibid., italics in original.
35 Ibid., at 777, italics in original. Cf. the 'remainders' in Honig's agonistic view on politics.

from outside the law are essentially non-legal and fall prey to a radical '*un*interpretability'[36] in terms of that legal order of which they want to be a part. So the claims from outside are also purely *de facto*. Lindahl, mobilizing Kelsen, argues that precisely those claims lead to an 'interpretative incommensurability'.[37] At some point the existing legal order must be torn down to make a claim interpretable: '*what cannot be said in one legal order can only be said by entering another order.*'[38]

Immigration provoking a state of exception

The previous steps revealed the *de facto* origins of the right to inclusion and exclusion. But they did not tell us why this is so problematic for the practice of law. Is it not just food for legal theorists? Is this *de facto* origin also reflected in the practice of immigration law and policy? What are its ramifications? At first glance the alleged *de facto* origins do not seem to present any problems. The sheer amount of domestic and international legislative and judicial activity and output in the field of immigration seems sufficient proof of the law's ability to capture properly this phenomenon. Yet there are forms of immigration which the law seems incapable of capturing. This is what Lindahl calls *de facto* immigration, 'i.e. a form of immigration that does not easily fit into the legal categories regulating border crossings'.[39] It is the way in which the legal authorities address *de facto* immigration that reveals in practice the *de facto* origins of the legal order. One response is the use of non-legal reasons to assess and justify the appropriate treatment of migrants. A case in point is the admission of aliens on humanitarian grounds. According to Lindahl 'humanity' and 'human being' are notions that are fundamentally non-legal.[40] It is 'by exercising a form of inclusion and exclusion that goes beyond that to which the law gives a right, [that] a polity obliquely betrays its *de facto* origins'.[41] Still, in these cases the response of the legal authorities is not purely *de facto* or a matter of effectiveness. The law tries to incorporate the non-legal notions of humanity and human being. In addition, the authorities appeal to reason. This suggests that immigrants may be able to hold the legal authorities accountable for the appropriateness of particular acts of inclusion and exclusion.[42] Yet there are settings where the response of the legal authorities is more radically *de facto*. There are cases where '*de facto* land appropriation catches

36 Lindahl (2003), at 778–9.

37 Ibid., at 792–5.

38 Ibid., at 795, italics in original.

39 Lindahl (2005), at 245. See also at 243: '[A] *de facto* immigrant raises a claim that cannot be qualified as legal, that is, as a particular case falling under a general rule of law.'

40 Ibid., at 243.

41 Ibid.

42 It is of my own interpretation that the appeal to human reasons suggests some form of accountability directed at the normal migrant, whereas the state of exception is about pure effectiveness.

up with a political community'.[43] These are the instances where the authorities address *de facto* immigration through purely *de facto* acts of border control.[44] So in response to the structural attempts by economic migrants to distort legal categories and apply for the legal status of refugee, authorities simply seek to prevent migrants from applying for refugee status. Any form of accountability is suspended and replaced by pure effectiveness. '[T]he *right* to inclusion and exclusion a polity claims for itself is suspended in view of recreating the conditions of normality under which this right can be exercised.'[45] Lindahl qualifies this situation as Carl Schmitt's state of exception.[46] It is precisely because the origins of the legal order are *de facto* that the non-legal claims expressed through *de facto* immigration challenge the foundations of that same order: '[*d*]e *facto* immigration poses a radical security problem because it contests the *right* claimed by the EU . . . to determine who, and what belongs within and without the EU.'[47] According to Lindahl, Schmitt would argue that in such circumstances the legal authorities are only accountable to those included in the original taking of land[48] and that 'the legal authorities could only be held accountable for enforcing the distinction between inside and outside, legally if possible, "effectively" if necessary'.[49]

Re-presenting the inside and outside

Up to now Lindhal's account seems to fully support the exclusion theory. It is the act of inclusion and exclusion that posits the legal order. This act is never pre-mandated, thus it lacks legal title. Worse, the inclusion and necessary exclusion are not restricted to the founding moment, but constitute a continuous process. The violence or the normative void in which the legal authorities determine whether or not something is a matter for the law (legal versus a-legal) can never be fully covered up. On the contrary, precisely *de facto* immigration recalls the *de facto* nature of our order, as it reveals our incapacity to address it through our normative (legal) categories. It is not so much that we do not want to justify the exclusion of normal migrants. Rather we have a fundamental incapacity to do so. The normal migrants not only challenge the denial of admission, they also ultimately question the legal nature of the right to exclude. This hits the foundations and existence of the legal order; it produces a state of exception. Still, Lindahl sees an opportunity for accountability and a limitation of the rule of inherent sovereign power precisely in the structure of inclusion/exclusion. It has

43 Lindahl (2005), at 243.
44 Ibid.
45 Ibid., italics in original.
46 Ibid.
47 Ibid., at 245.
48 Ibid.
49 Ibid., at 247.

to do with *representation* and *what counts as the inside and outside*. Determining the inside and outside – similar to determining the people in the paradox of politics – is always done by someone (or a group of persons) who *act in the name of something*. 'We, the People', our legal order, Europe, etc., they all must be represented, i.e. re-presented – made present again. The violence associated with taking up the space of any order is precisely the fact that someone has to stand up, seize the moment, and make a claim in the name of something. This person, the representative, is never pre-mandated to do so. By the same token, what is represented must necessarily precede the act of representation. If not, what would the representative be re-presenting? In fact the legitimacy of the representative is that he can show that he does not act in his own name, but in the name of what is represented. So quite pertinently Lindhal recalls that the founding Treaty of the European Community refers to a *prior*: 'an ever closer union among the peoples of Europe'.[50] The represented may be prior to its representation, but there is no *direct* access to this prior. It becomes only accessible thanks to its representation. Applied to the inside/outside distinction, the order only appears thanks to the authorities' representation of its inside and outside. There is no direct access to this inside and outside. This paves the way for an extra accountability for the authorities. Not only are they accountable for upholding the distinction between the inside and outside (e.g. of the European order). They are also accountable for *what counts* as the inside and outside. It may well be that the initial *de facto* claims of migrants seeking admission may in retrospect count as *de jure* claims.[51] In other words, the migrants are potentially insiders. However, one may argue that this does not pave the way for additional accountability, but rather produces a total normative void: anything and nothing can become an insider, so anything can count as Europe's inside. How can we ever tell we are dealing with Europe? How can we ever tell Europe is properly re-presented? Either Europe is misrepresented because it fails to account for the potential insiders, or it is not Europe anymore/any longer because anything can count as Europe. Lindahl's way out is to propose a form of representing Europe's self by drawing on two aspects of the self: character and agency. Character (idem-self) is supposed to remain the same over time as it reflects the qualities or properties of an entity. The agency aspect of the self allows a departure from past commitments while still being the self. To put it differently, it allows acts to be attributed to an entity even if these acts violate the past promises of that same entity. According to Lindahl, this is precisely what immigration policy is about. It represents (now) a prior inside, but by the same token it already must account for the fact that it will have to violate some of the aspects that made the inside: keeping promises to break them. Though Lindahl

50 Lindahl (2009), at 151.

51 'In response to an embryonic *de jure* claim by *de facto* immigrants, a distributive act can seize the initiative to redefine the boundaries of the collective, such that this *de facto* act retrospectively can be viewed as having been *de jure*.' Lindahl (2009), at 156.

does not really explain what precisely constitutes this breaking of promises, I guess we can think of the following. The authorities represent a (prior) Europe that upholds the commitment to values of universal human dignity and equality (see Area of Freedom, Security and Justice) while necessarily and knowingly breaking this promise when it comes to the many migrants seeking admission.[52] Alternatively, authorities represent a prior Europe that now includes as *de jure* insiders those that were at best *potential* insiders. This Europe no longer corresponds to earlier authoritative representations of the prior Europe (e.g. the enlargement of the EU with new Member States and competences).

In addition to the representation thesis and the idea of breaking promises to keep them, Lindahl identifies a closely related – but somewhat more concrete – opportunity for additional accountability. Taking the inside always presumes taking up a relation to the outside. The outsider is always included for purposes of its exclusion to establish the inside. But the outside is never simply there. Like the inside, the outside and its relation to the inside must be represented. Europe's representation of the outside happens to be one of a world market.[53] If so, this means that the migrant should be considered a player in this world market of which Europe is also a part. So not (yet) in his capacity of citizen but as an economic agent, the migrant is already part of Europe. If so, then Europe should be held accountable for its treatment of migrants *qua* economic agents.[54]

At first glance, Lindahl's account is very attractive. It reveals the structure of the exclusion thesis and it presents a way out. His suggestion of migrants being included as agents on a world market may have real institutional traction. Still, further inquiry is needed. First, Lindahl's way out does not get rid of the rule of inherent sovereign power. The proposed additional accountability does not mean that the exclusion must be justified *vis-à-vis* the normal migrants seeking admission. The authorities may have to justify what counts as inside and outside, but it does not follow that they should do so with regard to the excluded migrants. At best, they must justify the content of the inside/outside *vis-à-vis* those they deem insiders. More importantly, it seems that if one really takes Lindahl's powerful

52 Cf. Derrida and the inevitable breaking of the promise of hospitality. Jacques Derrida, *Cosmpolitanism and Forgiveness* (London: Routledge, 2003); Jacques Derrida and Anne Dufourmantelle, *Of Hospitality. Anne Dufourmantelle invites Jacques Derrida* (trans. Rachel Bowlby) (Stanford: Stanford University Press, 2000).

53 '[T]he Treaty also distributes space by separating the *world* from itself. In the same movement by which the Treaty splits Europe, it also splits the world, representing it as a market' (emphasis in original). Lindahl (2009), at 152.

54 '[A]cknowledging the political character of border crossings by immigrants, in particular so-called "economic" immigrants, requires creating mechanisms that account for their interests in how the EU structures the internal market and its relation to the external market. At stake, then, is devising venues of institutional participation of and accountability to those whom the EU, on its own terms, views as members of the proto-political community in which it participates.' Lindahl (2009), 154–5.

analysis of the right to inclusion and exclusion to heart, then there is simply no room for accountability (additional or not). The problem is the centrality of violence, decision, inclusion implying exclusion and *de facto* immigration as the state of exception. Lindahl is right that there may be many versions of Europe and that no representation can fully represent the self of Europe. Yet it does not follow that the authorities should be held accountable for *their version* of Europe's inside/outside. Accountability presupposes that the authorities made a *decision* on the many versions of Europe. But this also presupposes that a normative framework of (at least potentially) relevant versions of Europe's inside and outside is already available. If not, what is there to decide? The whole problem with the founding and re-affirmation of the legal order is that, each time, the *entire* order is at stake. Hence, the state of exception, which means that the *entire* order is suspended. There may be many versions of Europe and there may be many standards derived from numerous normative systems. The state of exception does not deny this. What the state of exception does deny is that these standards are relevant for the exercise of state power. The state of exception is precisely about picking the relevant standards against the background of an absence of relevant standards as long as the state of exception applies. So how can the authorities possibly account for their decision? Do they really decide? This is precisely the problem analyzed by Agamben. We will examine his contribution to the exclusion thesis to see what happens if one thinks through the logic of inclusion/exclusion, violence and the state of exception. Again, my point is not to discredit Lindahl's call for additional accountability (though it is too modest and not sufficiently legal). Rather the purpose is to show how Lindahl's own assumptions ultimately constitute an obstacle for any accountability or duty to justify exclusion.

Immigrant as state of exception and bare life. Agamben and the exclusion thesis[55]

Agamben's analyses correspond largely with Lindahl's discussion of the right to inclusion and exclusion. He also questions the basis of sovereign power. What constitutes the constituting power that establishes the constituted powers? What does sovereign power or the power of the sovereign consist of? Agamben gives a twist to Schmitt's assertion that the sovereign is he who decides whether there is a state of exception. According to Agamben sovereign power *is* the state

55 I draw on Giorgio Agamben, *Homo Sacer. Sovereign Power and Bare Life* (trans. Daniel Heller-Roazen) [1995] (Stanford: Stanford University Press, 1998); Giorgio Agamben, *State of exception* (trans. Kevin Attell) [2003] (Chicago: The University of Chicago Press, 2005). I will refer primarily to parts and chapters of the books as opposed to individual pages. For more detailed references see also my earlier discussion in 'Defending our Legal Practices: A Legal Critique of Giorgio Agamben's State of Exception', *Amsterdam Law Forum* vol. 1:2, pp. 113–25 (2009), with references to other reviews.

of exception. Sovereign power is about determining what belongs inside and outside the legal/political order.[56] But if this is true, it means that the sovereign cannot belong to the inside of the order itself. It would beg the question what determines the inside that determines the inside? Similarly, the sovereign cannot be outside because this is precisely what is to be determined. It means that the sovereign is necessarily in between inside and outside. It is the zone where neither inside nor outside are yet determined. It is a zone of the undecided (or the more radical 'undecidability'): a true state of exception where the standards of the inside (the normative order) do not apply. The state of exception makes the inside and outside possible, as it operates as its borders. In terms of legal order, the state of exception makes law possible precisely because it disconnects and connects law with non-law, i.e. the brute facts of life. But how is this in-between zone created? What is so special about the sovereign that he can constitute this zone of exception? It reminds us of Lindahl's category of the a-legal, where in the context of legal interpretation it must be decided whether or not an issue is to be considered in legal terms at all. Yet Lindahl simply assumes it to be a property of legal interpretation and the state of exception. By contrast, Agamben finds this insight so important he seeks to reveal how the sovereign is the source of this zone.

Bare life and the state of exception as 'undecidability'

The crucial step in creating the zone in-between is to create something that is neither governed by law nor the natural life. The quintessential vehicle to this effect is 'bare life'.[57] This is life that finds itself between law and natural (biological) life. It is not yet within the realm of the law, as it does not bear any rights and obligations. It is more than just brute natural life, because it has gained some political and legal relevance. Its relevance lies in the fact that the quality of bare life has turned the living into a matter susceptible to political/legal decisions. This decision is the most original aspect of political and sovereign power: life and death. In effect, bare life is life that is prepared or exposed to be killed. It is life that may be killed. As such it has the potential to be the subject of politics and law. Still, bare life is not within the legal realm because there is no obligation to kill it. Neither does the killing constitute a violation of law. In fact, the life that may be killed sets the stage for the most original and fundamental sovereign decision: to live or let die. Singling out bare life from natural life and law is the precise specialty of the sovereign. This is inscribed in his power over life and death. Agamben shows how the figure from ancient Roman law – *homo sacer* – reflected this notion of bare life, which makes it possible to separate and connect

56 Agamben (1998), 'Part One: The Logic of Sovereignty'.
57 Agamben (1998), 'Part Two: Homo Sacer'.

law and natural life. The *homo sacer* was the figure of the banned Roman citizen who could be killed, but could not be punished or sacrificed. The *homo sacer* represents a complex ban. He is banned from normal human law as he can be killed by any person and this killing would not be treated as homicide. In fact the *homo sacer* ceased to be a bearer of rights and obligations of human law. By the same token he was banned from divine law as he could not be punished and sacrificed. Yet human and divine law formulates this ban. So the *homo sacer* was both separated from and connected to human and divine law. Agamben goes on to demonstrate that the figure of the sovereign himself was also a kind of bare life. Rituals from the Roman period up to the Renaissance illustrated the importance of treating the body of those in power as if they were not subject to natural life. By the same token the killing of the sovereign was never treated as a normal homicide. In other words, what matters for the sovereign is to always take up a position between the inside and outside, the law and anomic life. The creation of this space is the essence of sovereign power and the state of exception. In a way, this is much more important than the decision by the sovereign. Actually, Agamben conceives of the state of exception in such a radical way that the decision does not really matter: the separation and connection of the law and anomic are only possible in a zone of true 'undecidability'. Hence, Agamben's critique of Carl Schmitt who does not pay due respect to the complexity and ambiguity of the state of exception. Agamben explains how Walter Benjamin points out how difficult it is for the sovereign to actually make the decision.[58] What is there to decide? From what perspective can the sovereign decide? Benjamin shows that even Schmitt underestimates the radical 'undecidability' of the state of exception. Schmitt recognizes that the state of exception is needed to allow for ultimate decisions to get the law off the ground, but in Schmitt's theory the environment in which these decisions are to be made seems still contaminated with law. In Schmitt's view, even in the state of exception, the law still functions as a point of orientation or reference. This is not good enough for Agamben. A more radical position seems inevitable.

One should think the state of exception in terms of a meaningful 'nothing', or rather a non-relation that still makes sense. To illustrate what is needed for an adequate theory of the state of exception, Agamben discusses several 'legal' phenomena that reflect how deeply rooted the state of exception is in Western European legal culture.[59] What all these phenomena have in common is that they show how two forces are continuously at work: (i) the law is trying to capture the non-law, the violence, the anomic; and (ii) the anomic is trying to break loose from the law. The true problematic nature of both law and anomie is that the two can only be understood in their (non-)relation. The law needs anomie to posit

58 Agamben (2005), Chapter 4.

59 Agamben (2005), Chapter 2 Force of law, Chapter 3 *Iustitium*, Chapter 5 The carnival and Chapter 6 Authority.

itself, like the anomic needs the law. The aporia that Agamben tries to address is that if one of the two forces takes over the other, both will vanish. For if the law were to fully capture anomie, it has no point to separate itself from. We simply could not tell anymore whether we were in a state of law or total anomie. Therefore, law must display – not as a matter of its shortcoming, a failure or imperfection – remnants or elements of violence and anomie. By the same token, anomie cannot exist without reference to the normal. A good illustration of this (non-)relation is Agamben's discussion of authority. Under Roman and mediaeval law, the quintessential property of the sovereign was his non-legal power. To make the order complete, the authority of the sovereign was needed. Authority was, in a sense, the mystical element of non-law that grants the legal order its full legal character beyond formalism. An essential feature of this authority is that it does not spring from the legal norm, but from the person of the prince. Authority springs from life, the anomic. If this were true, it also posed a serious problem of instability and continuity of authority as it was tied to the person of the sovereign, his life. To this effect mechanisms were designed to maintain the continuity of the authority, e.g. return authority to the senators and the two bodies of the deceased king. What matters to Agamben is that both Roman and mediaeval constitutionalists were fully aware of this necessary anomic ingredient for order and that they were keen to distinguish – institutionally – between authority and legal power. This is precisely where it goes wrong today. Facilitated by constitutional scholarship from the 1930s, authority was again recognized as a legal concept, but was immediately conflated with legal power. In other words, rather than untying the two forces, life and law, they are concentrated in one state organ. As a result, the very legal order it sought to substantiate vanishes.[60]

Exclusion thesis and the immigrant as **'homo sacer'**

Where does this leave the exclusion thesis and the rule of inherent sovereign power? Agamben's analysis seems to support explicitly one aspect of the exclusion thesis, i.e. the centrality of exclusion and the impossibility to justify. In fact, he goes further. It is not so much the exclusion in itself that is crucial but rather creating the zone between inclusion and exclusion: the state of exception. And its key characteristic is undecidability. This explains the fundamental absence and impossibility of accountability and justification. There is simply no framework for the decision. The focus on the state of exception also renders

60 Cf. 'As long as the *two elements* remain correlated yet conceptually, temporarily, and subjectively *distinct* (as in republican Rome's contrast between the Senate and the people, or in medieval Europe's contrast between spiritual and temporal powers) their dialectic . . . can nevertheless function in some way. But when they *coincide* in a single person, when the state of exception, in which they are bound and blurred together, becomes the rule, then the juridico-political system transforms itself into a killing machine.' Emphasis added, Agamben (2005), at 86.

the process of determining the inside and outside less central to establishing the legal order. The first question is not about the who, what, when and where of the 'we', but rather the space between those dimensions and natural life. The central point is not the phenomenon of representation of inside and outside. What matters is the creation of the zone in-between of undecidability, the state of exception. The state of exception does not refer to a preceding or prior entity. It cannot be represented. This is another way of explaining why (or rather how) there is no room for any (additional) accountability in the state of exception. If so, then there is one element of the exclusion thesis that Agamben's analysis cannot account for: namely the centrality of the exclusion of migrants. Indeed, the exclusion of migrants is already an attempt to fill out the inside and outside. It is not as such aimed at creating a zone of 'undecidability'. It already supposes a state of exception, but it does not necessarily create one. To put it differently, neither the act of characterizing someone as a migrant nor the quality of being a migrant produces *necessarily* a zone of undecidability. In short, there is nothing *per se* exceptional about the status of migrant. Historically, the migrant (or rather 'alien') is simply one among many legal categories of the person. However, Agamben describes developments in modern political thought and practices which seems to turn the migrant into precisely the bearer of bare life and as such the source of sovereign power.[61] In other words, these developments can explain how the exclusion of migrants has become central to modern legal order.

Again, what is crucial for a legal order is the zone between law and natural life. This was what the complex arrangements of old public law were supposed to do. It always kept the sovereign linked, but outside the legal order. Yet the advent of human rights radically changes this paradigm. First, political human rights – popular sovereignty – turned the sovereign into his own subjects. Previously the people constituted the inside and were subject to the sovereign who was (as such) in the zone between inside and outside. As the people became sovereign (their own ruler), the state of exception entered the inside. Since then it has no longer been possible to clearly locate the state of exception. Second, under the concept of human rights one becomes bearer of rights by the simple fact of being human. More precisely, the pure natural fact of *birth* gives rise to rights. So, natural life enters law directly. Worse, natural life produces law. Prior to human rights, the first step for having law was precisely the creation of a space between law and natural life, i.e. bare life. Bare life immediately recalled that the source of law is not so much life or birth but rather the capacity to be killed. Similar to the delocalization of the state of exception, human rights make it virtually impossible to locate bare life. However, according to Agamben, human rights did not get rid of the state of exception and bare life. They were merely covered up. Even our modern Western legal and political orders still

61 Agamben (1998), 'Part Three: The Camp as Biopolitical Paradigm of the Modern'.

live by the state of exception and bare life. The mechanism is too deeply rooted in Western legal thought and practice to simply vanish. This raises the question about today's state of exception and bare life. According to Agamben they are everywhere *within* the legal order. Agamben gives many examples of how the state of exception and bare life (through biopolitics) has penetrated the legal and political order. Bare life resurfaces through an inevitable mechanism that is the corollary of human rights. The mechanism may be understood in terms of the question: How do authorities deny and curtail rights if they are inalienable for living human beings? Well, one creates instances of human life that no longer qualify as human or alternatively do not count as a life worthy of living. One recreates the *homo sacer*. Agamben gives several modern examples of bare life. He describes the status of detainees in the Nazi death camps who were stripped of their rights and could be killed, but whose killing did not constitute punishment in legal terms. Another example was the status of the mentally ill under the Nazi euthanasia programs. These are very extreme instances of recreating a zone of undecidability (let live or kill), but less radical versions of bare life are equally significant. What matters is that the legal order cannot do without the *homo sacer* or states of exceptions, notwithstanding human rights. This brings us to *de facto* immigration. I believe Agamben would agree with Lindahl's contention that the above-mentioned forms of *de facto* immigration create a state of exception. But the point is not that they challenge the legal order by questioning the distinction between inside and outside, as Lindahl puts it. By contrast, I think Agamben would argue that the *de facto* migrant *qua* person constitutes the state of exception.[62] The *de facto* migrants are themselves the zone of undecidability; they are the bearer of a kind of bare life. Different aspects may point to this. First, many *de facto* migrants are in long asylum procedures where their definite status remains undecided. Second, when entered illegally, they are under the constant threat of being expelled, i.e. banned from the legal order. By the same token there is the possibility or prospect of a rather comprehensive regularization of the illegal migrants. This is not a right but a kind of mercy – the sovereign's grant of mercy. The paradox is that the longer the illegal alien remains in this precarious situation, the better his chances of being part of a regularization scheme. So his condition is clearly one of long undecidability: illegal versus regularization. Third, a lot of *de facto* immigrants have left their country of origin (outside) but fail to enter the EU (inside). They linger in the so-called transit countries. In a way these transit countries constitute precisely the experience of the zone between inside and outside. This image of a zone in-between is reinforced by the increasing extra-territorialization of border controls. The factual borders of Europe are constantly moving inside and outside the transit countries, turning

62 Agamben does not really address the status of *de facto* migrants. He speaks primarily of refugees. Yet I believe it is safe to understand *de facto* migrants in terms of the *homo sacer*.

these zones into states of exception. This is also reflected in the extremely poor legal protection the migrant enjoys in these transit countries. Finally, from a legal perspective, the migrant is really banned, i.e. an exclusive inclusion: he is included as a norm subject of the migration laws to keep him out of the rest of the legal order.[63]

The disturbing conclusion is that thanks to the (*de facto*) migrant we are still more or less able to single out bare life and the state of exception. Thanks to the migrant we still have the bare life and state of exception *more or less outside* our legal order. We need him. As long as there is some kind of sovereign power there will be bare life and states of exception. For our own sake, we ought to keep the bare life out of our order. Otherwise we may all end up as *homines sacri*. In a way, this is already happening with the phenomenon of border police controlling the inside of the territory following the abolition of internal border controls and the failure to keep *de facto* migrants physically at bay. Identity checks and checks for title of stay take place not at the border of the legal order, but inside the territory. Only after these checks have been carried out can one determine whether or not those inside really belong inside. As a result, everyone on the inside is potentially both legal and illegal. The status of the insiders is undecided until the official check. The analysis of the 'logic' of human rights completes Agamben's version of the exclusion thesis. It explains the centrality of the migrant in the exclusion thesis. The advent of human rights turned the migrant into the quintessential bearer of bare life. His capacity to be excluded saves the rest from becoming *homines sacri*, because the migrant is the zone in-between, his treatment (inclusion/exclusion) is ultimately beyond justification.

No justification. Just 'an open space of pure human praxis'

Agamben's thesis is what you get when thinking through radically the assumption that law is a matter of distinguishing inside from outside. It inevitably points to the state of exception as the source of sovereign power. Equally inevitable is the conclusion that in the state of exception there is no room for justification, not even the accountability through representation proposed by Lindahl. Fully consistent with his own radical analysis Agamben does not believe there is a way out – or at least a way out that comes anything close to the practice of justification. It is clear to Agamben that the state of exception is inescapable. There is no point in taming the state of exception by bringing it under the aegis of the law. This conflation is precisely what created the killing machine.[64] By contrast, the way out is to recognize and unmask the forces of violence in

63 See Chapter 5 on the authority of migration law.

64 See n. 60.

the state of exception. By that same operation these forces may be reused to create different meanings of life and law. How is this possible? From where do we get the instruments to move the forces around, instead of the forces moving us? How can we stop the machine? First, since law and life can only be understood thanks to their non-relation, it follows that there is no true life or true law that pre-exists law and life. Though effective, the two forces and their creation of the order are – literally – a fiction. Yet, this fiction has potential, or rather presumes and requires potential. According to Benjamin, precisely because law and life can only be understood in their non-relation it follows that there is a way of understanding life and violence as a purely relational manifestation. It means that there is an instance of violence where the content is not pre-determined, it depends on the way one uses it. To put it differently, since it is all a matter of fiction one needs building blocks, instruments to construct it. Like Lego-blocks that do not serve any predetermined end or form, but are pure means. But if there is a possibility for pure violence, Agamben thinks that there is equally a possibility for pure law. This law that has deposed of a particular connection with a particular violence and life, holds the potential or promise of a different relation to violence.[65] Hence, it is the means to a different meaning of life and law. In other words, moving the elements is possible because there are conceptual instances where we can untie the law from life (and vice versa) so they become mobile again. As a result, an open space of pure human praxis is created where we can play with the elements and be truly politically active.[66] Now, whatever, this open space of pure human praxis is supposed to be, it is clearly not a practice of justification or the mobilization of legal constraints.

We have seen how Agamben's analysis departs from Lindahl's account in an important way. Lindahl believes that there is still some potential for additional accountability, while Agamben only sees a way out through a radical open space of human praxis. The difference in outcome can be explained by where the authors locate the true source of the legal order and sovereign power. Lindahl locates the essence of the legal order in the taking of the inside and outside (dimensions of spatial unity, the taking of land, representation of the 'we' and 'they'). Agamben goes one step further. The source of sovereign power is not the creation of the inside and outside, but the creation of the state of exception that constitutes the zone between inside and outside. To put it more plainly, Lindahl still locates the source of the legal order in *what* is decided *in* the (inevitable) state of exception. Accordingly, he seeks to finds ways to produce some form of accountability (through the re-presentation thesis) *within* the state of exception. In contrast, Agamben locates the source of the law not so much *in* the state of exception but rather in the *creation of* the state of exception. There is no point in looking for

65 Agamben (2005), at 63.
66 Ibid., at 88.

additional accountability. This is what you get for radically thinking through the state of exception.

Carl Schmitt and the exclusion thesis

Whatever their differences, the previous contemporary contributions to the exclusion thesis share two important points. First they understand law and legal order as a matter of determining inside and outside. This taking of the inside necessarily implies taking the outside. Second, they deal with this 'implication' in a highly philosophical, almost metaphysical way. It is precisely this philosophical character of their accounts that raise some questions as to the status of the implication 'no inclusion without exclusion'. Lindahl seems to suggest that the implication is ultimately a matter of the phenomenology of determining a 'we'. This always involves taking up a relationship with a 'they'. Similarly, Agamben argues that it is in the core of Western political thought and practice to create a state of exceptions and bare life. As long as there are political and legal orders, we will have a state of exceptions and bare life. We cannot get rid of them. At best we may reveal (locate) them. The worse we can do is covering up (dislocating). Let us assume that Lindahl and Agamben provide us with a correct account of the phenomenology of political order and the tradition of Western political thought and practice. We still can ask what makes our phenomenology and Western traditions such that we cannot include without excluding. Is this also something necessary and inevitable? This question brings us to another aspect of the exclusion thesis which we have not previously addressed. There is something about the exclusion thesis that echoes 'common sense' and the really concrete: 'good fences make good neighbors'; 'everyone's friend is nobody's friend'; 'there must be a limit'. This is not a matter of metaphysics or high-brow philosophical analyses, but simple lessons from life, like locking your door at night. In fact, I will speculate that the intuitive appeal and persuasive force of the exclusion thesis (and the rule of inherent sovereign power) are partially explained by its very concrete, physical and down-to-earth connotations. So if we want to do justice to the exclusion thesis we must account for all these features. We will turn to Carl Schmitt to explore the concrete and more down-to-earth reasons for the implication 'no inclusion without exclusion'. This may seem ironic because it is probably Schmitt himself with his political–theological and philological approach to law and politics who somehow paved the way for high-brow philosophical accounts of the exclusion thesis in particular, and political and legal theory in general. Yet the salient Schmittian notions mobilized by Agamben and Lindahl can be understood in a way that is less philosophical and sophisticated. The reasons for the implication 'no inclusion without exclusion' may be much more straightforward. In what follows I will reconstruct a kind of Schmittian contribution to the exclusion thesis that should reveal the concrete and practical reasons behind the implication. To this end I will discuss some of Schmitt's key notions (e.g. unity, order, state of exception, friend/enemy, taking of land) from the perspective of his preoccupation with how to avoid and curtail absolute destructive war (*Hegung des Krieges*). To be sure this reconstruction is not a philological and exegetic exercise aimed at revealing the most adequate interpretation of Schmitt's political and legal theory.[67] The purpose is to show how with Schmitt we can discover the possible pragmatic and concrete reasons for maintaining that inclusion implies exclusion. Of course, I do not believe that the reasons are sound and we will try to refute them in the next chapter. Yet the value of discussing Schmitt is that it makes the reasons transparent. Moreover, since the motive of the *Hegung des Krieges* is a genuine and a legitimate concern, it urges us to conduct a charitable reading of what could be Schmitt's contribution to the exclusion thesis.

'Hegung des Krieges' and law as concrete order

The main concern for Schmitt was finding a way to curtail the excesses of political struggle and war. He seeks to put limitations to warfare (*Hegung des Krieges*). He wants to avoid at all costs long-lasting absolute and total war.[68] According to Schmitt, this is the historical task of the (sovereign) state and the law: neutralize the bloody conflicts.[69] How does this neutralization take place? The (sovereign) state and the law ensure that conflicts are no longer expressed in ideological and theological terms that claim absolute truth over the other. Instead, the conflicts are expressed in terms of the law that does not decide on the moral truth but distributes the tools of power, through a system of constraints. In a sense the law recognizes that each may have an equally valid claim to the moral truth,

67 The reconstruction adopts only one perspective, the *Hegung des Krieges*, inevitably leaving out others that were also crucial to Schmitt. For example, it does not incorporate Schmitt's underlying concern for how to understand secular power in the context of Paul's remarks on the so-called katechon (see for an excellent and accessible account of this highly complex topic: Marc de Wilde, *Verwantschap in Extremen. Politieke Theory bij Walter Benjamin en Carl Schmitt*, Ph.D. Dissertation (Amsterdam: Amsterdam University Press, 2008)). Furthermore, the reconstruction does not respect the chronology of Schmitt's writings, as it applies the perspective of the *Hegung des Krieges* to Schmitt's writings of both after and before the war. Neither does the reconstruction contrast different scholarly interpretations of Schmitt's works. My general understanding of Schmitt's thinking and its emphasis on the *Hegung des Krieges* is primarily shaped by Jozef Van Bellingen's comprehensive and elaborate study *De Rechtsfilosofie van Carl Schmitt* (Brussels: Ph.D. thesis VUB, 1988), Faculty of Arts and Philosophy, supervisor: Prof. Dr M. Weyembergh, p. 356 (hereafter: Van Bellingen) and a separate volume 'Noten and Bibliografie', p. 97. An indication of the comprehensiveness is that Van Bellingen consulted and used 40 of Schmitt's published monographs and 53 of his articles. Unfortunately from the perspective of international scholarship, Van Bellingen's thesis is written in Dutch and not commercially published. It is available at the VUB library and on file with the author.

68 Carl Schmitt, *Der Nomos der Erde im Voelkerrecht des Jus Publicum Europeanum*, (Koeln: Greven Verlag, 1950) (hereafter: *Der Nomos*), at, inter alia, 66, 69, 112–15 (for the scope of the curtailment compared to the bloody religious wars).

69 Van Bellingen, at 60.

and this is precisely why matters will not be decided in such terms. The state does not decide in favor of one party, but rather places itself with the law above the parties and the conflict.

But how do we get to such a neutralizing legal system? To answer this question it is a prerequisite to understand the characteristics of law in the first place. Schmitt identifies three components: the general norm (normativism), decision and concrete order. If we do not understand which of these three components is the most important we obtain a distorted view of the law and accordingly fail to see what may establish and threaten the legal system. Schmitt believed that, in his time, too much priority was given to normativism which degenerated into legal positivism, which he sometimes equated with legal formalism. The degenerated form of normativism understood law in terms of a system of norms to be distinguished from facts: we may connect the norm to the fact, but the fact is not constitutive to the norm or the law. Instead Schmitt argued that facts do create and shape the law in the sense that the content of a decision in a particular application of the law cannot be derived from the norm.[70] In fact, judicial decisions are not to be fully derived from the norm but rather from the stable, constant and verifiable praxis of the judiciary.[71] Crucial as the decision may be, the primary component of law is the concrete order.[72] For the decision – even in its ultimate and salient instance, i.e. the state of exception – is always aimed at establishing or re-establishing the concrete

70 'Jede konkrete juristische Entscheidung enthaelt ein Moment inhaltlicher Indifferenz, weil der juristische Schluss nicht bis zum letzten Rest aus seinen Praemissen ableitbar ist, und der Umstand, dass eine Entscheidung notwendig ist, ein selbstaendige determinierendes Moment bleibt.' Carl Schmitt, *Politische Theologie. Vier Kapitel zur Lehre von der Souveraenitaet* (Munich/Leipzig: Duncker & Humblot, 1934), at 41. See also Van Bellingen, at 112–13.

71 Carl Schmitt, *Gesetz und Urteil. Eine Untersuchung zum Problem der Rechtspraxis* (Berlin: Verlag von Otto Liebmann Buchhandlung fuer Rechts- und Staatswissenschaften. Verlag der Deutschen Juristen Zeitung, 1912):

> 'Eine richterliche Entscheidung ist heute dann richtig, wenn anzunehmen ist, dass ein anderer Richter ebenso entschieden haette. "Ein anderer Richter" bedeutet hier den empirischen Typus des modernen rechtsgelehrten Juristen.', at 71.
>
> 'Nicht davon ist auszugehen, dass der Richter rueckwarts auf einen Willen oder einen Befehl schaut; sondern er benuetzt eine Norm (d.h. ihre Wirksamkeit) als Mittel, um zu berechnen, was heute, bei diesen positiven Gesetzen, bei diesem Einfluss der ausserpositiven Normen, bei diesen Praejudizien, von der Praxis des Rechts allgemein als richtig betrachtet wuerde.' at 98.

72 Carl Schmitt, *Ueber die drei Arten des rechtswissenschaftlichen Denkens* (Hamburg: Hanseatische Verlagsanstalt, 1934):

> 'Die Norm oder Regel schafft nicht die Ordnung; sie hat vielmehr nur auf dem Boden und im Rahmen einer gegebenen Ordnung eine gewisse regulierende Funktion mit einem relative kleinen Mass in sich selbstaendigen, von der Lage der Sache unabhaengigen Geltens.', at 13.
> 'Eine Aenderung der Norm [ist] mehr die Folge als die Ursache einer Aenderung der Ordnung', at 24 with reference to Santi Romano, *L'ordinamento giuridico*, in footnote.

See also, Van Bellingen, at 3–4.

order. The decision under *normal* conditions per the definition presupposes stable institutions, hierarchy and authority.[73] Where the decision is secondary to the concrete order, the status of the norm is even more subordinate.[74] The norm is to be understood as a function of the concrete order. The order is what generates the norm, not the other way around.

Jus publicum Europeanum: Sovereign Power and 'Justus Hostis' in Europe

As the concrete order is the central starting point, Schmitt is particularly interested in the *content* and *origins* of such concrete order. Now, Schmitt has of course in mind a specific concrete order, namely the *jus publicum Europeanum*. This order allegedly existed for more than 200 years following the Peace of Westphalia (1648). It was the response to the endless and excessive religious – civil and interregional – wars that kept Europe in a state of disorder. The key characteristic of the new *jus publicum* was the neutralization of conflicts, by creating European *sovereign states*. The sovereignty of a state meant that within a designated territory the state had the ultimate authority to decide on the conflict. The state had the authority to do this, not because it was in the best position to decide on who holds the truth in the ideological conflict. It had the authority because it put an end to the conflict by determining itself what is right, irrespective of any theological conflict.[75]

Since at the interregional level there is no ultimate authority to end the conflict, the neutralization takes a different form. While internally the conflict is fully pacified in the sense that no warfare is allowed, at an interregional level the war is allowed, but limited. The main vehicle to this effect has been the introduction of the notion of the legitimate or just enemy (*justus hostis*).[76] This allowed warfare to be regulated without having to decide on the moral right of the belligerents. Previously, the focus was on whether there was a just cause for the war. In Christian Europe, the Pope had the ultimate authority to decide on this issue, however, as soon as the Reformation had become a stable reality of the European political and theological landscape, the Pope had lost this authority.[77] In fact, whether or not the cause of the war was just may have been precisely the reason for war in the first place. If the legitimacy of the war is denied then it means that the fighting parties may consider each other as ordinary criminals, or worse, as agents of evil. When fighting evil there is ultimately only one objective: total destruction. According to Schmitt this explains the excessive and everlasting nature of the religious wars.

73 Van Bellingen, at 4.

74 '. . . die Regel [ist] nur ein Bestandteil und ein Mittel der Ordnung.' Carl Schmitt, *Ueber die drei Arten*, at 13.

75 Van Bellingen, at 36, 60–1.

76 Ibid., at 33–47.

77 Schmitt, *Der Nomos*, at 25–36.

The *justus hostis* notion seeks to address this problem by introducing a non-discriminatory or formal notion of the just war.[78] This can be contrasted with the theological or moral soundness of the motives of the parties at war. The formal notion does not pertain to causes of war, but to the parties themselves. The most important requirement is that the armies must be public, i.e. acting for and on behalf of the state or sovereign. In other words, the fighting can only take place between those armies; civilians are excluded. The exclusion not only applies to the lives of civilians, but also to their property. Thus, private property is, in principle, exempt from the victor's claim to the bounty. That is why a comprehensive law on bounty has been developed coevally. Furthermore, the war must be preceded by a declaration stating particular demands. This is an extremely important limitation of the scope of the war, because it means that fighting is only allowed to the extent necessary for the realization of these demands.[79] Another element of the *justus hostis* concept, is the peace treaty including an amnesty. The aim is not the elimination of the enemy as such. Furthermore, the hostilities are to take place at the borders of the sovereign states to guarantee that the violence does not spill over to the inside.[80] According to Schmitt, this scheme of an inside of friends and an in-between of conventional enemies is only possible if the conflict with the potential absolute or real (existential) enemies can be exported to an outside. Hence, the importance of the seizure of a space outside the European sovereign states: the taking of the high seas and the discovery of the 'New World'.[81] This was the space allocated to the absolute enemies, unrestrained violent conflict can take place that is not governed by the *jus publicum Europeanum*.

So, according to Schmitt, the starting point for any order is seizure of space. Through an etymological and historical investigation, he traces the origins of every order (Nomos) back to a physical taking of land,[82] the underlying idea being that the exploitation or use of land and its resources is always preceded by a distribution of the land, which in turn, is preceded by a taking of the land. The taking of land creates the life of the order. It enables the distribution of resources and provides each his place. This place is crucial for the *Hegung des Krieges*. Not only friends, but also legitimate and absolute enemies need a place. Accordingly, with respect to the European order, Schmitt identifies *at least* two kinds of borders and thus three zones.

78 Schmitt, *Der Nomos*, at, inter alia, 112–15, 124–5, 129, 133–4.

79 Moreover, the notion of a demand already excludes the possibility of the total destruction of the absolute enemy or evil. Firstly, total destruction is incompatible with a 'demand', because it is generally beyond practical reasoning to ask someone to destroy himself. Second, the notion of 'demand' excludes the possibility of the opponent being an agent of evil; for one does not ask something from, or negotiate with, the devil. Third, the notion of demand also shifts the conflict from truth to material reality, because you cannot as such 'demand' someone to accept the truth: he must 'see' or 'believe' it.

80 Van Bellingen, at 44.

81 Schmitt, *Der Nomos*, in general Chapter II 'Die Landnahme einer neuen Welt', 53–109, and for a clear summary of the central tenets at 120–1.

82 See Schmitt, *Der Nomos*, paragraph on 'Das Recht als Einheit von Ordnung und Ortung', at 13–20, and paragraph on 'Die Landnahme als konstituierender Vorgang des Voelkerrechts'at 48–51.

The first border lies between the sovereign European states. The inside of each state territory is friendly and pacified. The outside lies in another European state who is a potential legitimate enemy. The second border distinguishes between the territory of the European states and its outside. Here the outside is made up of absolute enemies. Schmitt's emphasis on territory and borders now becomes clear. The sovereign states must seek to keep their borders impenetrable. This maintains the pacification inside and keeps the violent (but regulated) conflict outside. This is precisely why and how military conflict can be fought at the borders of the state, as opposed to inside the state, which would necessarily implicate the civilian population. The same rationale applies to upholding the border between Europe and the outside. Within Europe violent conflict is still possible (or rather necessary), but thanks to the *justus hostis* there is a *Hegung des Krieges*. This is not the case outside Europe. Out 'there', no curtailment is possible for want of any order. It also means that enemies from outside will not respect the principles of the *justus hostis*. If so, allowing the 'other' enemies to enter Europe will bring back total and absolute warfare to European territory (as during the religious wars). This explains why taking the inside must involve the creation of an outside. Inclusion involves exclusion; without it one runs the risk of allowing in (civil) war through the back door. The relationship between borders and the *Hegung des Krieges* also explains why taking land is not an act of pure violence. Though it cannot be derived from any pre-existing legal order, it is nonetheless connected to order and the law. How then is taking land to be distinguished from a simple act of violence such as robbery, oppression etc.? It derives its legitimacy from the sole fact that it aims to establish an order that distinguishes between the inside and the outside. It creates the conditions for eliminating excessive violent conflict by exporting it to an outside. In short, the European *Hegung des Krieges* was fully dependent on the existence of three different relationships with corresponding bounded spaces. These can be depicted schematically as follows.

Relationship	*Conflict*	*Space*	*Law*
Friends	No violent conflict	Territory of sovereign European state	Domestic private and public law
Conventional enemies	War is possible, but restrained	At the borders between European states	*Jus publicum Europeanum*
Absolute or real enemies	Absolute war	Outside Europe	–[83]

83 This box is left blank intentionally. It would be inexact to simply say that the zone outside Europe was a complete legal void; in particular the legal regime of the high seas was much more complex. '. . . nach dem Utrechter Frieden [1713] gelingt eine Hegung. Sie besteht darin, dass die Kontrolle der Regierungen ueber die kaperschiffe ihrer Untertanen staerker wird, so dass der Freibeuter alten Stils zum kriminelen Piraten absinkt.', Schmitt, *Der Nomos*, at 153. See in general the paragraph 'Von der elementaren zur geordneten Freiheit der Meere', at 153–6.

Still, we are left with an important question. How does taking land create such order as opposed to other acts of violence? To put it differently, what if the taking of land in itself involves a lot of excessive and destructive violence to put an end to the disorder? It must be noted that not every instance of the state of disorder is necessarily violent. There may be periods of relative calmness. The problem with the state of disorder (or nature) is that when the conflict becomes violent there is no way of curtailing it, let alone stopping it. In other words, is the prospect of a *Hegung des Krieges* so much better than disorder if it takes a long, bloody and destructive war to get there? Schmitt was aware of this problem, which is precisely why he was against a world peace.[84] The creation of a pacified inside that comprises the entire world is only possible through an extremely violent and long-lasting war. The disagreements between peoples are simply too great. But how much struggle is justified? How can we be sure that the same level of violence is not needed to maintain the order? The justification and safeguard for the taking of land and maintaining order is homogeneity. It must refer to a certain unity. This unity also presumes continuity: the future must be directly connected to the past order. If not, the future order would be new, which implies an end to the unity. In effect, according to Schmitt, authority is a matter of tradition. For Europe the tradition and the elements of homogeneity and unity are Christianity and the social institutions of the family and property (including the relationships of economic corporatism).[85] Thus, sovereign states can establish and maintain an order without too much violence to the extent that they refer to the values and convictions associated with our Christian society. Actually, the term 'refer to' is not correct, because it suggests that the authorities have a rather passive and transparent role. Instead Schmitt uses the term representation, which is much more creative. The notion of re-presentation involves an act of making something present and real. By the same token this 'something' already exists because it is *re*-presented. It is this act of representation that produces the unity that is necessary for any order to rise above and neutralize the conflicts of private interests.[86] According to Schmitt, for the taking of land and order to be effective (i.e. become a reality without continuing excessive violence) the authorities must reflect and at the same time realize the unity: they must represent the structures of solidarity, i.e. homogeneity. That is why according to Schmitt legitimate authority is ultimately

84 Schmitt, Carl Schmitt, *Der Begriff des Politischen* [1932] (Berlin: Duncker & Humblot, 1963), at 77–8.

85 See n. 86.

86 Cf. Carl Schmitt, *Verfassungslehre* (Munich/Leipzig: Duncker & Humblot, 1928):

> 'Was nur Privatsache und privaten Interessen dient, kann wohl vetreten werden . . . aber es wird nicht in einem spezifischen Sinne repraesentiert. Es ist entweder real gegenwaertig oder es wird durch einen abhaengigen Beauftragten, Geschaeftstraeger oder Bevollmaechtigten wahrgenommen. In der Repraesentation komt eine hoehere Art des Seins zur konkreten Erscheinung', at 210.
>
> 'Die Repraesentation bewirkt erst die Einheit', at 214.

a matter of tradition and it must appeal to the values associated with the social structures.[87] Legitimate authority is about having the conviction to represent and thus realize unity.[88]

So, state authorities will be successful in keeping the peace within their territory to the extent that they truly represent the tradition of the society. It also means that the structures are susceptible to unity. If not they can only be held together by extreme and long-lasting violence. Therefore, Schmitt adheres to the notion of a 'pluriversum' of sovereign states each representing 'its' relative unity. How then is the order between those sovereign European states possible? To put if differently, the pacification within the state is possible by the sovereign authority, which is based on the state's ability to represent the unity. The order between European states is based on the *justus hostis* principle.

But what is the unity at the European level that entices the sovereign states to consider the other European state as a legitimate enemy as opposed to a criminal and evil state? There is, of course, some common Christian basis. However, the religious wars have shown that the ideological differences between Catholics and Protestants are too great to foster any *Hegung des Krieges*. Schmitt argues that the *Hegung des Krieges* between sovereign European states was only possible thanks to a concrete spatial order that consisted of a concrete balance of powers. Although the European states take their decisions in freedom and independence, the decisions will be taken against the background of a sentiment of a common fate as a

87 This genuine unity relies on the basic fabric of the social and cultural order. In other words, the trick for the authorities is to represent the order that is in a way already present. Schmitt does not have in mind the 'natural' order informed by the rules of coordination ('Verkehrsgesellschaft'), but a more institutionalized, probably ethical order. Cf. Carl Schmitt, *Ueber die drei Arten des rechtswissenschaftlichen Denkens* (Hamburg: Hanseatische Verlagsanstalt, 1934).

> 'Es gibt andere Bereiche menschlichen Daseins, fuer welche die Uebertraegung eines derartigen Funktionalismus der Regelhaftigkeit gerade das spezifisch rechtliche Wesen der konkreten Ordnung zerstoeren wuerde. . . .
>
> Das Zusammenleben der Ehegatten in einer Ehe, der Familienmitglieder in einer Familie, der Sippengenossen in einem Sippenverband, der Standgenossen in einem Stand, der Beambten eines Staates . . . kann weder in den Funktionalismus vorherbestimmter Gesetze, noch in Vertragsregelungen aufgeloest werden.
>
> [Die konkrete innere Ordnung jeder Institution] stellt jeden Gesetzgeber und jeden, der das Gesetz anwendet, vor das Dilemma, entweder die mit der Institution gegeben, konkreten Rechtsbegriffe zu uebernehmen und zu verwenden, oder aber die Institution zu erstoeren.' at 19–20.

88 Schmitt then goes on to explain that it follows from this that the authority is ultimately a matter of personal authority. The reason is that the unity or structure of solidarity is not directly accessible, and there is no general standard from which the particular content of the unity can be derived directly. In other words, the personal acts and *decisions* of the sovereign are necessary (like in the norm applying activity) to *shape* the content of the unity. This means that ultimately the content of the unity depends on the *person* who decides. The focus on personality will ultimately bring Schmitt to contending that the model of personal leadership (Fuehrer Prinzip) is the only legitimate form of authority.

result of the equitable balance of powers. In fact, it is the concrete spatial balance of powers that constitutes the guarantee of that same sovereign freedom.[89] In other words, what matters for order in Europe is not so much the intentions expressed by the sovereign states, but rather the balance of powers: the capacity of each state to control and protect the unity within its territory against internal conflict and threats from other states. And if this balance of powers is distorted then it will ultimately bring down the *Hegung des Krieges*.

The end of the European Nomos

As concrete spatial inclusion/exclusion, representation of unity and the balance of power are the necessary ingredients for a successful creation of placement and order; their absence inevitably equates with the end of the European order. This is precisely what has been happening especially since the end of the First World War. At the internal level within the European states, e.g. Germany under the Weimar constitution, the unifying and ordering functions of the law have been abandoned and substituted for the purely technical neutralization of the opponents. Schmitt identifies fundamental ideological disagreements which go to the heart of the order (e.g. socialism, communism). These are conflicts that have no place within the state that is pacified and they should be dealt with not among friends, but among enemies. To the extent the Christian and European placement is questioned, it should be a matter of war between absolute enemies. But instead of exporting these conflicts to the outside of the sovereign state or even the European space, they kept within the state where violent combat is not allowed. Still, the battle continues. This time the weapons are not swords, but the words, i.e. the law. The power of the law is not used to end the conflict, but rather to neutralize the opponent. The law is not used to maintain the order, it is used to put a new order in place. In other words, the law is cut off from its place and order and it no longer functions as a vehicle for the *Hegung des Krieges*. The law is disconnected from its founding order and the underlying political conviction and social traditions. It ceases to have any legitimate authority and becomes purely a technical instrument serving the particular interests of the parties in a concealed war.

89 See Schmitt, *Der Nomos*:

> 'Was aber in der Wirklichkeit an konkreter neuer Ordnung und Hegung des Krieges voelkerrechtlich entstand, hat sich nicht nur aus der Weiterfuehrung moraltheologischer und ebenso wenig nur aus der Verwendung roemisch-rechtlicher Begriffe und Normen entwickelt. Es entstand aus der damals sich bildenden konkreten Raumordnung Staat und der Vorstellung eines europaeischen Gleichgewichts dieser Staaten', at 96–7;
>
> 'Nicht die prekaeren Bindungen des 'sich selbst bindended' souveraenen Willens, sondern die Zuegehoerigkeit zu einem als gemeinsam empfundenen, raumhaften Gleichgewichts-System und die dadurch ermoeglichte Hegung des europaeischen Krieges machten den eigentlichen Halt dieser voelkerrechtlichen Ordnung aus', at 137.

At an external level, the *Hegung des Krieges* comes to an end due to a demise of its founding factors. The constitutive elements of the European order were sovereign states impenetrable borders, a concrete balance of powers, and a European outside. The Treaty of Versailles and the creation of the League of Nations formally recognized the principles of state sovereignty and the outline of the impenetrable borders. However, through exceptional provisions they radically compromised these founding notions. Schmitt has in mind the so-called rights granted to some states (e.g. the allied forces) to intervene in the internal affairs of another 'sovereign' state. These intervention rights blur the distinction between war and peace, which equals the end of the *Hegung des Krieges*. The physical killing will now take place under the cover of civilian or pacifistic notions.[90]

Schmitt not only identifies the end of the European sovereign state with its impenetrable borders and its clear distinctions between war and peace, he also observes the end of the European zone. The real powers determining the order are no longer in continental Europe but are located in the zone outside Europe, i.e. England and especially the USA. In fact, what happens outside Europe from now on determines what happens inside. The problem is that rather than exporting the extreme conflicts to the zone outside Europe, the blurred order of the USA (with its quasi-sovereign Latin American satellites) is introduced into Europe. What Schmitt criticizes is the total incapacity to establish a legal system that corresponds with a concrete order. There is neither a real occupation of European states by the US, nor an attempt by the US to represent a new order within European states. At the same time, the European states are not allowed to remain fully sovereign and maintain their own order. The exploitation strategy used with regard to the satellite states is in a way imported in Europe (in particular the Rhineland).[91] In short, the crumbling of the European order and its beneficial

90 'Fuer die Anwendung solcher Mittel [i.e. modern weapons and techniques aimed at physical killing] bildet sich allerdings ein neues, essentiell pazifistisches Vokabularium heraus, das den Krieg nicht mehr kennt, sondern nur noch Exekutionen, Sanktionen, Strafexpeditionen, Pazifizierungen, Schutz der Vertraege, internationale Polizei, Massnahmen zur Sicherung des Friedens.' Carl Schmitt, *Der Begriff des Politischen*, at 77. But this precisely paves the way for the demise of the *Hegung des Krieges* because surely these civilian and pacifistic techniques are *de facto* acts of war:

> 'Wie ist eine Jurisprudenz moeglich, die angesichte blutiger Kaempfe, angesichts der Zehntausende von Toten immer noch von "friedlicher Besetzung" zu sprechen wagt und dadurch das Wort und den Begriff des "Friedens" dem grausamsten Hohn und Spott ausliefert?'

[Carl Schmitt, 'Voelkerrechtlichen Formen des modernen Imperialismus' [1932], in *Positionen und Begriffe. Im Kampf mit Weimar-Genf-Versailles 1923–1939* (Hamburg: Hanseatische Verlagsanstalt, 1940), at 177.

91 'Der kontrollierende Staat sichert sich alle militaerischen und wirtschaftliche Vorteile seiner Annexion ohne deren Lasten.' Carl Schmitt, 'Die Rheinlande als Objekt internationaler Politik' [1925], in *Positionen und Begriffe. Im Kampf mit Weimar-Genf-Versailles*, at 31.

Hegung des Krieges are a direct consequence of the incapacity to uphold the crucial distinction between inside and outside.

The restoration of the Nomos: state of exception

The previous paragraph indicated the main cause for the demise of the European order: failure to uphold the distinction between inside and outside. This is precisely why Schmitt suggests that we must return to the 'original' concept of law and legal order that has inclusion and exclusion as its central theme: the state of exception. The state of exception is the situation where legal norms (and principles) are suspended for the authority to restore the legal order.[92] In the state of exception it is decided what belongs inside and outside the law. In the state of exception it becomes clear that the content of law is matter of a decision that cannot be derived from general legal norms. Schmitt observed that the end of the European order was the result of the abuse of the neutralizing language of domestic and European public law. Decisions that were in reality political and even constituted acts of war were concealed and justified by the law of a pacified order. In fact, by using the legal provisions of the European order, interested parties were creating a new order by stealth.

In the state of exception *covert* politics is impossible. First, he who decides in the state of exception cannot hide the true content of his decisions behind legal norms: the whole point of the state of exception is that the legal norms are suspended. Second, in the state of exception it is impossible to secretly decide on the order, new or old, because the one and only *theme* of the state of exception is order. In other words, that what is decided in the state of exception equals order. There is no way in doing this covertly. The positive upshot is that the state of exception allows us to evaluate the true authority or legitimacy of the decisions and thus the legal order. Stripped of its false justifications, the true content of the decided becomes clear. This allows us to answer two fundamental questions. First, does the decided order adequately represent the tradition and homogeneity of the norm subjects? If not it means that the order can only be upheld by the use of excessive violence and war. Second, does the order correspond with a concrete order expressed by the balance of powers within the pluriversum of orders? If not, the order will not survive and will be an invitation to a continuing war between states. Only if the two answers are answered positively, can the decisions be considered truly to effectuate a stable order in which

92 The analogy with the Landtaking is of course that according to Schmitt the *entire order* is at stake: 'Denn nicht jede aussergewoehnliche Befugnis, nicht jede polizeiliche Notstandsmassnaheme oder Notverordnung ist bereits Ausnahmezustand. Dazu gehoert vielmehr eine prinzipiell unbegrenzte Befugnis, das heisst die *Suspendierung der gesamten bestehenden Ordnung*' (emphases added), Carl Schmitt, *Politische Theologie*, at 18.

the *Hegung des Krieges* is possible. Only then can we truly speak of legitimate authority.[93]

Hegung des Krieges and the exclusion thesis

The *Hegung des Krieges* offers a different perspective on the central elements of the exclusion thesis. It gives a concrete explanation of why inclusion implies exclusion. Also it explains the relevance of territorial borders. Territorial borders, territorial inclusion and *exclusion* are crucial for locating the different types of conflicts and relationships: friend, legitimate enemy and absolute enemy. This is not so much a matter of a particular phenomenology or metaphysic, but a concrete historical fact. 'No inclusion without exclusion' is not a conceptual but a practical implication. Determining the outside is needed not for defining the inside, but for protecting it. Moreover, it turns the state of exception into a much more concrete and practical notion rather than one that is epistemic and metaphysical. The legal order is suspended because it no longer corresponds with what is happening on the ground. Either the legal norms are simply ineffective, because they are structurally ignored and violated, or they are enforced effectively, but cease to be neutral favoring some factions on the ground and oppressing others. In the state of exception authorities have to make afresh an articulation between the legal and the concrete order. An update is needed of the distinction between friends, legitimate enemies and absolute enemies. The law must be brought back to conform with the concrete order by changing either the scope of the legal order or the concrete balance of powers. On this account the state of exception is indeed a rare thing. There are also explicit criteria for evaluating whether the authorities have the effective authority to declare and decide in the state of exception. The litmus

93 We all know that Schmitt had in mind a particular homogeneity, i.e. the German nation. He also believed that the institution most capable of concretely representing such unity was a real embodiment of personal authority, i.e. the Fuehrer. ('Der Staat als besondere Ordnungsreihe innerhalb der politischen Einheit hat nicht mehr das Monopol des Politischen, sondern ist nur ein Organ des Fuehrer der Bewegung.' Carl Schmitt, *Ueber die drei Arten des rechtswissenschaftlichen Denkens*, at 63). And 'die Bewegung' pointed at the history and fate of the German people (see Van Bellingen, at 236). Van Bellingen points out that by adopting the Fuehrer principle Schmitt clearly departs from his own legal and political theory. In Schmitt's own theory the state of exception is temporary for the purposes of restoring the legal order. In other words, restore the distinction between law and politics. By contrast, the Fuehrer principle may actually lead to a situation whereby the Fuehrer not only decides *in* the state of exception but also decides whether there is a state of exception in the first place. This may lead to an entire suspension of the law Van Bellingen, at 235–6. Therefore Schmitt distinguishes between the dictator as 'Aktionskommissar', and the sovereign dictator. The former depends on his principal, the sovereign (for Schmitt the people). He has a precise task: restore the pre-existing order. The latter, the sovereign dictator, also has a task, but no principal. His task is to create a new order not restore an existing one. Schmitt initially preferred the former (see Van Bellingen, at 121–3, with reference to Carl Schmitt's *Die Diktatur*).

test is the proper representation of unity, the balance of powers and ultimately, the realization of the *Hegung des Krieges*. So there are criteria in the state of exception, but they are clearly not legal. This then explains why exclusion is, at crucial moments, beyond (legal) justification.

With Schmitt we can offer a rather down-to-earth and common sense explanation of the central elements of the exclusion thesis. However, there is one link missing: immigration and normal migrants. It is interesting to note that though exclusion is central to Schmitt, he does not deal with the inherent sovereign power rule, let alone admission laws. As an erudite legal scholar of public law he must have known the treaties and case law that reflect the inherent sovereign power rule (see Chapter 1). The rule should serve Schmitt's purpose well. Inherent sovereign power may be understood as one of the few things left over from the 'great' European order, because it expresses the importance for every sovereign state to ensure a homogeneous inside. It gives the state the sovereign power to decide who stays outside. In other words, it gives the state the power to keep out those who may bring violent conflict into its territory.

To put things in a more concrete way: with the inherent sovereign power rule, Schmitt can keep out the dangerous communists from the East. Why then did he fail to take advantage of this legal vehicle? Obviously, we can only speculate, but doing so may shed some light on how to understand sovereignty and exclusion. Schmitt was worried about what was happening with the people already inside. The inherent sovereign power rule does not give states the right to expel their citizens, even if some of them pose a threat. So, the sovereign power rule would not help to restore the peace in the inside.

Another explanation may be that Schmitt remained loyal to his own account of the *justus hostis* and state of exception. Aliens simply do not pose a threat to the order. First, they are not agents of a *justus hostis*; they are not soldiers of a public army of another state that declared war on the receiving state. Second, the aliens do not form a group or party that makes a claim and pursues a strategy of creating a new order through the existing one. In effect, these explanations correspond with our objections from positive law discussed in Chapter 2. Indeed Schmitt, who is mainly interested in the big picture of states and what happens to their peoples, cannot in fact really cope with a displaced person who does not fit into a larger group. We must recall that for Schmitt the concrete order is the product of the social structures and traditions of a people already located in a territory. This basis is for Schmitt a given. It is the starting point of any order, not a variable. The individual migrant defies this logic. So in Schmitt's theory there is no real place for individual migrants. This may all mean that as long as the individual migrant fits (or will fit) into the homogenous society, it does not make trouble or provoke too much disagreement, there are no grounds for excluding him. How could the authorities have reasons beyond the order? How could there be reasons other than the maintenance of the homogeneity? It would be illegitimate for the authorities to have a will or reasons of their own beyond the unity. So, this concrete and practical Schmittian contribution to the exclusion thesis makes it difficult to explain why the exclusion of normal migrants is so crucial for the legal order.

Recapitulating the central tenets of the exclusion thesis

The main thrust of the exclusion thesis is that the exclusion of (normal) migrants is essential and constitutive to the legal order to the extent that it is inescapably beyond justification. We have been looking for such a strong thesis because anything weaker cannot account for the rule of inherent sovereign power. Again, this rule is our main concern as it legally sanctions the current practice of exclusion without justification. In this chapter we reconstructed elements of the exclusion thesis based on the works of Schmitt, Agamben and Lindahl. In their attempts to really think through the centrality of exclusion for legal order, these authors provide the strongest, most fundamental arguments in favor of the exclusion thesis. First, law is a matter of determining the inside and outside. Already the foundation of the legal order requires an initial determination of what belongs to it and what does not. The same goes for the further business of law: it cannot but continuously set boundaries between legal and illegal and legal and a-legal. The need for an outside and thus exclusion can be explained as a matter of the phenomenology of determining a 'we' which always involves determining a 'they' (Lindahl). Similarly, law can only be understood in its relation to non-law, natural life. So if the two are not separated we simply cannot tell what is law and what is not (Agamben). Alternatively we may understand the need for an outside in a more physical and concrete way as protection for what is inside (Schmitt). In any event, there is an inescapable implication at work: 'no inclusion without exclusion'. Second, a crucial dimension of the inclusion and exclusion is territory. The taking of land is the basis for any form of distributive justice and order (Lindahl, Schmitt). A territorial outside also guarantees that there is an actual *place* to locate the legitimate and absolute enemies of the legal and political order (Schmitt). Furthermore, the inclusion and exclusion are not pre-mandated by the legal order: they are essentially beyond the legal. However, there may be some form of accountability. When taking the inside and outside the authorities cannot but re-present a prior inside and outside. By the same token nobody has direct access to the inside and outside. Hence, the authorities can be held accountable for their version of the inside and outside (Lindahl). Alternatively, they may be held accountable for effectively representing unity, the actual balance of powers and ultimately realizing the *Hegung des Krieges* (Schmitt). Conversely, it may be argued that accountability and justification are impossible because there is no relevant framework of reference. At best we can hope for an open space of human praxis (Agamben). At any rate, it is clear that inclusion and exclusion are ultimately beyond normal legal and political standards of justification. Third, the exclusion of migrants is crucial because, migration policy is ultimately a matter of border policy which involves positing and enforcing the inside/outside (Lindahl).

Furthermore, the way we treat migration – in particular *de facto* migration – reveals the special and non/pre-legal nature of inclusion and exclusion. It cannot be captured by the *normal* categories of law. The *de facto* migrants challenge the foundations of the order and, as such, provoke a state of exception (Lindahl). Even stronger, the migrant is the state of exception. He is the quintessential bearer of the inescapable bare life. This bare life and state of exception are the necessary conditions for our Western legal and political order. Ironically, without the precarious status of migrants, we would not have our order (Agamben). Finally, the basic assumption of law as a matter of determining inside/outside and the implication 'no inclusion without exclusion' point to a deeper logic: namely law and legal order as unity (Schmitt, Lindahl and, less explicitly, Agamben). In fact, as will be discussed in Chapter 4, the need for boundaries and the inside/outside is premised on the picture of order as unity. Unity only makes sense if there are complete boundaries. The notion of unity explains why each time the entire order is at stake and how the migrant can be understood as constituting or provoking a state of exception.

Chapter 4

Orders without borders

Refuting the exclusion thesis

This chapter will try to refute the exclusion thesis. By doing so, we hope to debunk the strongest possible justification for the rule of inherent sovereign power. The critique is structured as follows. First, it challenges the exclusion thesis for its emphasis on the origins of order and its explanation of taking the inside/outside, especially land, as the necessary condition for the creation of order. Here, the critique seeks to demystify the apparent common sense and empirical aura of the exclusion thesis. Second, the refutation addresses the more philosophical aspects as it reveals the conceptual flaws in the commonly held belief 'no inclusion without exclusion'. Finally, we take up what is probably the deeper flaw underlying the exclusion thesis, i.e. understanding legal order in terms of 'unity' and 'oneness'. This will also tackle the special ontological status that the exclusion thesis grants to the exclusion of migrants.

Order without land and taking

The exclusion thesis starts from the idea that law is a matter of determining the inside and outside. This idea immediately directed attention to the origins of the order: the first act of determining the inside and outside. Hence, the inquiry into a *prima causa* of societal life, which almost seamlessly leads to life's essential activity, i.e. the use, or exploitation, of resources. Under the exclusion thesis, the exploitation or use of resources is necessarily preceded by distribution, which in turn is preceded by a physical taking, the taking of land being the most fundamental. In liberal political theory these elements – taking, distribution and property – are often dealt with in the context of property theory. It involves a regress towards the 'original' title to an asset. In law this has been developed into a sophisticated system of succession of title, including special provisions regarding prescription to cover invalidities. However, that is not what is meant by the exclusion thesis. The land-taking-distribution-exploitation sequence is a *precondition* for the legal regress or succession of legal title. Neither does the exclusion thesis fit the standard approach of liberal political theories on property and the distribution of resources. These theories are primarily understood in hypothetical terms to test our moral intuition about current schemes of distribution. Yet, the sequence land-taking-distribution-exploitation is not presented as a hypothetical one; its intuitive appeal lies in its historical or empirical pretension. Who cannot see this historical self-evidence? Take by force, divide the resources among those worthy of trust and yield. Is this not the logic of the rise (and fall) of empires throughout history (from the Hellenistic and Roman Empires to the 'Conquest' of the Americas and European colonial empires)? However, a closer look at these clear-cut cases may show a different picture. The roll out of the 'empires' involved war, physical occupation and the taking of land. But more often, the taking has been preceded by distribution. In fact, most battles have been a matter of alliances. Few powers could deploy sufficient armed forces to go to war without an ally. The distribution of enemy resources was typically a central theme of the terms and conditions for an alliance. In other words, acceptable distribution arrangements were a precondition for an alliance and thus a precondition for the taking. The different stages of the conquest of the 'new world' constitute another very important case in point. Often titles of dominion (ownership and authority) were distributed prior to actually taking and occupation of the 'new' land. The same goes for concessions and trade monopolies in the 'new world'; here, in fact, it is the distribution that initiates the taking.

Perhaps I am not taking the notion of distribution ('Teilen' in Schmitt) sufficiently literally in the sense of division or cutting up into parts. If distribution is to mean the physical act of making divisions in the asset, then surely one must first take the asset. Yet if distribution is understood physically and not normatively, then the second part of the sequence (distribution → exploitation) does not obtain *necessarily*. More than often the exploitation produces a concrete physical division, not the other way around. In fact, all resources that undergo an irreversible change when exploited will be divided by the mere fact of exploitation. Indeed, this is precisely the problem with ecological issues, where the exploitation entails a *de facto* distribution over generations. Finally, often the exploitation not only produces distribution, but it also constructs *what* is included in the taking. To put this another way, often the use defines the object taken. If so, then taking does not *necessarily* precede the meaningful exploitation.

The exclusion thesis is not only mistaken (or too emphatic) in its focus on taking, but also on its focus on land. The focus on land is expressed in the status of the land taking as the quintessential form of taking. In fact, it is the taking of land that founds the order. As a result every order is, in essence, territorial. From an empirical perspective this contention does not hold. We have already indicated that territory in terms of *property* does not play an essential role in the notion of sovereignty (see Chapter 2). Nor should we overstate the founding role of territory in terms of physical land. Early European legal history gives us important counter-examples, whereby each person was governed by his or her 'own' law ('statuten'). This situation lasted for three centuries up to the ninth century AD.[1]

1 John Gilissen and Frits Gorlé, *Historische Inleiding tot het Recht*, I (Antwerpen: Kluwer rechtswetenschappen, 1991), at 157–9.

Studies in contemporary cases of legal pluralism have convincingly challenged the alleged prerequisite of territorial unity.[2] In the field of criminal law, crimes against humanity show that the notion of territory is not a necessary ingredient in understanding the *normativity* of a legal order.

Canonic law is another case in point. It certainly reflects a legal community and, for a long time, a political community, but the claim to a territory in the sense of land taking is absent.[3] In addition, due to its proselytism and general universalistic pretensions, the Catholic Church does not define itself by exclusion, but by inclusion. If the Catholic Church has an enemy, it is not legitimate, but an absolute, i.e. Satan. Finally, the teachings of the Church through its ideas of a boundless sharing (cf. the miracle of the multiplication of the loaves of bread and the fish) also go against the notion of an exclusive land taking. This counter-example is particularly interesting because to Schmitt, the Roman Catholic Church was the quintessential instance of a legitimate legal order, because it fully respected the notion of personal authority, tradition and conviction.

Another counter-example is the relationship between borders and territory. To Lindahl the European border policies are a reflection of the need for a spatial unity. Yet, empirical analyses show that the border policies are not located at the borders. The policies of remote control move the *de facto* borders of Europe into third countries, where European and foreign official and private institutions perform the actual enforcement.[4] At the same time, due to the 'abolition' of internal borders (control), the controls by border officials are no longer taking place at the internal borders, but inside the territories of the Member States.[5] These are all indications that the sense of space becomes purely conceptual and ideological.[6] This is not necessarily problematic, but it must be noted that the intuitive force of the exclusion thesis was precisely its empirical or physical connotation: land taking and unity correspond with a physical reality and practice.

2 See the case studies of the *lex mercatoria*, regulations issued by multinational enterprises, mega-insolvencies, labor law and human rights referred to in Chapter 2, n. 5.

3 Gilissen and Gorlé (1991), at 215–32.

4 Elspeth Guild, 'The Border Abroad – Visas and Border Controls' in Kees Groenendijk, Elspeth Guild and Paul Minderhoud (eds), *In Search of Europe's Borders* (The Hague/London/New York: Kluwer Law International, 2003); Virginie Guiraudon, 'Before the EU Border: Remote Control of the "Huddled Masses" ' in Kees Groenendijk, Elspeth Guild and Paul Minderhoud (eds), *In Search of Europe's Borders*.

5 Kees Groenendijk, 'New Borders Behind Old Ones: Post-Schengen Controls Behind the Internal Borders and Inside the Netherlands and Germany' in Kees Groenendijk, Elspeth Guild and Paul Minderhoud (eds), *In Search of Europe's Borders*, at 146; John Crowley, 'Locating Europe' in Kees Groenendijk, Elspeth Guild and Paul Minderhoud (eds), *In Search of Europe's Borders*, at 34.

6 It corresponds with the positive law analysis of Chapter 2 where not the territorial in terms of land, but the competence or jurisdictional aspect of state territory (and thus borders) became clear.

However, evidence points in a different direction: legal order in general and border policies in particular have little to do with spatial unity, let alone a territorial one.

Arguably, the attractiveness of the exclusion thesis is not so much its capacity to explain law in terms of a concrete order, but rather in terms of *a particular* concrete order. In fact, the whole notion of the founding act of land taking presumes an actual and relevant beginning of a particular order. In addition to the novelty of an order, the exclusion thesis also identifies the continuity and the ending of an order. Schmitt, of course, had in mind a particular order, i.e. *jus publicum Europeanum* that came about as of 1648 (the Peace of Westphalia) and lasted for more than 250 years up to the Treaty of Versailles and the League of Nations. Lindhal's version of the exclusion thesis is less explicit about the particular order, but his idea of the entire order being at stake clearly presupposes a 'dialectic' of novelty, continuity and ending. The problem, however, is that from an empirical perspective it is extremely difficult to establish the beginning, continuity and demise of an order. Hereafter, we will restrict ourselves to pointing out some important historical events that clearly do not fit the assumptions about the novelty, continuity and ending of the *jus publicum Europeanum*. Again, the argument here is not comprehensive and exhaustive, but it should suggest that more thorough historical analyses can easily debunk exaggerated ideas about the 'radical life' of an order. The contemporary contributions of the exclusion thesis, may seem less affected by this flaw because they are, as indicated earlier, less empirically oriented. Yet, the focus on order and the state of exception reflects a strong presence of a genuine novelty, continuity and ending of order.[7]

According to Schmitt, the *jus publicum Europeanum* started with the Peace of Westphalia, which established the notion of internal and external sovereignty. From then on the ruler was sovereign in its territory and, in principle, free sovereigns were to respect each other's territorial sovereignty. This interpretation, indeed, corresponds with the traditional reading of the Treaties by political scientists.[8] However, a closer reading of the Treaties of Westphalia in combination

7 It may be that this sequence is purely conceptual or mythical, and as such not susceptible to any empirical counter-examples. If so, the exclusion thesis will also lose much of its intuitive appeal.

8 Schmitt explains that the basis for this new order was laid at least 100 years earlier with the Peace of Augsburg (cf. *cuius regio, eius religio*) (Carl Schmitt, *Der Nomos der Erde im Voelkerrecht des Jus Publicum Europeanum*, (Koeln: Greven Verlag, 1950)). This suggests that Schmitt himself may be aware of how in fact the coming about of an order may be a more gradual and transitional matter. For Schmitt it makes sense to exclude the Peace of Augsburg from the *jus publicum Europeanum* because it only included the Lutherans and not 'other' Protestant movements. As a result it could not prevent the 30-years war that preceded the alleged beginning of the *jus publicum Europeanum*. But the fact that there was war is, of course, not an argument for or against an order. What matters is the *Hegung des Krieges*. Schmitt assumes that, from a polemological perspective, after the Peace of Westphalia wars were constrained.

with their 'geo-political' background reveals that the treaties constituted a confirmation of traditional power and empire in Europe rather than the establishment of a new order.[9] Again, it is probably a typical tendency to observe novelty in 'successful' social and political arrangements, whereas thorough historical analyses establish continuity rather than novelty.[10]

Now, Schmitt also claims that there has been a continuity of the *jus publicum Europeanum*. Even though I believe that indeed the practice of law has little room for 'radical' novelty, it is very odd that Schmitt who himself found revolution a necessary and inherent possibility of law, does not treat the French Revolution as the arrival of a new order. In fact, he treats the Napoleonic wars as a kind of exception, because of its partisan (i.e. guerilla) nature, as opposed to wars between regular armies.[11] Indeed, the Spanish wars were particularly brutal as Goya's drawings can tell us; the Russian campaign was equally harsh. However, as soon as they were over, everything went back to normal with the Treaty of Vienna. The problem, however, is that this important period is treated as an exception, while it may be a crucial counter-example of the continuity of the order. Probably, more important is the impact of the French Revolution and the Napoleonic Empire on the law. If it makes sense to speak of legal revolution at all, and if there is an event that deserves the label revolutionary, then Napoleonic civil and public law seem

9 In these texts [the Treaties], the idea of a territorially based system of independent states is nowhere to be found. These documents dealt with questions of religious toleration, territorial settlements, and the power to make treaties, but never with the kind of wholesale reconfiguration of the political order which we have been led to believe by so much modern scholarship. In fact, these documents went a long way towards preserving the power and prerogatives of empire in Europe.

Jens Bartelson, 'The Concept of Sovereignty Revisited', 17 *European Journal of International Law* 463 (2006), at 472–3. This follows the de-construction of the Westphalian Treaties by Stéphane Beaulac, *The Power of Language in the Making of International Law. The Word Sovereignty in Bodin and Vattel and the Myth of Westphalia* (Leyden/Boston: Martinus Nijhoff Publishers, 2004), at 67–97.

10 See for example Johan Huizinga's account of the Dutch civilization of the seventeenth century. Instead of being the result of a radical new social and economic order, the basis for the success of the Dutch economy was nothing more than the old (outdated) late medieval corporate system.

> 'De welvaart van het land [Nederland] is ontstaan binnen de beperkingen van een bedrijfssysteem, dat men veeleer *verouderd* zou moeten noemen, en dat in omringende landen bezig was, plaats te maken voor strakkere en meer moderne vormen van organisatie. Het stelsel waarin Nederland zijn grootheid verworven heeft, was in feite nog het laat-middeleuwse, praemercantilistische bedrijfssysteem.'

Johan Huizinga, *Nederland's Beschaving in de Zeventiende Eeuw. Een Schets en Hugo de Groot en zijn Eeuw* (Groningen: Open Universiteit/Wolters-Noordhoff, 1984) [1941], at 20.

11 Carl Schmitt, *The Theory of the Partisan: A Commentary/Remark on the Concept of the Political*, [1963] (trans. A.C. Goodson) (Michigan: Michigan State University Press, 2004).

to be the most obvious candidates. Yet, they are considered as a mere continuation of the *jus publicum Europeanum*.[12]

Another case in point is the extension of the suffrage to an increasing number of groups in society as of middle of the nineteenth century. What can be more radical and concrete than a change in the number and nature of those who may ultimately decide the state of exception? And we could go on like this. The point is not that I personally believe these events revolutionary in the legal sense. Rather, it is difficult to substantiate any claim about the novelty and thus continuity of an order.

Though Schmitt's observation about the blurring of boundaries between war and peace is correct and especially relevant in today's geo-political environment, it does not follow that conflicts today are more cruel than, say, 150 years ago. The Holocaust is probably a typical example of the demise of the *Hegung des Krieges*, because it defies any logic of the *justus hostis* principle. Yet, the war itself during the First and Second World Wars was not aimed at total destruction of the enemy. Virtually all the crucial fighting took place between regular armies. Even the use of atomic weapons against a civilian population (surely against the laws of war) was used to end the war and to avoid more bloodshed on both sides (military and civilian), or at the least that is the official story. I do not want to downplay the horrible effects of both world wars. But I just wanted to point out that both wars may actually still fit Schmitt's model of the *jus publicum Europeanum*. If so, then even these almost unimaginable events do not reflect a demise of order. It means that order may be much more resistant to the logic of novelty, continuity and demise. As a result, there are strong indications that one of the basic assumptions underlying the exclusion thesis simply does not fit our practices.

Under Schmitt's version of the exclusion thesis the taking of the outside was in a way empirically necessary for the *Hegung des Krieges*. The outside territory

12 Still, Schmitt understands the French Revolution in truly revolutionary terms when it comes to the identity of the constituting power. Schmitt argues that with the French Revolution the nation gives to itself a constitution for the first time. By doing so it represents a new political unity. (Carl Schmitt, *Verfassungslehre* (Muenchen/Leipzig: Duncker and Humblot, 1928), at 49–51). Still, Schmitt does not explain whether this revolution has any *legal* consequences for the *jus publicum Europeanum*. Probably, he believes that the French Revolution is still an internal affair that does not affect the legal relations with other states in the context of the *European* public law order.

In terms of legal consequences of a revolution, it may be recalled that, strictly speaking, a new regime need not abolish or declare invalid the laws of the previous regime. If the new regime is truly constitutionally revolutionary, then previous laws, which were obviously not issued through this newly constituted power, simply do not count as law unless explicitly provided for by the new constitution. By the same, token if previous laws get a 'second life' under the new constitution, which is almost always the case, then it suggests that, from the perspective of legal practice, the new orders may be not so new after all. This impossible exercise simply goes to show the difficulties and often irrelevance of determining the beginning (and end) of a new order.

must be taken in order to keep the (legitimate) enemies away from the inside. Furthermore, the outside is needed precisely because, under the *Hegung des Krieges*, the objective is *not* total destruction of the enemy. If so the enemies must also have a place to live. So it is consistent with the exclusion thesis that a territorial outside is a necessary condition for viable inside. What does not follow is the 'taking'. It presupposes an intentional and creative act, which establishes something that did not exist before (cf. 'good fences make good neighbors'). But according to Schmitt, the adequacy of the borders is determined by the concrete balance of powers and the homogeneity of the inside. This has not been created, it was already there. It simply must be respected. If so, what is there to take? Either the outside is taken by a creative and authoritative act, which means that it does not correspond with a concrete balance of powers, or it is simply a matter of conforming to the concrete balance of powers, which leaves out the creative and authoritative aspect.

Inclusion does not imply exclusion

'Here' and 'there'

While the preceding critique concentrated on the 'empirical' aspects of the exclusion thesis, the contemporary contributions by Lindahl and Agamben represent a more conceptual strand. They seem to echo persistent and common conceptual intuitions. In normal colloquial language, it is not unusual to use antonyms. Arguably, the same goes for the notions 'here' and 'there': 'if something is not *here* it must be *there*, and vice versa'. From this perspective, it is perfectly understandable to state that the spatial inclusion ('here') implies a spatial exclusion ('there'), and vice versa. Below we will refute the implication inclusion/exclusion in general logical terms, for now we may want to concentrate on how we actually use the terms 'here' and 'there'. A closer look at even our common, colloquial, use of here and there, reveals that they are not implicating terms. In fact when I say 'here', you cannot tell, without further contextual information, what I mean by 'there'. Also, if I am saying something is not 'here', it does not mean that it is 'there' either: the something may simply not exist. Furthermore, even if the something exists and is located in the there, I should specify the 'there'. If not, the 'there' simply means not 'here'. This may be meaningful or rather useful, but not more useful than saying 'the something exists and it is not here'.

The reverse scenario is even more obvious. If I am saying something is 'there', you will not know where 'here' is. Depending on our respective locations 'here' and 'there' may even be in the same place. More importantly, if I am saying that something is not 'there', it would be very odd for you to assume that the something is 'here'. What all this shows and on which we will elaborate below, is that exclusion does not determine the inside, and inclusion does not determine the outside, if what is included in the outside is not specified.

A similar flawed implication governs the idea that borders fulfill a special role in determining whether or not one is located in the inside or outside. In reality (or rather in practice) we do not orientate or locate ourselves through the frontier between inside and outside. Probably, in virtually every case of spatial location people orientate between two or three points, which they know to be located inside. As long as they situate themselves between the two points or within the triangle made up by the three points they know they are inside. It is not necessary to locate *a* border, let alone *all* the borders. The two or three points can be located in an identical way through other *points*. In other words, we locate ourselves not through any form of spatial unity (implying borders) but rather through a spatial coherence of connections between *particular* points that are *at least* inside.

'Us' and 'them'

I agree with the exclusion thesis that in order to establish a legal or political community it must be known what and who belong to it. In other words, membership must be determined. Accordingly, closure establishes this inside or membership. Under the exclusion thesis closure involves not only inclusion but also exclusion. Here I do not agree. I believe that inclusion is needed to determine who and what belongs to the community, but I do not think that one must know who is *not* a member to establish the community. To make my point I should find an instance where a community can be established through inclusion only. I will consider the 'modern' quintessential political act of inclusion, i.e. the assertion 'We the people'. Such inclusive assertion always involves some 'founding fathers' who claim that there is a 'we'. To make sense and to have any effect, it must be known who is meant by 'we' in concrete contexts. As of the moment the founding fathers or other officials have specified this, the 'we' or community can start to operate and function. It can make rules and decisions about the distribution and exploitation of goods. It can organize public services etc. There is no need to tell *ex ante* which persons are excluded from the 'we'.

But what about the people that are not included in the 'we'? Well, their status is simply unknown. They are neither included nor excluded. This situation is not at all problematic; it is a basic feature of human organizations. We are all latently included in, or excluded from, organizations. In other words, we must distinguish three statuses: being included; being excluded; or being neither included nor excluded. To create an order or group you only need statuses 1 and 3. In other words, to constitute a legal and political order the founding fathers just need to decide on who is *at the least* included. 'We the people' is to a large extent an open-ended act of inclusion that doesn't involve any exclusion per se. It doesn't follow from its formulation that certain persons are necessarily excluded. But what if the founding fathers stated that only White Anglo-Saxon Protestants are included in the 'we'? It seems that here inclusion necessarily implies excluding those who do not meet these criteria. The 'others' are not some abstract notion, but real concrete identifiable people. However, this merely shows that the word 'only' combines inclusion and exclusion. It does not mean that you need exclusion to make a successful inclusion. Of course if your purpose is to exclude some then you must exclude, but if you include to create a meaningful group, it suffices to know who are *at the least* the members of that group.

Exclusion and distribution

There is still another argument in favor of exclusion: justice. For purposes of distributive justice it seems that exclusion is required, for, we must fix the number of people that will be taken into account for the distribution of a particular resource.[13] If distributed to all persons on the planet, most resources will be broken down into shares so small that they become insignificant to their beneficiaries. In addition, if the number of beneficiaries is not fixed but under constant revision, the current beneficiaries cannot rely on their share. This will provoke uncertainty and make it virtually impossible for people to organize their lives and commit their assets and themselves to their life projects.

Distributive justice seems to involve at least three types of exclusion: persons excluded from benefiting from the resource; exclusion of possible uses of the resource other than the one selected; and the exclusion of other possible meanings of what counts as a resource. The first person who took the resource defined it as a resource, ascribed it a certain use and must have defined a concrete or hypothetical repartition of the resource. My general objection to this line of reasoning is that it overlooks the normative, or rather the intentional, nature of inclusion and exclusion.

To appreciate my point we should first turn to the meaning of the terms. To exclude means quite literally to shut out a person or to hinder a person from entering a place, enclosure, society etc.[14] Exclusion then refers to the action of excluding, or the fact or condition of being excluded.[15] To include means to shut in, or to enclose and refers to the action of including, while inclusion means the fact or condition of being included.[16] So both exclusion and inclusion refer to actions namely by an excluder and 'includer' respectively. Both actions are intentional, i.e. the intention to bar or enclose the person is a constitutive element of the action. The intentional aspect of the action helps us to explain two things. First, it makes clear why the fact that somebody is present in a place does not mean that the person is necessarily included. Similarly, the fact that somebody is absent from a place does not necessarily mean that the person is excluded from that place: having access and not having access are not per se instances of

13 This argument was brought to my attention for the first time by Bert van Roermund during a discussion of a paper on the state's power or right to exclude aliens.

14 *The Shorter Oxford English Dictionary* (Oxford: Oxford University Press, 1973).

15 Ibid.

16 Ibid.

inclusion and exclusion. Second, it explains why inclusion and exclusion only pertain to the persons who are the object of the inclusion or exclusion. This is why the inclusion of at the least *someone* is possible without the necessity to exclude some other.

Let us consider the trivial case of John holding a cake[17] and inviting five friends to have a cake party. Obviously the five invitees have become member of the cake party, but does this mean that all other persons are excluded? What if a sixth friend of John drops by who did not receive an invitation to join the cake party; is he excluded? It depends. The sixth person may be excluded if John intended the invitation to be exclusive. It may also be the case that John was more or less expecting the sixth friend to drop by anyway (he might be his neighbor). John may simply have forgotten about the sixth person, or he may have thought that the sixth person was abroad and so he did not bother to send him an invitation. Also it may be the case that John wanted to have at the least the first five friends to join the party and that he was indifferent about sharing the cake with other people. So from the invitation we cannot derive any exclusion, because the inclusion does not express any intention to exclude others.

Of course there are limits to the party. First the cake cannot be preserved for longer than a determinate period of time. So the party members must eat the cake within that period of time; anyone wanting to join the party afterwards misses out on the cake. Second there is an implicit understanding, or common use, among John and his friends that a piece of cake should have a particular minimum weight. If not, eating the cake loses its point. It follows that the cake can only be shared between a limited number of people. These are clearly inevitable limitations, the effect of which means that a lot of people will not have access to the cake. But are these really instances of exclusion? Did John, when holding the cake and deciding to throw a cake party, intend to deny access to all the other people? Does the fact that others do not have material access to the cake help us to understand who is to join the cake party? I believe that the limitations merely reveal the material constraints and limitations inherent in most resources. Inferring acts of exclusion from these material limitations inflates the notion of exclusion. There is a serious risk of inflation because if material limitations become a matter of exclusion, everything we do constitutes an act of exclusion. Playing field hockey becomes an act which excludes drinking beer (one cannot drink beer and play field hockey at the same time). I believe that most amateur field hockey players prove each weekend that playing field hockey does not exclude drinking beer!

The exclusion thesis not only inflates the notion of exclusion, it also gives it too much credit. It was said that one must fix and thus limit the number of beneficiaries of a resource to avoid constant revision of the distribution, which would provoke uncertainty. Fixing the number of people to be accounted for does not stabilize the actual distribution. There are still countless contingencies that affect

17 In our example, no statement is made as to John's title to the cake; John *holds* a cake.

the size and the quality of the beneficiaries' share of the resource. Even if fixing the number of beneficiaries is necessary, it does not mean that the actual fixation is beyond justification. So in the case of the cake party, the minimal weight of a piece of cake, as John and his friends understand it, determines the maximum number of beneficiaries. And John (and his friends) must have this understanding of the maximum number of beneficiaries prior to throwing the cake party; if they did not, they would not know whether or not they could have the party in the first place. If there were no cake party, there would be nothing for other non-invitees to join. So the distinction between the members and non-members of the cake party and the decision to have the cake party in the first place are in a sense beyond justification. This is what the exclusion thesis wants us to believe. However, the fact that the initial (or hypothetical) distribution is prior to the cake party does not render it beyond justification. There is no particular reason why John and his friends should not justify the minimal weight of a piece of cake. What if someone drops by who is starving? What if John and his friends can satisfy the cake needs of 20 additional people just by giving up 2.5 per cent of their minimal share? I am not saying that John and his friends can never stick to their minimal distribution. I am just saying that the distinction between member and non-member is not beyond justification. Furthermore, the exclusion thesis seems to suggest that it is thanks to the cake party that others can make a claim to the cake in the first place. But this need not be the case. The claim can be made at the exact moment there is something which other persons consider to be a valuable resource. It does not matter whether or not there is a cake party, it does not matter whether or not John has any title to the cake, it does not even matter who holds the cake.

Exclusion and corrective justice

If not distributive justice, then at the least corrective justice seems to require exclusion. It is obviously the case that what is right cannot be wrong at the same time. Murder cannot be both just and unjust. Hence Lindahl's claim that '*Closure is indispensable* for normative orientation by the members of a community; in its absence, they would not know how they ought to behave.'[18] Since the reasons for approving or disapproving a particular behavior is ultimately linked to the values endorsed by a community, some values are necessarily excluded from a community. According to Lindahl, this is the whole point of the distinction between the legal and non-legal. In effect, the argument pertains to the two levels of exclusion associated with legal interpretation: legal vs non-legal (values) and legal vs illegal (behavior). Of course, some things are discarded by legal systems because they are believed to be bad, or simply irrelevant, and no particular

18 Hans Lindahl, 'Dialectic and Revolution: Confronting Kelsen and Gadamer on Legal Interpretation' 24 *Cardozo Law Review* (2003), at 777, emphasis added.

legal norm can account for all relevant values. However, this does not mean that the exclusion of values is constitutive for the legal order. Rather it seems that the central business of law is not so much excluding values, but rather mediating between values that are included but incommensurable. The quintessential case in point in modern liberal legal systems is, of course, the difficult balancing exercise between freedom and equality.

'In' and 'ex'

The previous argument showed that a successful inclusion only requires a statement and decision about what is *at the least* included. So in terms of establishing the community, the closure should only involve inclusion and not exclusion. Does not the notion of inclusion in itself entail exclusion?[19] Imagine that the founding fathers for the purposes of establishing (or representing) the 'we' included at the least 'x' – or in short: I(x). Now, I(x) obviously means that *it is not the case* that *inclusion is not the case*, in short: I(x) = ~ ~ I(x). But this may be rephrased in terms of exclusion: the *inclusion of x* means that *not inclusion of x* is *excluded*, in short: I(x) = E (~ I(x)). So, there is some exclusion after all. Yet this exclusion is purely tautological, it does not say much about what is exactly excluded. It does not capture the 'other'. Neither does it define in any sense the 'they' as opposed to the 'we'. It only says that some instance of inclusion is excluded. In addition, this reasoning does not explain where the exclusion is coming from in the first place.

Perhaps, the exclusion can be argued from the premise that the inclusion of x is not identical to the exclusion of x, in short: I(x) ≠ E(x). We may infer that the opposite, i.e. I(x) = E(x), is not true at the same time: in short: ~ (I(x) = E(x)). From this we can probably derive that when there is inclusion of x there is no exclusion of x, in short: I(x) = ~ E(x). This argument is more convincing since it does not presuppose an implication; it simply starts from the premise that inclusion and exclusion are not identical. Still, the statement does not say much about what is excluded; it does not capture the 'other'. It simply says that it is not the case that x is excluded. The exclusion thesis claims that inclusion

19 Cf. for the persistence of the intuitive appeal of this 'logic' Gregor Noll, 'The Exclusionary Construction of Human Rights in International and Political Theory' in Zenon Bankowski (ed.), *Epistomology and Ontology*. IVR Symposium Lund 2003, (Stuttgart: Franz Steiner Verlag, 2005). He quite pertinently identifies the problematic status of the refugee: 'The refugee brings out the radical crisis in the *concept* of human rights, included solely by means of exclusion.' (116). He then goes on to cite Wilhelm Rasch to explain the inevitability of this situation, which is due to the logic of law: 'Just because one can observe the excluded as excluded does not mean the excluded can now be painlessly included, for this logical observation also operates by way of exclusion and can only see a former exclusion, a "latency", by way of exclusion. Try as we might, we have not developed alternative logics, ones that could promise exclusion-free inclusion' (116, fn. 69. Cited from Wilhelm Rasch, 'The Limit of Modernity: Luhmann and Lyotard on Exclusion' in *Observing Complexity, Systems Theory and Postmodernity* 199 (2000), at 203–4 (emphasis omitted)).

necessarily means capturing the 'other'. Instead of the statement $I(x) = \sim E(x)$, the exclusion thesis asserts that $I(x) = E(\sim x)$; the *inclusion of x* means the *exclusion of not x*.

(1) $I(x) \neq E(x)$ Prem
(2) $\sim (I(x) = E(x))$
(3) $I(x) = \sim E(x)$
(4) $\sim E(x) = E(\sim x)$
(5) $I(x) = E(\sim x)$

Proposition (4) is flawed and as a result renders statement (5) incorrect. The move from ~E(x) to E(~x) is flawed for two related reasons: reiteration of the notion 'only' and introduction of the concept 'all' or 'everything'. The proposition ~E(x) says that it *is not* the case that x is excluded. It does not say *what is excluded.* Conversely, the proposition E(~x) says what is excluded, namely not x. But what does not x mean? It means 'that what is not x', which means 'all things but x' or 'everything but x'. But if all things but x are excluded, it means that *only x is included.* So the proposition simply reiterates the notion of 'only', which by definition combines inclusion and exclusion. Yet this reiteration only begs the question, for we want see whether inclusion entails exclusion, not if both can be combined, which is obviously the case.

In the previous objection I have showed that there is no reason why we should accept the move from 'inclusion of *at the least* x' to 'inclusion of *only* x'. The introduction of the concepts 'all things' or 'everything' also renders the proposition equally problematic. While the inclusion of x only constitutes a modest act of defining and categorizing x, the exclusion of 'all things' renders it into ambitious operation of literally cosmic proportions. We cannot confine ourselves to determining x, we must also determine the meaning of 'all things (but x)'. The problem of the notion of 'all things' is that it purports to include the universe and beyond. Normally for a notion to be meaningful (at the least in terms of practical knowledge) a minimal set of features must be determined in light of the context in which the notion is used. So, not all features must be determined. The idea is that in light of the context there is some content without which the notion cannot be understood properly and which at the same time suffices to understand it. This is only possible to the extent that a notion purports to mean *some*thing. Yet the notion 'all' or 'everything' cannot be captured by *some* content. The whole point of the notion 'all' or 'everything' is that it does not purport to be *some*thing(s) but rather *all things* and *every*thing. It follows that we cannot seriously understand what the notion 'all' means until we have understood all that is captured by it. This is an ever-expanding enterprise that has no end.[20] It renders the notion

20 The simple fact of thinking about 'all' produces a thought that belongs to the 'all' (to the extent the thought is not a part of *x*).

meaningless, or at the least useless for the purposes of practical knowledge. In other words, the notion of not-x, or ~x, is problematic if it means all things but x.

Now, one may argue that ~x does not mean 'all things but x', but simply means that '*some* things that are not-x are excluded'. Now the proposition becomes I(x) = E(a, b, c), given that neither a, b or c is identical to x. To understand this proposition we do not have to understand the notion 'all' or 'everything'; it seems sufficient to know that x is excluded and that neither a, b nor c is identical to x, therefore they are not included and thus excluded. Yet this restatement simply reiterates the notion 'only'. For as argued earlier, I(x) means the inclusion of at the least x. It does not follow from the inclusion of x that a, b or c is excluded. It may well be the case that both x and a, b or c are included.

A final argument in favor of exclusion is the contention that exclusion explains or defines what is included: the 'we' is partially defined through the 'they'. Let us imagine the exclusion of x, in short: E(x). What does this tell us about what is included? This case is simply the reverse of the question what does the inclusion of x tell us about what is excluded. We have seen that I(x) = ~E(x). Similarly, the exclusion of x only leads us to the proposition that *the inclusion of x is not the case*, in short: E(x) = ~I(x). Any stronger inferences are incorrect. The inference E(x) = I(~x) is flawed for the same reasons as I(x) = E(~x) was proven to be wrong. In other words, the only things exclusion can tell us about inclusion are purely tautological, meaningless or constitute a reiteration of the notion 'only', which simply combines exclusion and inclusion.

Order as connections: orders without borders

The deeper problem: law as unity

The previous paragraphs challenged the basic elements of the exclusion thesis from the empirical, conceptual and even logical perspective. The challenges are not exhaustive and we have been rather modest, especially in the area of the empirical counter-examples. The counter-examples should be at least sufficient to put the ball back in the court of the proponents of the exclusion thesis. Yet my expectations are that the proponents of the exclusion thesis will not be really bothered about our challenges. I guess the commitment to the centrality of exclusion is largely informed by an equally strong, if not stronger, commitment to an understanding of order and law in terms of unity. For Schmitt, the law represents not only law, but also rather law as political unity. It is the unity reflected in the law that allows making a decision in the name of the law (and thus political unity) which terminates the (violent) conflict. Since the decision is made in the name of the law and not in the particular private interests of rival parties, it is possible to rise above the conflict. If the law represents political unity, it presupposes that elements that compromise this unity are removed or kept out, i.e. excluded. So, the exclusion of the 'other' is necessary to safeguard the order.

The exclusion is not only necessary to create and maintain the order, but it also *defines* the order. Again, the order Schmitt had in mind is one where internal conflicts are fully pacified. Constrained violent conflict is only allowed at the borders between civilized states. Outside these borders there is the disorder of the unlimited and excessive violent conflict. Yet according to Schmitt, the mere empirical observation that no physical fighting is taking place is not sufficient to establish that there is order. The Weimar experience showed that internal factions may pursue their struggle by abusing the neutralizing and pacifying force of the law and overthrowing the order from the inside. The absence of violent conflict may simply constitute a prelude to the most horrible form of disorder: civil war.

What then distinguishes the apparent order and the real order? Not the absence of overt violent conflict but the *absence of claims for a different order* distinguishes the real order from covert violent conflict. Unity is the absence of claims for another order. This corresponds exactly with Lindahl's observations on the radical '*un*interpretability'.[21] It is important to note the shift from the empirical to the speculative or definitional. Where initially the order is a matter of the (empirical) absence of (excessive) violent conflict, the order now becomes the *absence of claims for another order*. But how do we know that the 'other' order is not in fact 'the' order? How can we, in fact, distinguish them in the first place? This is precisely why the other is necessary: if there is no other we simply cannot tell an order if we see it. We need the other for the purposes of excluding it. It is the guarantee that our worst enemy is still outside and that our order is really an order. Thanks to the (illegal) migrant who functions as the zone of exception, there is the possibility of sovereign power that makes the insider a true insider. It is the continuing reassurance that it is not a snake we are holding in our bosom. 'Order as unity' and 'unity as exclusion' are the flipside of a Schmittian anthropological pessimism; man is not only incapable of coming to terms with fundamental disagreements, he is also incapable of dealing with peace and order. If man does not see any enemies on the outside, restlessness and suspicion will urge him to find them among his friends.

Unlike Schmitt, Lindahl does not rely on any simplistic anthropological reductionism. Yet he is equally emphatic about unity. Both see the law as an attempt to represent unity. For Schmitt it is the only way for the law to legitimately overcome the conflict and decide in real neutral terms. For Lindahl the representation of unity is a matter of how to bring particular cases and actions under the aegis of the law. If indeed the business of law is interpretation and interpretation involves decision, how can we possibly move from the general legal norm to the particular, and back again? Arguably, decisionism leaves us with particulars, a life of heteronomy instead of *a* Nomos.

In this respect unity offers an attractive picture. It can bridge the gap between the particular and the general. If law is understood as a whole, then each of its

21 Lindahl (2003), at 778–9.

manifestations in particular cases entails and mobilizes the 'entire' law. By the same token, each of law's manifestations through general legal norms entails particular cases. The law is always one and the same thing. It is another way of stating that in each legal interpretation the entire order is involved and thus the omnipresence of the founding decision, i.e. the initial land taking. Again, this also explains the importance of the state of exception for the legal order. From this emphasis on unity necessarily follows the necessity of exclusion and an outside. As of the moment one seeks to represent the law as a whole, one not only seeks to represent what is *at least* included, but *all* that is included. If so, then one must also seek the confines of the law, i.e. its borders. Not only *some* of the law's borders are implicated, but *all* the borders of the law; if they are not, one runs the risk of including what does not belong there or keeping out what ought to be represented. In other words, the act of representing the law as unity necessarily involves representing what lies outside it, i.e. what is excluded.

Another way to understand the necessary connection between an emphatic – or rather speculative – notion of unity on the one hand and exclusion and an outside on the other, is to point to the meaning of unity as 'oneness'. It was said that the law is always one and the same thing. This means that there is in principle no particular or general element of law that is more essential than the other:[22] every general norm implicates as much the particular, as the particular implicates the general norms (also horizontally: general norms implicating other general norms and particulars implicating other particulars). There is as such no relevant general distinction between the centre and its extensions. If so, such conflation of centre and extension implies that from the perspective of the law there is no way to tell if the legal order is extending or contracting. In fact, it may be that the law has exploded or imploded. We simply would not know. To make sense of the 'oneness', it must be a 'oneness' of something. To identify this something, the 'oneness' needs an 'other', an outside. In other words, the unity as 'one' needs something else to identify the 'one'. Hence, the importance of exclusion.

Alternative: open system and connections

The previous paragraph suggests that the statement 'no inclusion without exclusion' is not the root of our problem with the exclusion thesis. It is just the 'logical' or conceptual consequence of a deeper logic: law as unity. It poses a serious challenge: how can we determine the inside, bridge the gap between the general and the particular and maintain an order without exclusion and without law as unity? The remainder of this chapter attempts to present a picture of the law that successfully addresses this question. The picture consists of the following three elements and academic representatives:

22 Or at the least there are many elements that are on an equal footing.

- Law as an *open system* (Paul Scholten).
- Legal statements as counter-facts (Foqué and 't Hart).
- Law as the practice of imputing connections (Bruno Latour).[23]

In the following short but powerful passage, Scholten indicates how the law can be a system, an order, compatible with decisionism, but without any recourse to emphatic notions of exclusion and unity.

> In the end, the decision always involves a leap. He, who realizes this, also understands that the decision is never a deduction from a closed system. Still without a doubt, the law constitutes a system, a whole of logically fit arrangements. Yet a system that displays hiatuses here and there, not because it is the product of defective human labor, but because by its nature it is never complete and never can be, since it constitutes the foundation for decisions that add something new to the system. I believe that this is best expressed if we speak of an open system.'[24]

The thrust of the picture lies in the notion that law is a system that constitutes the foundation for the decisions that change it. This simple thesis accounts for the decisionism and legal change. By the same token, it makes the decision fit into the system itself without the need to create a state of exception or an open space. No 'additional' open space is needed because the system itself is open. The

23 These authors are not necessarily the first or the most famous to have produced these perspectives. Others have come up with similar accounts: the more, the better. I picked these authors because they fit a particular narrative. Scholten sets the stage by going to the heart of the matter: how can the general and the particular, the norm and the decision be reconciled? Though a contemporary of Schmitt and aware of the legal debate in Germany, Scholten deals with the problem of decision without ending up with a hyperbolic understanding of order and law. His account is not only extremely clear, it also seems to correspond best with legal practice. The fact that Scholten was a judge himself may have played a role. Foqué and 't Hart, the latter also both scholar and judge, are equally deeply rooted in the legal practice. Unlike Scholten, they mobilize quite some philosophy. Still, their thesis can be understood as an abstract description of how Scholten's 'open system' operates. Latour, the only non-lawyer in the line-up, nicely completes our selection of authors. While Foqué and 't Hart give an abstract account of how the law connects the facts and the norms, Latour describes how judges actually make the famous leap. We will see that rather than a leap, the decision is more like a long passage.

24 My translation of:

> 'In de beslissing zit ten slotte altijd een sprong.
> Wie dit inziet, begrijpt ook, dat de beslissing nooit de deductie is uit een gesloten systeem. Toch vormt het recht ongetwijfeld een systeem, een geheel van logische passende regelingen. Maar een systeem dat niet, omdat het gebrekkig mensenwerk is, hier en daar hiaten vertoont, maar dat uit zijn aard niet af is en niet af kan zijn, omdat het de grondslag is van beslissingen, die aan het systeem zelf iets nieuws toevoegen. Ik meen, dat dit het beste uitkomt, indien we van een open systeem spreken.'

Paul Scholten, *Algemeen Deel – Mr. C. Asser's Handleiding tot de Beoefening van het Nederlands Burgerlijk Recht* (Zwolle: WEJ Tjeenk Willink, 1974), at 76.

problem with Agamben's open space and Lindahl's state of exception is that the connection with the law is purely oblique. Again the whole point of the state of exception is that the law (or its relevant parts) is suspended in order to restore (Schmitt) or re-establish (Lindahl) order. By contrast, under Scholten's system the legal constraints are applicable each time the 'something new' is added. Not anything goes. Why? The only way to add something new by a decision is to ground the decision on the legal system, which 'constitutes the foundation for decisions'. In other words, interests, morality, religion, power cannot turn a decision into a new statement of *law*. For sure these factors play a role. What is really at stake is the effective capacity (not mere potential) of the decision to find grounds in the system. This is quite the opposite of a state of exception, where an appeal to the legal constraints does not constitute any privileged foundation for one's claim. To put it differently, the legal constraints must apply; if not, it is impossible to show that the decision was a legal one, not a mere matter of power and private interest.

Things may be different if making statements of law were reserved for a single set of persons, who do not make any statements other than legal ones. If so, then there would be no trouble identifying the law. However, this is not what our legal practice is about. In fact the peculiar aspect of law is that it is essentially de-monopolizing: nobody owns it exclusively. Statements of law belong to all. In this respect we may consider briefly Laurent De Sutter's interesting observations on the role of legal theory.

> 'If the core of any legal practice is to make emerge a possible that could be named or qualified with regard to the name "law", it *does* mean that every kind of discourse that assumes this act of qualification, every kind of discourse that shares the same concern about the question of the name and the force of it, *is legal by nature*. That also means that there is no real difference between all the possible types of discourses around the name "law", precisely because all of these discourses are legal discourses. Every legal discourse is the discourse of the law and the other way around, *but nothing else*. There is no difference between "levels" of discourses, or levels of reflexivity, when time comes to talk "law". That means, furthermore, that there is no meta-discourse in law, as Bruno Latour perfectly puts it.'[25] (emphasis in original)

> 'When lawyers pronounce a word as a word of law, this word *does not belong to them anymore*.'[26] (emphasis in original)

> '[L]aw does not adapt itself to social change: law *is* the language of social change.'[27]

25 Laurent De Sutter, 'How to Get Rid of Legal Theory', in Zenon Bankowski (ed.), *Epistomology and Ontology* (2005), at 44.

26 Ibid., at 46.

27 Ibid., at 47.

The way I understand these passages is that the law is without privileges. The simple act of making a claim 'in the name' of the law disowns the speaker of those same words, in the citation the lawyers. In other words, the law resists being monopolized by particular persons. Neither is there a metaphysical privileged position to understand and speak of the law. There is no meta-discourse when it comes to making statements of law. Indeed, the discourse is about what counts as (valid) law. Of course, not every legal discourse produces valid statements of what the law requires. To be successful one must ground one's claim (and the corresponding decision) on relevant and weighty legal statements of the system. Why? Nobody has a monopoly or even a genuine privileged status to make claims in the name of the law. The decision only becomes legal to the extent it is supported by sufficient legal material. This is precisely why the decision cannot take place outside the constraints of the law in the state of exception or the open space of human praxis. It must take place not in any kind of human praxis, but a very particular one: legal practice.

Law between real and ideal

The upshot of the exclusion thesis is that it allowed so much room for real politics in the business of law setting and law making, that there is hardly any point in explaining how the law informs the actual decision taken. What matters to the exclusion thesis is that the law must be capable of creating a space where it can be decided what counts as the law. The legal aspect of this phenomenon is the fact that the law creates such space and that what is produced in this space will tell us what belongs to the law and what does not. By contrast, if we opt for the law as an open system, then the whole business of deciding – the so-called leap – is constrained by the law itself. As a result we must provide a picture how the law informs and constrains the decisions. If not, we run the risk of ending up with a state of exception.

The notion of the counter-factuality of law as elaborated by Foqué and 't Hart offers us a useful abstract description of how the law can inform and constrain decisions.[28] The counter-factuality of the law roughly means that the legal

28 A.C. 't Hart, *Recht als schild van Perseus. Voordrachten over strafrechtstheorie*, (Arnhem: Gouda Quint, 1991) and R. Foqué and A.C. 't Hart, *Instrumentaliteit en Rechtsbescherming. Grondslagen van een Strafrechtelijke Waardendiscussie* (Arnhem: Gouda Quint, 1990). For an interpretation of their work I relied primarily on Serge Gutwirth, 'De toepassing van het finaliteitsbeginsel van de Privacywet van 8 december 1992 tot bescherming van de persoonlijke levenssfeer ten opzichte van de verwerking van persoonsgegevens', *Tijdschrift voor Privaatrecht*, (1993), at 1419–21; Serge, Gutwirth, *Waarheidsaanspraken in recht en wetenschap. Een onderzoek naar de verhouding tussen recht en wetenschap met bijzondere illustratie uit het informaticarecht* (Brussels/Antwerp: VUBPress/MAKLU, 1993), at 349–61; Mireille Hildebrandt, *Straf(begrip) en procesbeginsel. Een onderzoek naar de betekenis van straf en strafbegrip en de waarde van het procesbeginsel naar aanleiding van de consensuele afdoening van strafzaken* (Sanders Instituut/Kluwer, 2002), at 126–31.

concepts, vehicles or the statements of law (this includes general norms but also particular rulings) are constructs that go against the facts, i.e. they are a kind of fiction. An important example in this respect is the legal concept of '*rechtssubjectiviteit*', which I will translate as (individual) legal agency, i.e. the capacity to have legal rights and obligations. It is clear that legal agency is not identical to being a person of flesh and blood. When asked about their identity, not many people would answer that they are an autonomous legal agent who is a holder of rights and obligations. So the notion of legal capacity is artificial and idealist. By the same token, the notion presumes and pertains to real flesh-and-blood people. If not, there would simply be no use for the notion. It is precisely this hybrid nature (idealist and factual) that offers two levels of constraints on the legal decision-making process (Foqué and 't Hart speak of protection of the individual).

First, the fact that legal agency appeals (per definition) to a notion of autonomy means that even if a person is in fact not autonomous, the law must treat the person as such. The upshot being that a legal decision must always ensure that the autonomy of a person is safeguarded, even if people are not in position to deploy their autonomy. Even if in terms of effect, it would not make much difference whether or not autonomy is respected, the decision must comply with the constraint. In other words, the idealist aspect operates as an important legal constraint on decisions purely inspired by efficacy considerations. It keeps the possibility open to legally act against the facts. However, if legal concepts were to be considered only from their artificial perspective, they could easily become a cold theoretical excuse for unsound practices. This is offset by the realist aspect of legal concepts. The connection must be made with the particular case. In the case of autonomy, it means that idealists or naïve notions of free choice must be refined when an idealist application of the rule actually fosters dominance rather than autonomy (cf. the advent of labor law as a derogation of the normal principles of freedom of contract). In other words, a kind of mediation must take place. This mediation is characterized by the fact that we cannot tell beforehand where the equilibrium will be fixed. But we can tell where most of the legal constraints will affect the equilibrium.

The second level of constraint is precisely the fact that the law *cannot* coincide with reality. There is no 'real' truth about the law. There is no identity between reality and law. This has two important implications. First, he who allegedly holds or controls the truth about our reality does not control the law. For instance, the truth about the logic of technological development does not mean that the law must follow suit and put everything in place to support any form of progress.[29] The same goes for the alleged truth of the enormous costs associated with the legal protection of aliens seeking admission. The second implication – the reverse – is that the law does not monopolize reality. It follows that nobody can claim an

29 Cf. Gutwirth, *Waarheidsaanspraken*.

absolute truth in the name of the law. This is, of course, a safeguard for diversity, but more importantly, it means that each time the law affects reality it must show how it does so *legally*. To put it differently, those acting in the name of the law must show how they make the connection between law and reality. If the connection is made too easily or automatically there may be a problem.[30] Counter-intuitively or paradoxically, those acting in the name of the law must show that their actions did not come about as a matter of a true sense of reality. If not, they raise the suspicion of confusing law as counter-factuality with law as factuality (e.g. concrete order, state of exception, etc.). To avoid such suspicion, they must indicate that they were bound by legal constraints. In other words, rather than moving away from the legal constraints, the key characteristic of the legal decision – the new something to be added – is its direct connection (not an oblique connection like the state of exception) with legal constraints.

Law as passage and connections

The previous discussion showed how the counter-factual nature of law is searching for legal constraints. We also pointed out that making a legal decision should not always come too easily; it raises suspicions of an identity between law and reality. In this paragraph we would like to say a bit more about how the constraints actually work. What does it look like to move into the constraints of the law rather than away from them? Scholars have of course examined law in action (cf. legal realism and critical legal studies) which have produced very important – and often disturbing – insights. However, the actual physical acts involved have not been a subject of study. When asked about his profession, a lawyer would typically speak of the output he produces. Rarely, would he say that he reads texts, underlines passages, puts papers on his desk, hesitates (i.e. really waiting before saying or writing something down), etc. Yet this is precisely what Bruno Latour has done. This is what we need to render tangible how legal decisions and their constraints go hand in hand. The following is a brief discussion of aspects of Latour's account of the law that are relevant for our purposes.

In *La fabrique du droit. Une Ethnographie du Conseil d'Etat* Latour seeks to paint a picture of the law (with a lower case 'l') through an anthropological study of the French Conseil d'État. Latour's study is situated in his general investigation into the core of the 'modern' society.[31] Law is one of the central forms of 'truth-diction' ('*véridiction*') that characterizes our society among other forms already treated by Latour such as science, technology, politics and religion.[32] As in his earlier studies, Latour wants to disclose the salient features of a form of

30 Cf. the importance of hesitation in the path of law (see *infra* discussion of Latour).

31 Bruno Latour, *La Fabrique du Droit: Une Ethnograhie du Conseil d'État* (Paris: Découverte, 2002), at 265.

32 Ibid., at 265 and 271.

véridiction, and point out what makes them so valuable in terms of our own society. The underlying idea being that for want of one objective nature and due to the pressure from cultural pluralism/relativism there is no fixed standard to describe and evaluate our societies. Therefore, we must, according to Latour, investigate afresh our own society in its own terms to establish how we can relate to other societies: 'Voilà, selon nous, ce qui constitute *notre* humanité, qu'en est-il de la vôtre?'[33] Hence, the objectives of *La fabrique du droit* can be briefly stated as follows: (1) investigation into the features of our law '... idée du véritable mode existence de notre propre Etat de droit ...'[34] and (2) show that our law is valuable and deserves respect from other cultures. For the purposes of this book, I will only draw from Latour's observations regarding objective (1). We will restrict ourselves to Latour's discussion of the judicial branch of the Conseil, which acts as a kind of Supreme Court in administrative litigation in the sense that it only reviews the legality of decisions, not the merits of the case. As a result the procedures have a high juridico-technical character, but that does not mean that the justices themselves are from the legal profession. Though some of them trained to be lawyers, most of them held senior positions in the French administration.

Latour selected the Conseil, because it is the stage where the law is presented in its purest form. Most lawyers would not agree with such a notion of 'purity', but after publication of his book, Latour proposed a very modest and pragmatic understanding of 'purity'. To Latour, the procedure before the Conseil was one where almost all the different steps that amount to a legal decision have been *documented.* In other words, for purposes of a field study, the Conseil offered him relatively easily accessible data which allowed him to retrace the path of the law.[35] The advantage of the Conseil is that the justices make a collective and unanimous decision; this allowed Latour to document the deliberations without scrutinizing what goes on in the minds of the justices.[36] The actual field research took two periods of six months and covered activities in all kinds of departments (library, cafeteria, offices of the justices, archives) and all kinds of meetings. In fact, Latour claimed to be embedded like a 'mouche sur le mur'.[37]

Having described the activities, the backgrounds, the attitudes, the physical movements, utterances and the spatial environment of the justices and the other employees of the Conseil, Latour comes up with following description. Law is a matter of making connections, whereby the law has a particular binding effect. This binding force of law is best described as a passage through which the 'dossier' must move. Going through this trajectory whereby the dossier is

33 Latour (2002), at 264, emphasis in original.

34 Ibid., at 265.

35 Explanation given by Latour during brainstorm session at the VUB on 5 February 2004 organized by the Center for Law, Science, Technology and Society Studies.

36 Ibid., at 271.

37 Ibid., at 16.

confronted with the different typical features of the law turns the decision about the dossier into a legal decision, i.e. a statement of what the law requires in a particular case.

Laws as connections

Facts, persons and legal texts are being linked to each other. Or rather, the texts that pertain to facts, persons and law (in the sense of written statements of law) are being connected. Latour relies for this analysis on his descriptions of what the case managers are doing and the physical trajectory of the dossier. Latour shows us how the case manager physically puts the different texts on his desk side by side,[38] compares them, writes down the (relevant) excerpts and summarizes them in an opinion. These texts all make certain connections with people, facts and past legal decisions (legislative and judicial). This process of making connections is also reflected in the trajectory of the dossier. The physical trajectory (where the file is located) in a sense determines by whom, what kind of and when, connections may be added. For example, it matters for the type of connections and thus the final outlook of the decision whether the dossier pursues the easy or hard case trajectory.

Law as something binding

Latour also observes the special binding force of the law. He does not derive this observation from the wording of the legal materials, but from what the justices are saying. During their deliberations they indicate that they are constrained: 'on ne peut pas rejeter le moyen';[39] 'il nous est difficile d'annuler';[40] 'ça nous pose un vrai problème'.[41] It can be summed up by the words of one the justices: 'Nous sommes là pour dire le droit'.[42]

Law as a passage

Having established the constraints of the law, one would expect Latour to address the perennial question: What gives the law its binding force? What makes the judges feel the constraints? However, Latour stays away from any investigation into the mental state of the justices or their reflective methods.[43] He restricts himself to an anthropological study of what happens when justices are discussing;

38 Petition, evidence (i.e. the expert reports), written pleadings of the parties and legal materials (laws, regulations, case law, doctrine).
39 Ibid., at 37.
40 Ibid.
41 Ibid., at 38.
42 Ibid., at 63.
43 Ibid., at 141.

he follows the course of the dossier. According to Latour, the course of the dossier may be described as the circulation or transfer of objects of value, analogous to the analysis of a dynamic novel.[44] These objects of value undergo a change during the course of the case and especially during the deliberations of the justices. The 'objects of value' refer to what the justices find important in the process of their decision. In a sense the objects of value affect (constrain and inform) the justices' point of view on the dossier, and at the same time their points of view express the objects of value. In fact, the changes in the objects of value are being expressed in the words of the justices ('*phrases prononcées*') during their deliberations.[45]

Though it may not be fully clear how one should describe the nature of the value objects, it is clear how Latour sees the business of judging cases: judicial review ('*dire le droit*') is a complex and dynamic process, whereby the different value objects in a way bump into the dossier. For example, the interesting aspects of the dossier may be of great influence on how the justices formulate their opinions. The coherence becomes crucial when a case 'requires' the justices to revisit their own case law. The list of value objects should make it clear that to Latour, it is of little relevance to divide the value objects into essential or secondary ones. They all play a part, and from the empirical material one cannot conclude that one object is more dominant than another.

What matters to Latour's picture of the law, is that change in the value objects (or rather their role) during the passage guides the outcome of the case rather than specific reasoning: 'Les juges ne raisonnent pas: ils sont aux prises avec un dossier qui agit sur eux, qui les presse, qui les force, qui leur fait faire quelque chose'.[46] It seems that the dossier makes its way through the value objects like the metal ball in a pinball machine: the bumpers or the bouncers in the machine are both an obstacle (constraint) and an impetus (guidance) for the ball. Thus, judicial review is not a matter of a logical chain of ideas or a simple connection of texts.[47] The

44 Latour identifies about ten objects of value: 1. Authority of the justices. It matters who says what when; 2. Course/progress of the petition. It is impossible or at the least unusual that a petition leads to a decision without encountering any obstacles; 3. Organization of dossiers. An important consideration is the pace of a dossier in the logistical organization of the Conseil; 4. The interesting aspects of the dossier in terms of its complexities and difficulties. This partially determines the involvement of the justices; 5. The weight of the legal materials to which the dossier is connected; 6. Quality control, which verifies to what extent the conditions for adequate treatment of the dossier have been satisfied; 7. Hesitation, which allows the justices to maintain some distance from the existing and proposed connections to the dossier, before making a decision; 8. 'Moyenne' or legal argument, which forces the justices to connect certain legal texts with the case; 9. Coherence of the law, the justices see it as their task, irrespective of the scope of their ruling, to situate their decision in the context of the system of existing legal rules and judicial rulings; 10. Limits of the law, which determine whether or not a case should go through the passage of the law in the first place.

45 Ibid., at 141.

46 Ibid., at 201.

47 Ibid., at 150–1.

connection is crucial, but the connection is both the outcome of the decision and the making of it. This process cannot be simple or clean as logic. It is heavy and laborious. In fact, the value objects are like concerns that confront the dossier and turn it into a problem. They slow down and complicate the process. But it is precisely due to this process of moving through constraints and revealing them, that we come to consider the decision on the dossier as a legal one, as opposed to one of politics or economics.[48]

There are obviously some critical comments to be made on Latour's study,[49] but this is not the place and, in any event, the critiques will not pertain to the aspects of Latour's account that are relevant for our purposes. We should retain from Latour's discussion how the decisional aspect of the law is really a matter of constraints. Also, the notion of making a multitude of connections is extremely important. This is a clear indication of the fact that the passage of law is not one that ultimately aims to make a connection with and re-affirm the foundation of the law (basic norm or land taking). Instead, when the coherence is at stake, the existing rules and past decisions that pertain to *similar* cases are considered, not the entire order.

The whole point is to make connections *up to certain points*, but not up to a central point. Conversely, the existence of a central point in law would indeed justify the legal process as an expression of a logical chain. Similarly, if there were a foundational point in the law, then the multitude of connections would be, in reality, just an expression (probably a defective one) of a single, unique, one and the same connection ('*e pluribus unum*'), between the particular case and the foundation of the order. If indeed this foundation (e.g. land taking) is one that is ultimately not constrained by the law, then the same should apply to any decision connecting to it. Hence, the state of exception or its milder version, Agamben's open space. But Latour shows us that this is not what happens.

The Conseil displays a very particular practice, that does not fit Agamben's far too general 'human praxis' or whatever other version can be called a state of exception. The state of exception cannot account for the objects of value that Latour identified. An extremely important value object is 'hesitation'.[50] This object goes fully against the whole notion of a state of exception, concrete order or any form of physical reality. It is a deliberate attempt to create distance from what is clear, true, evident, etc. Hesitation is incompatible with the urgency and emergency that provokes the state of exception. Yet, hesitation is a key aspect of a legal decision. More generally, it is interesting to note that the concrete order and any form of effectiveness of the law is something about which the law is much less demanding than its theorists. If effectiveness and the actual and concrete

48 The analogy with the inversion of scientific process and scientific fact is of course not a coincidence.

49 See Laurent Sutter and Serge Gutwirth, 'Droit et cosmopolitique. Notes sur la contribution de Bruno Latour à la pensée du droit', *Droit et société*, 259 (2004).

50 See object No. 7, n. 44.

reality were so material for the meaning and pretension of the law, it would be extremely difficult to give a place to the very long prescription terms (statute of limitations) in both civil and criminal law. This is a clear indication that the law deliberately distinguishes between constraints on the one hand and effectiveness or reality on the other. To put it differently, so-called disorder and the apparent ineffectiveness of a legal order does not suspend the law: the law always takes its time. In other words, we must not give up too easily on the law.

Let me summarize the relevant findings from Latour's analysis. First, the legal decision does not take place ultimately in a state of exception or an open space, but rather in a process shaped by constraints. Second, coherence is an important aspect of what makes the legal decision legal, but the coherence does not involve unity or the re-affirmation of the order and its foundations. Rather coherence (and a successful legal decision) is a matter of a multitude of relevant connections. Third, these connections extend to certain points, but not to a central or foundational point. Fourth, another important aspect of the law is hesitation. The law takes its time. This also means that alleged disorder in society, or rather gross violations of the law, does not equal a state of exception.

Orders without borders

It has been argued in this chapter that there is neither empirically nor conceptually a necessary connection between exclusion and identity, law or 'inside'. Furthermore, it has become clear that unity (as sameness, wholeness or oneness) and the state of exception cannot account for what happens when 'something new' is added to the law. Law as unity meant that each decision ultimately implicates the *entire* legal order and thus a complete inside and outside, hence, the necessity for borders and exclusion. The new decision involves the order self, the normal constraints of law cannot apply anymore. Hence, the state of exception or the 'open space', in which it must be decided afresh what belongs to the inside and the outside. This then is allegedly the positive upshot of the exclusion thesis. The advantage for the normal migrant seeking admission is that since the inside is decided (partially) afresh, and nobody has any privileged access to what belongs to the inside, the migrant has the *potential* to become an insider. I have argued that this gives far too little protection to the normal migrant. By contrast, when the law is understood not as unity, but as an open system, we can see that taking a legal decision regarding *something* is not to move away from the legal constraints but to openly and deliberately submit to the normal constraints of the law. The *something* may be new, but it becomes legal because it respects the constraints of the system.

Law as connections and passage presented us with a tangible picture of how such a submission to the constraints actually works. Latour's analysis showed that an important aspect of the legal decision is to make connections to *particular points* in the law. There was no attempt to mobilize the entire legal system or to look for a single and unique connection to the heart of France's legal order or political unity. What matters is the capacity to make a multitude of relevant connections. This also explains the logical impossibility of determining what is included through exclusion: exclusion cannot tell you what connections are available. Law as connections and passage provides us with a much more realistic and plausible picture of the borders of a legal order than law as unity. Under law as connections, the importance of borders is brought back to more modest proportions. The borders do not operate as a separator between the inside and outside of a legal order; at best they are the expression of a failure to make relevant connections between two points whereby at least one is already part of the legal order. It is possible that the other point does not connect to the point already inside. Still this does not necessarily disqualify the other point as being outside the legal order. It may make connections to alternative points that are part of the legal order. In other words, the border cannot tell you what points are successfully connected to each other, only the connections between the points can! It is only after failing to make the connections that we can picture the so-called outside and the borders.

Again, the question is not whether a point lies on the wrong side of the border, but rather what it takes to make the relevant connections. This all explains what is typically called the contextual, relative and porous nature of borders (of a legal order). Law as unity can only account for porous borders by qualifying them as a constant defect of an imperfect order. Law as unity must, by definition, adopt an emphatic notion of borders. Failure to do this compromises the notion of unity. If law is to be understood as unity then the borders must be complete and perfect. The borders must surround and completely contain the entirety of the legal order; if not, the unity dissipates into an 'other'. Consequently, though borders may expand and contract *over time*, at any given *point in time* borders must be perfect. This means that at every point in time we must have a perfect idea of the entirety of the legal order, if not we are always in *complete uncertainty* whether or not we are in the order.

Since unity is an absolute and 'all or nothing' concept there is no room for more or less (un)certainty. In fact, law as unity cannot account for (porous) borders of a legal order in the real world. To somehow save their position, proponents of law as unity introduce a separate sphere: the state of exception. The contingencies of the real world are dealt with in the state of exception which functions as an annex or backroom of the order as unity. As a result, we can still speak meaningfully of order as unity and as a result we should be emphatic about the role played by borders. By contrast, if we adopt a more plausible and practice based understanding of the legal order, the primacy of borders, exclusion and the state of exception vanishes. Order without border? Yes and no. Legal orders will always have their borders, primarily as a reflection of the intended scope of jurisdiction. However, setting and enforcing the borders are not constitutive for the order.

Where does this leave the normal migrant? If indeed we discard the hyperbolic understanding of law as unity then the centrality of exclusion and the state of exception disappears. Hence, there is no reason to consider migration as provoking or constituting a state of exception, which either challenges (Lindahl) or enables (Agamben) the existing legal order. Neither is the exclusion of migrants constitutive for the order. What then does the phenomenon of migration tell us? How should we understand the authorities' treatment of normal migrants? For one, it should be clear that migrants seeking admission do not challenge the foundations of the legal order. They do not challenge the authorities' *right* to exclusion. If they challenge anything it is of course the exclusion itself and probably the way in which the exclusion is carried out, i.e. without justification. In short, there is no point in substantiating the centrality of the exclusion of migrants, because 'exclusion' is simply not central. Still, if the challenge of the migrants seeking admission is not special or exceptional, surely the official response to especially '*de facto* migration' is. Both Lindahl and an extended reading of Agamben do point to the exceptional way in which migrants are treated. Lindahl is partially right in emphasizing the use of typical a-legal categories for admitting migrants, e.g. humanitarian reasons. The exceptional nature of the migrant's 'inclusion for purposes of exclusion' is problematic. However, the point is that the exclusion thesis seeks the cause for this allegedly extra-legal treatment of migrants in the structure, concept and phenomenology of the law. Worse, it is the inevitable flipside of the advent of human rights. In contrast, having abandoned safely law as unity, we may reiterate a much more plausible characterization of the authorities' treatment of migrants. Rather than being an inescapable state of exception revealing the violent – almost mysterious – origins of sovereign power, immigration policy simply violates the basic standards of law and legal practice. The most fundamental legal standard violated is probably the principle of proportionality. Yet under the exclusion thesis it is impossible for the authorities to violate this principle or any other legal standard for that matter. Under the exclusion thesis, one may report that the authorities use violence and inflict harm in the name of the law. But one can never establish that the authorities invoke the law falsely. There are ultimately no legal standards of reference because any determination of the law boils down to a kind of state of exception, which involves the establishment of the entire order afresh. At best, one can hope for an additional accountability that is clearly not legal (Lindahl) or worse an 'open space of human practice' (Agamben). The exclusion thesis with its focus on unity and thus the state of exception puts the law out of service too easily. When things are getting tough and the law is most needed, it is put aside. For Schmitt this is not a problem because if it is really getting tough, there is actually a fundamental disagreement. Under conditions of fundamental disagreement, law lacks legitimate authority because it will then simply operate as violence in disguise. Of course, Schmitt does not mean to say that in a system of political unity citizens have ceased to disagree. On the contrary, law is the civilized vehicle used to settle disagreements between citizens. Yet the law is incapable of dealing with *fundamental* disagreements. But when does a civil disagreement really turn into a fundamental one? In the abstract we can easily define instances of disagreement that the law is incapable of addressing.[51] But in practice the law hardly ever fails to address important disagreements. *When pushed hard enough* the law always makes a kind of connection to the effect that the most radical and unexpected phenomena – such as genocide and universal suffrage[52] – are brought under its aegis. So, in practice Schmitt's fears of fundamental disagreements rarely materialize. Or in any event, the disagreement is not so fundamental to the effect of compromising *per se* the legal order. In short, the idea that the order is at risk or is challenged is a very strong image, but it rarely occurs in the practice of law and political life. As a result there is no reason to keep the exclusion of migrants out of the legal realm. The only 'legal' justification for not justifying the exclusion is the rule of inherent sovereign power. But this rule is without any foundation. Its only support is the intuitively attractive but deeply flawed exclusion thesis. In short, the current practice of exclusion without justification is legally untenable.

51 For example one could define a fundamental disagreement as follows. Opposing and mutually exclusive positions (e.g. on economics, family life, religion) that rely on views about what counts as the legal order, whereby each view covers the *entire* legal order (and thus not merely economics, family life, religion) and adopting the position of the other requires a *total* rejection of one's order.

52 Genocide is used as an example because it can be argued that its radically heinous and inhumane character puts genocide 'out of our legal order': conventional criminal law can never account – not even partially – for the motives and effects of such acts (leaving aside 'technical' problems of retroactivity) (cf. Hanna Arendt, *Eichmann in Jerusalem: A Report on the Banality of Evil* (New York: Penguin Books, 1994)). Universal suffrage, though a most welcome phenomenon, is in this sense equally radical and unexpected: the *conceptual* basis for legitimate political and legal authority changed radically from pluto- and aristocratic to democratic.

Chapter 5

Inclusion for the sake of exclusion

The authority of immigration laws

In the preceding chapters the main target of our investigation has been the rule of inherent sovereign power. This rule is crucial as it legally sanctions the current practice of exclusion without justification. The aim of the critique was to show that the rule does not find any basis in positive law when it comes to the other powers associated with sovereignty (see Chapter 2) and that its sole support comes from the deeply flawed exclusion thesis (see Chapters 3 to 4). It has become clear that there is nothing exceptional about the exclusion of normal migrants that should prevent it from being subject to normal legal constraints. Consequently, there is simply no legal basis for the authorities to exclude normal migrants without proper justification. The rule of inherent sovereign power and thus exclusion without justification is legally untenable. So far, the argument is essentially one of competence. Authorities need a legal basis for their actions, and in the case at hand they happen to lack this competence. The reason is that such an absolute discretionary competence relies on hyperbolic notions of order as unity, exclusion and the state of exception, which do not fit the structure of law. There is another argument from the structure of law against the current practice of exclusion without justification. Ironically, the exclusion thesis points to this argument as it identifies a painful anomaly: the migrant is included for the purpose of his exclusion. However, as the exclusion thesis focuses so much on order, it overlooks two crucial closely related elements. First, not only does the law grant the authorities the power to exclude migrants,[1] but the authorities also use the law to organize the exclusion. This is not self-evident because authorities could have organized the exclusion without the use of migration laws. They might have opted for just putting up fences and giving orders to their officials to keep out aliens by all means not prohibited by law. Yet in addition to such measures, states have also issued immigration laws. In other words, states use the law to organize the exclusion of migrants. Second, migrants are officially the norm subjects of the immigration laws. The immigration laws are not only directed at the officials

1 My claim is not that there is no right to exclude migrants. I just deny the right to exclude migrants *without justification*.

responsible for executing the exclusion of migrants, but they are also directed at migrants; the migrants are expected to obey the immigration laws. The admission laws contain provisions directly addressed to migrants, e.g. they cannot enter and reside in the territory without the proper documentation, and risk (penal) sanctions if they violate such interdictions.

In this chapter, I take these two elements as a promising route for showing that our admission practices, or rather admission laws, are legally untenable. My argument is based on a particular analysis of the role of authority in law, namely the authority thesis as developed by Joseph Raz. The central idea is that if admission laws are to count as laws they must meet some minimal requirements that are inherent to the *structure of law*. I shall contend that current admission laws cannot satisfy these minimal requirements. The starting point is the observation that the law claims authority. To seriously claim authority the law must at the least have the *capacity to have legitimate authority*. This capacity depends on whether the law or the relevant area of the law can meet the conditions set by the so-called normal justification thesis. According to this thesis, the law must *reflect the reasons that are directly applicable to the relevant individuals* from whom it requires obedience. It does not mean that the law must satisfy the wishes and desires of the relevant individuals. Nor should the law give priority to the reasons applicable to them. The law should just reflect that it constitutes a judgment on all those reasons. To put it in (too) simple terms: if the law can show that it took into account the reasons that concern the relevant individuals, it has the capacity to have legitimate authority *vis-à-vis* those persons. When it comes to admission laws, this capacity is missing, precisely because of the discretionary character of exclusion without justification. This, then, turns admission laws into incoherent, paradoxical and ultimately illegal instruments: the legal community only considers the migrant as a relevant individual for the purposes of excluding him from that same community. As a result, the authorities cannot seriously claim that the migrants have any reason to obey the admission laws. Consequently, the authorities lack even the capacity to claim authority: the admission laws fail to count as law *vis-à-vis* the excluded migrants.

Preliminary remarks on the use of Raz' authority thesis

Legal scholars have produced many theses and concepts about the nature of law, many of which seem relevant for our attempt to challenge the legal tenability of current admission policies. Those theses that contend that normative principles play a role in identifying the existence and content of law seem promising, as current admission practices may find it hard to satisfy some of these principles. However, I have opted for a thesis about law belonging to a strand of legal theory which holds the exact opposite view: moral evaluation can never be an element of identifying the existence and content of law. In effect, the authority thesis is used by Raz to defend his exclusive legal positivism as reflected in the sources thesis.[2] I do not support exclusive positivism, but my choice for the authority thesis is somewhat strategic. As a kind of *a fortiori* argument, I will try to show that even the most – morally neutral or empty – thesis about law will already demonstrate that current admission practices are legally problematic. Furthermore, it is quite possible to reject (exclusive) legal positivism, and still accept the authority thesis. Almost all dominant strands of legal theory (or philosophy) believe that the authority of law is a crucial element to be accounted for. For example, our main opponent in the previous chapter, Carl Schmitt, despised legal positivism (or probably formalism) precisely because of its failure to produce genuine authority. Even contemporary (neo-classical) strands of legal positivism's alleged arch-enemy, i.e. natural law as advocated by the likes of John Finnis, is fully in line with the authority thesis.[3] Raz' authority thesis has attracted some criticism, but this has mostly to do with Raz' intention to use the authority thesis to prove the sources thesis.[4] Few contemporary scholars have challenged the fact that the law claims authority – their objections are primarily concerned with the scope of the authority claimed. Now, more 'empirically' oriented strands of legal theory, e.g. law and economics, or critical legal studies, may find the law's claim for authority of lesser interest and even consider it a kind of sham. And closer to empirical reality, practicing lawyers may have little dealings with ideas about law's claim for authority. Still, those academics and practicing lawyers do not deny the fact that the law *claims* authority and that in law's *own terms* authority is an important feature.

More important than virtual consensus in academia, is that the legal authorities – the officials – cannot openly and seriously contest the authority thesis, as to do so may be self-defeating. The claim for authority is nothing less than the claim for general obedience from the relevant individuals. It is difficult to imagine a government which claims that its own rules and regulations do not deserve obedience from the relevant individuals. In other words, authorities must at least pretend to have authority over these relevant individuals. So, the mere fact of using the law triggers a claim for authority over the relevant individuals. By the same token, the authorities – by using the law – take up another crucial commitment: they pretend that there are *reasons* other than the threat of coercion to comply with the directives. If not, the authorities can only claim obedience to the extent they can

2 E.g. 'The main purpose of this essay is to defend the sources thesis . . .' (Joseph Raz, 'Authority, Law and Morality' in Joseph Raz (ed.), *Ethics in the Public Domain: Essays in the Morality of Law and Politics* (Oxford: Clarendon Press, 1994), at 195) 'We will concentrate on two features which must be possessed by anything capable of being authoritatively binding. These two features will then be used to support the sources thesis.' (Ibid., at 202.)

3 John Finnis, *Natural Law and Natural Rights* (Oxford: Oxford University Press, 1980), at 233–7, 261.

4 For my use of Raz in the context of the perennial controversy between normative jurisprudence and descriptive conceptual legal theory, see Bas Schotel, *Protecting the Alien's Interest in Immigration. Arguments from Law and Political Theory for Changing Our Admission Laws and Practices* (2008), Vrije Universiteit Brussel, Ph.D. dissertation.

effectively enforce compliance. Modern regimes, including oppressive ones, do not openly state that their directives should be complied with *only if and when* non-compliance will be punished by force. Both coercion and repression are elements of enforcement, but they do not constitute the official reason for obedience. Instead the typical official reason for obedience is *the law*: the legal directive should be obeyed because it is the law.

It must also be noted that Raz would probably not approve of the way in which I use the authority thesis. First, I will make an extended reading of the authority thesis. I will try to argue that authorities cannot simply *claim* authority. In my view, to *claim* authority, they should at least have seriously considered the reasons that apply to the individuals over whom they claim authority. Raz does not go this far. Second, I will also try to show that the failure to seriously claim authority compromises the legal validity of the legal norms. Contrary to Raz, I believe that sometimes our theses about the nature of law (in the case at hand, the authority thesis), also affect what we think is valid as law.[5]

The authority of law: an extended reading of Joseph Raz' authority thesis[6]

Authority, obedience and reasons

The starting point of the authority thesis is the observation that the law or legal officials claim authority over individuals. To put it in more technical terms: the

5 Raz himself has been very emphatic about distinguishing between the conceptual analysis of law and theories of adjudication or the legal validity of norms: 'There is something inherently implausible in adopting the lawyer's perspective as our fundamental methodological stance.' ('Authority, Law and Morality' in Joseph Raz (ed.), *Ethics in the Public Domain: Essays in the Morality of Law and Politics* (Oxford: Clarendon Press, 1994), at 203.) Or, as La Torre has phrased it perspicuously: 'Raz believes that the "nature of law" is independent from legal practice, hence also from the internal point of view, that is, the point of view of judges, lawyers, other officials, or citizens, who use and apply the law.' (Massimo La Torre, 'On Two Distinct and Opposing Versions of Natural Law: "Exclusive" versus "Inclusive"', 19 *Ratio Juris* 197 (2006), at 214.) In that same contribution, La Torre has convincingly shown that Raz' position in this respect is untenable. It takes us too far to elaborate on this issue, but it easy to see how one's concept of law must determine what one believes counts as valid law. For example, if one holds the view that conceptually law is necessarily a system of directives, then clearly one must accept that a system made up exclusively of non-directives (e.g. forecasts, historical time tables,) cannot count as – valid – law. See Bas Schotel, *Protecting the Alien's Interest in Immigration*, (2008), Ph.D. dissertation.

6 The following discussion draws on Raz' presentation of the authority thesis in the following works: Joseph Raz, *The Authority of Law. Essays on Law and Morality* (Oxford: Clarendon Press, 1979); *The Morality of Freedom* (Oxford: Clarendon Press, 1988); 'Authority, Law and Morality' in Joseph Raz (ed.), *Ethics in the Public Domain: Essays in the Morality of Law and Politics* (Oxford: Clarendon Press, 1994), 194–221. For Raz's discussion of law as a system of practical reasons I drew on *The Concept of a Legal System. An Introduction to the Theory of Legal System* (Oxford: Clarendon Press, 1980); *Practical Reason and Norms* (Oxford: Oxford University Press, 1999).

law claims authority over its norm subjects. Authority means that an individual has a duty to obey the entity that has authority over him. The individual must do what the authorities require of him. What is special about the concept of authority and obedience is that what is required by the authorities constitutes a reason in itself for what an individual must do. By 'in itself', we mean that the individual must not consider other reasons for determining what to do. In the context of the law, authority means that an individual must do what the law requires *because* it is the law. For instance, traffic laws require you to stop if there is a stop sign. In concrete cases there may be good reasons to stop because it would be dangerous for you (or others) not to stop. Also, often there may be overriding reasons for you not to stop (maybe you are in a real hurry or there is no traffic). The point of law's claim of authority and obedience is that you should not consider these other reasons for stopping or not stopping. The fact that the law requires you to stop should be the one and only reason for determining what to do. It means that according to the law, you need not consider so much the merits of what the law requires from you. The law provides a kind of content independent reason for determining what to do. Its demand for obedience implies that you should not consider other reasons that may guide your action; the law excludes other reasons for determining what to do. Raz speaks of exclusionary reasons. At first glance, the idea of content independent and exclusionary reasons suggests that the law's claim for obedience denies the rationality of individuals. By contrast, the whole point of the authority thesis is that it understands the law as a subset of practical reasoning. First, it recognizes that individuals have many reasons that can guide their actions. The only thing the authority thesis asserts is that the law demands that individuals only consider legal norms when determining what to do (not what to think). Second, according to the authority thesis, the law purports to be a *reason* for action in itself. It claims to constitute a reason, not just an instance of coercion.

Having and claiming authority

According to the authority thesis the law *purports* to have authority; it *claims* obedience from individuals. The authority thesis does not say that legal authorities have authority. To have authority, i.e. *legitimate* or *de jure* authority, means that there *are* (overriding) reasons for an individual to do what the law requires because it is the law. So we must distinguish between having and claiming legitimate authority. Just because legal authorities *claim* legitimate authority does not mean that they actually *have* legitimate authority. As a matter of fact Raz asserts that '. . . it is all too plain that in many cases the law's claim to legitimate authority cannot be supported'[7]. What is the point of the authority thesis if authorities lack legitimate authority? It seems that authority is just a very high normative standard, which legal systems simply do not meet. What can we

7 Raz, 'Authority, Law and Morality' (1994), at 200.

possibly learn about the law if we understand it only through this unrealistic notion of – legitimate – authority? First, though most, if not all, legal authorities may not have legitimate authority they must at the least have effective or *de facto* authority. A person or a system has effective or *de facto* authority 'only if the people [or some of them] over whom he has that authority regard him as a legitimate authority'.[8] It refers to an almost empirical observation that minimal effectiveness of a legal system requires that at least some relevant individuals believe that the authorities have legitimate authority. It follows that the notion of legitimate authority is also central to understanding *de facto* authority. Second, it happens to be the case that legal officials themselves claim legitimate authority: doing otherwise would be almost self-defeating. No lawmaker will officially state that its laws must only be followed insofar as individuals think they have good reasons for doing so. Neither do lawmakers publically declare that an individual must only follow their laws insofar as the authorities can effectively enforce compliance. In short, while legal authorities may not have legitimate authority, in reality they still rely heavily on its concept.

The link between legitimate authority and *de facto* authority becomes even clearer if one considers what it means to *claim* something, in particular to claim authority. Raz argues that claiming authority and having *de facto* authority are not only a matter of the law's aspiration but also a matter of the law's accomplishments in fact.

> It could be that, in order to be able to claim authority, the law must at the very least come close to the target, i.e. that it must have some of the characteristics of authority. It can fail to have authority. But it can fail in certain ways only. If this is so, there are features of authority that it must have.[9]
>
> [O]nly those who can have authority can sincerely claim to have it, and [. . .] therefore the law must be capable of having authority.[10]

In other words, the legal authorities should at the very least have the capacity to have legitimate authority. In a way, we now can distinguish three stages regarding authority: having legitimate authority, claiming legitimate authority and having the capacity to have legitimate authority. For want of an adequate shorthand term, we will use the acronym CLA for the 'capacity to have legitimate authority'.

What does it take for the authorities to have CLA? In Raz' own view it does not take much: '[T]he fact that the law claims authority for itself shows that it is capable of having authority.'[11] In an almost tautological sense, it seems that 'claiming authority' is a condition of being capable of having authority. Raz

8 Raz, *The Authority of Law* (1979), at 28.
9 Raz, 'Authority, Law and Morality' (1994), at 200.
10 Ibid., at 200.
11 Ibid., at 201.

seems to suggest that it is also a sufficient condition. In contrast, in my view more is needed for having CLA. Rather, for the authorities to 'have some of the characteristics of authority' one must look at what it takes to have legitimate authority. In other words, the legal authorities must move, one way or the other, towards satisfying the conditions for having legitimate authority. In Raz' own words 'the law must at the very least come close to the target'. The law may not fully succeed 'but it can fail in certain ways only'. To put it differently, to have CLA, the authorities must come close to having legitimate authority. Again, the notion of legitimate authority is central for determining whether legal authorities have CLA. It also means that to determine what it takes to have CLA we must understand what it takes to have legitimate authority. Why should an individual obey the law? Why should an individual only consider the law for determining what to do and exclude other reasons that could guide his actions?

At the basis of the legitimacy of (legal) authority lies the service conception. According to this, the authorities are at the service of individuals in the sense that the authorities are 'mediating between the people and the right reasons which apply to them, so that the authority judges and pronounces what they [the people] ought to do according to right reason'.[12] The service conception reflects that authority is about reasons. It recognizes that there are reasons for action that apply to (count for) individuals directly. A legitimate authority asks an individual to put these reasons aside (when determining what to do) because the authority has already considered those reasons for the individual. In a sense the directives issued by the authorities reflect a judgment of the reasons that apply to individuals directly. This may be explained by two theses, which operate as conditions for having legitimate authority: dependence thesis and normal justification thesis (NJT).[13] Dependence thesis states that there are right reasons and they should function as a point of reference: 'All authoritative directives should be based . . . on reasons which apply to the subjects of those directives and which bear on the circumstances covered by the directives.'[14] Again, the starting point is that there are right reasons for actions that apply to individuals. However, individuals may act for the wrong reasons. The idea of the service conception is that authority helps people to act for the right reasons. This is reflected in the NJT:

> The normal and primary way to establish that a person should be acknowledged to have authority over another person involves showing that the alleged subject is likely better to comply with reasons that apply to him . . . if he

12 Raz, 'Authority, Law and Morality' (1994), at 198.

13 For our discussion we have left out the preemption thesis. The three theses have been advanced by Raz for the first time in 'Authority and Justification', *Philosophy & Public Affairs* (1985), and reprinted in Part I of Raz, *The Morality of Freedom*. But it is in Raz, 'Authority, Law and Morality' (first published in 68 *The Monist* 3 (1985)) that Raz links the three theses explicitly to the legitimacy of legal authority.

14 Raz, 'Authority, Law and Morality' (1994), at 198.

> accepts the directives of the alleged authority as authoritatively binding, and tries to follow, than if he tries to follow the reasons which apply to him directly.[15]

The NJT introduces a kind of efficiency standard: the individual will better comply overall with the reasons that apply to him directly if he does what the directives require, rather than assessing what to do on the merits of the reasons directly applicable to him. There are some typical justifications why an individual may do better in acting for the right reasons if he obeys the law. The legal authorities may have more expertise. The authorities are in a better position to address coordination problems. Also, further to a logic of (soft-) paternalism, the law may prevent individuals from acting against their own rational self-interests.

Authority is a matter of degree

To have CLA, the authorities need not fully satisfy the conditions set out in the dependence and normal justification theses. They must come close – but how close is close? It is beyond the scope of this book and probably impossible to come up with a comprehensive answer. Yet we can point out two things that are relevant to our discussion. First, authority is a matter of degree. Second, it seems possible to indicate when in any event the law does or does not come close to target. Authority is a matter of degree precisely because it is linked to the reasons that apply to individuals directly.

> The government may have only some of the authority it claims, it may have more authority over one person than over the other. The test is as explained before: does following the authority's instructions improve conformity with reason? For every person the question has to be asked afresh, and for everyone it has to be asked in a manner which admits of various qualifications.[16]

In other words, the law may have authority over *some persons* with regard to *some areas* of the law. Raz speaks here about having *legitimate* authority. Yet it follows from the direct connection between legitimate authority and CLA, that having CLA ('coming close to target') is equally a matter of degree. So, the law may have CLA with regard to some individuals and not with regard to others. Now, when is the law so off-target that it not only fails to have legitimate authority but also lacks the capacity to have legitimate authority? We can identify at least two instances. The first is the situation whereby the law deliberately operates *against* the reasons that apply to the individuals directly. The most salient examples are areas of the law that aim to oppress and even destroy (groups of) individuals.

15 Raz, 'Authority, Law and Morality'.
16 Raz, *The Morality of Freedom* (1988), at 74.

Though sometimes difficult to accept from a moral point of view, one should distinguish these areas from other areas of the law within the same legal system. It may be the case that a legal system contains areas that clearly do not even come close to target because it is oppressive and destructive, while other areas may even have legitimate authority (cf. traffic code under the Nazi regime).[17] The second instance whereby an area of the law lacks CLA is more subtle. While the first situation was about the law deliberately acting *against* the reasons applicable to the individual, in the second situation the law simply does not consider those reasons. The problem here is that the law does not even get into the business of what the service conception is all about. Again, the starting point is the reasons that apply to the individual directly. If the authorities do not seriously consider these reasons, they simply cannot claim authority over the individuals to whom those reasons apply. To put it in Razian terms: legal directives must reflect a judgment on the reasons that apply to the norm subject directly. It may be that this judgment is wrong. If so, the directives lack legitimate authority. The judgment may even be fundamentally wrong in that it deliberately seeks to act against 'vital' reasons. If so, the law does not even come close to having legitimate authority. However, in the second situation, the law lacks CLA, not because the judgment on the reasons is wrong, but because there is just no judgment on the reasons that apply directly to the individuals. The reasons were not seriously taken into consideration.

Absence of CLA, de facto *authority, existence of law and legal validity*

The previous paragraph explained how an area of the law may not only lack legitimate authority, but may also fail to come close to target. As a result, it will lack the capacity to have legitimate authority: it cannot seriously claim to have authority. What are the consequences of a lack of the CLA? Raz himself does not really discuss the ramifications of an absence of CLA.[18] Nevertheless, we may identify the following sequence of consequences associated with the absence of the CLA. First, a condition for claiming authority is CLA. The absence of CLA makes it impossible to claim authority. The legal authorities can deliver the speech or write down the act of claiming authority, but they are conceptually mistaken or simply acting in bad faith when doing so. There is no CLA when the authorities, or an area of the law, fail to come close to satisfying the normal justification thesis. This is the case when an area of the law does not reflect a judgment on the reasons that apply to individuals over whom authority is claimed. Second, it is a

17 See for this example Scott Shapiro, 'Authority' in Jules Coleman and Scott Shapiro (eds), *The Oxford Handbook of Jurisprudence and Philosophy of Law* (Oxford: Oxford University Press, 2002), at 395 with reference to Robert Landson 'In Defence of a Hobbessian Concept of Law'. In this respect it is noteworthy that the directives that were directly associated with the Endloesung were secret and, as such, were not part of the official public legal system.

18 This is probably due to his focus on the sources thesis.

necessary feature of *de facto* authority that the legal authority can claim legitimate authority. To regard the authority as legitimate authority, it must be able to claim legitimate authority over at least those individuals who are to regard the authority as legitimate.[19] Since the authority is not capable of claiming authority, it actually fails to have *de facto* authority. Third, if there is no *de facto* authority, there cannot be any legitimate authority because legitimate authority also requires minimal effectiveness. The absence of legitimate authority also directly follows the lack of CLA; the absence of CLA means that the authority radically fails to come close to having legitimate authority. Raz argues convincingly that the conditions for having legitimate authority may be satisfied with regard to some individuals, but not others. It depends on the personal circumstances of the particular individual and the reasons that apply to him directly. By extension, I suggest that CLA and – as a consequence – *de facto* authority also depend on the personal circumstances of the relevant individuals. It means that the same area of the law has different normative effects on different individuals.[20]

The next step is to establish the consequences of not having CLA and *de facto* authority. I contend that if an area of the law lacks CLA and thus *de facto* authority, its legal validity is directly affected. Though Raz would surely not agree with this extended reading, he offers us some passages that point to a connection between authority and validity. According to Raz 'necessarily law, every legal system which is *in force* anywhere, has *de facto* authority'.[21] So, all law that exists must have *de facto* authority. And the existence of law – or it being in force – means that it is legally valid: 'A rule which is not legally valid is not a legal rule at all. A valid law is law, and invalid law is not.'[22] And also: 'A valid rule is one which has normative effects. A legally valid rule is one which has legal effects.'[23] In short, legally valid law necessarily has *de facto* authority. We can turn this assertion around. Not only does valid law necessarily have *de facto* authority, but having *de*

19 Now, there may be a system in place that consists of practical statements (i.e. propositions on what to do) that do not purport to constitute protected reasons (e.g. a system of health warnings or expert recommendations). Yet some may believe wrongly that the statements are legal directives. Does this system have *de facto* authority? Probably not. It matters (among other things) what the system claims for itself. A tree cannot have *de facto* authority, even if some regard a tree as a legitimate practical authority.

20 There is a complication that has to do with the notion of *de facto* authority. A condition for *de facto* authority is that some norm subjects consider the authorities or area of the law to have *legitimate* authority. So, if nobody for whatever reasons believes that the authorities have legitimate authority, then the authorities cannot have *de facto* authority. It is a kind of 'perceived effectiveness' criterion. The complication is that it may be the case that an area of the law comes close to satisfying NJT with regard to some norm subjects and accordingly has CLA. But it still may fail to have *de facto* authority because there are no norm subjects that believe the area of the law has *legitimate* authority.

21 Raz, 'Authority, Law and Morality', (1994), at 199 (first emphasis added).

22 Raz, *The Authority of Law* (1979), at 146.

23 Ibid., at 149.

facto authority is a condition for legal validity. To have *de facto* authority, an area of the law must have CLA. It must have the capacity to *claim* its normative effects: 'A legally valid rule is one which has the normative effects (in law) which it *claims* to have.'[24] If an area of the law cannot claim normative effects it surely lacks legal validity. This establishes that there is a direct link between CLA and legal validity. If an area of the law fails to come close to satisfying the normal justification thesis, its lacks CLA and legal validity. It is not legally valid because it cannot even pretend to be law. This is not a matter of morality, but rather a matter of the law's own conceptual pretensions.

Relative legal validity

If indeed having CLA affects legal validity, an awkward legal concept emerges: relative legal validity. Having CLA and *de facto* authority is a matter of degree and context. An area of the law may have CLA and *de facto* authority with regard to some individuals, but not to others. If so, then it follows that an area of the law may be legally valid with regard to some, but not to others. However, legal validity is typically understood as operating *erga omnes*. In this respect, relative legal validity seems an oxymoron. Yet a closer look may reveal that relative legal validity has a place in both the theory and practice of law. The starting point is to realize that the concept of relative legal validity does not replace general legal validity. It only kicks in when an area of the law cannot achieve full legal validity, i.e. legal validity regarding all relevant individuals. So, relative legal validity recognizes that general legal validity is the normal and superior legal status. However, relative legal validity is preferred over general legal *in*validity, i.e. an area of the law that is legally invalid with regard to *all* individuals. Thus we may rank the preferred legal status of an area of the law as follows:

- *general legal validity*: area of the law is legally *valid* with regard to *all* relevant individuals;
- *relative legal validity*: area of the law is legally *valid* with regard to *some* relevant individuals, and legally *in*valid with regard to *others*;
- *general legal* in*validity*: area of the law is legally *in*valid with regard to *all* relevant individuals.

Showing that relative legal validity makes sense and is useful means demonstrating that it is indeed superior to general legal *in*validity. We must make a plausible argument that it makes a difference if an area of the law has relative legal validity rather than general legal invalidity. How can the differences between them be established and evaluated? I suggest we look at the functions of law. We may consider some of the central functions legally valid norms purport to

24 Raz, *The Authority of Law* (1979) (emphasis added).

perform: coordination and control.[25] It is clear that, in these matters, general legal validity does a better job than relative legal validity and general legal *in*validity. However, the question here is whether an area of the law that is struck by relative legal validity does better in terms of guiding the action and distribution of desert and entitlements than general legal invalidity. The threshold is not as high as it may seem. It suffices to establish 'instances' where relative legal validity does a better job than general legal invalidity in 'servicing the functions of law'. We have run different scenarios to see if and under what circumstances, relative legal validity makes a difference. It goes beyond the scope of this book to get into those analyses, but it is not difficult to see that, depending on how the scenarios are framed, relative legal validity can be meaningful.[26] When it comes to guiding action and solving coordination problems there are instances where relative legal validity is just as sub-optimal as the absence of a legal valid norm. However, there are also scenarios where relative legal validity produced outcomes that were inferior to general legal validity but were still superior to the absence of a legal norm, i.e. general legal *in*validity. There are also instances where the relative legal validity does just as well as general legal validity. What matters was how the following three dimensions were set. First, the 'compliance appetite' of the agents to whom the general or relative legal norm applies. Second, the need for cooperation. Third, the agents' awareness of each others' compliance appetite, the need for cooperation and the validity of the norm. Since law in the real world is confronted with all sorts of combinations of these three variables (and many others!) it is safe to say that there is clearly a place for relative legal valid norms when it comes to guiding behavior and addressing coordination problems. Again, this does not mean that we can now get rid of general legal validity. On the contrary, it is only when general legal validity is compromised that relative legal validity kicks in. Depending on the case, relative legal validity can make sure that the compromised legal norm still has (some of) its coordinative effect.

When it comes to the control function of legal norms, relative legal validity is less productive. The problem is of course that the control function of law typically involves norms that favor the interests of some at the expense of others. What is lacking is the interest in cooperation. Worse there may not even be a possibility of cooperation and coordination. We are dealing with norms that have a zero-sum character. This is the case of norms where the only benefit[27] of compliance is the absence of sanctions (of criminal, administrative or civil law). In these cases

25 See for this categorization of the functions that rules may perform Tom D. Campbell, *The Legal Theory of Ethical Positivism* (Aldershot: Dartmouth Publishing, 1996), at 50–2.

26 See Bas Schotel, *Protecting the Alien's Interest in Immigration* (2008), Ph.D. dissertation, at 136–50.

27 It does not mean that the norm subject has no reason to obey. It simply means he does not benefit from compliance. For example, in terms of short-term self-interest, a professional burglar clearly does not benefit from not stealing, but he may still have a moral reason not to steal.

the law must determine for all parties involved what the law is. These are ultimately matters of desert. Normally, a rule of tort that is valid for the applicant but not the defendant does not work.[28] The same goes for a rule of property. The situation is similar but more complex if we consider the enforcement by officials of a rule struck by relative legal validity. Imagine the rule is not legally valid for a private individual, but legally valid for an official. The official is justified in enforcing the rule and, by the same token, this rule does not count (legally) for the individual. How should we understand legally the situation whereby the officials enforce a rule that does not count as law *vis-à-vis* the private individual? It is clear that this is a legally imperfect situation. However, the imperfection associated with relative legal validity is not a failure of its concept, but a failure of the particular area of the law struck by relative legal validity. Relative legal validity highlights the normative shortcomings of some laws, and at the same time it explains why these same laws can still perform their typical functions *vis-à-vis* some individuals. Maybe this is best understood in the context of legal invalidation. This is a situation whereby legal authorities, mostly (constitutional) courts, decide that a legal norm is legally invalid. The perennial problem is what to do with those who relied on the invalidated legal rule. It bears on the issue of retroactivity. Easy cases of legal invalidation are properly captured by the dichotomy of general validity and general invalidity. Either the rule was manifestly illegal and thus was never to count as law. In this case the existing legal framework offers sufficient indications beforehand that the officials should not have relied on the rule. Or the rule is not manifestly illegal. In this case the officials could have relied on the legal validity to the extent that the rule was issued by the competent authorities in accordance with the existing legal framework (i.e. systemic validity). After further scrutiny the rule must be invalidated, but the effects of the invalidation only operate *ex nunc* (i.e. from the moment of invalidation onwards). In these two scenarios general legal validity does well. It becomes problematic when a rule is not manifestly questionable on the basis of the existing legal background, but the existing legal background itself is legally questionable for a group of individuals. In this case there is a *systemic* flaw in an area of the law regarding some individuals. How can the normative force of such an area of the law that structurally excludes a category of individuals be explained? Can the officials rely on such a rule? Should this systemic flaw not give rise to a chain reaction of regressive invalidations of all acts that were directly or indirectly based on this area of the law? In short: legal revolution. Yet, in practice, legal revolution is rare. Even the most abject legal arrangements (e.g. slavery, apartheid, GDR border guard instructions) did not lead to the legal invalidation of the background system that explicitly supported it. The law organizes legal transformation, but always in

28 One can imagine a more complex scenario where the applicant simply has to establish that he did not commit a tort to benefit under an insurance scheme. In such a case it does not really matter whether or not the rule is legally valid with regard to the defendant.

the sense of continuity, not revolution or generic invalidation.[29] This is precisely what relative legal validity does. It will accept that (lower-ranked) enforcement officials were justified in relying on the rule, but it does not provide legal cover for senior officials who designed and issued it. Enforcement officials cannot be held liable by the individuals with regard to whom the rules are struck by relative legal validity. However, senior officials may be held liable and can be prosecuted. The private individuals are legally justified in not obeying the rule. The same goes for the enforcement officials. So, disciplinary measures against disobedient officials must be invalid. In short, relative legal validity helps to understand how a compromised area of the law can both succeed and fail to fulfill the functions of law.

The plausibility of relative legal validity and its value for making sense of legal practice depend on its exceptional nature. It recognizes that general legal validity and invalidity (or absence of legal norm) are the normal cases. Furthermore, it must be noted that in terms of its effects, the law has quite some experience with relativity. We must not confuse legal *validity* of a rule with its *application*. Still, many laws prohibiting or permitting a particular behavior have relative *effect*. They may apply to some individuals but not to others.

Recapitulating central tenets extended authority thesis

Law claims obedience from individuals. This means that the law claims that individuals have reasons to do what the law requires *because it is the law*. There may be other reasons for doing or not doing what the law requires, but the law's claim for obedience requires that individuals *exclusively* consider the law for determining what to do. However, the law can only make this claim if it at least *purports* to have legitimate authority: that the law is *in fact* a sufficient and exhaustive reason for action. Why should an individual have reasons to abandon his own judgment and rely 'blindly' on what the law requires? It seems that the individual should *normally* do a better job of complying with reasons that *apply*

29 A relative recent case in point is the GDR border guard cases. The prosecution of the border guards was rendered possible by a legal transformation: namely the reunification of the FRG and the GDR. The legal basis for the reunification is the Unification Treaty between the two States – the Treaty between the Federal Republic of Germany and the German Democratic Republic on the Establishment of German Unity of August 31 (1990) 30 *ILM*. 457. According to Article 9 of the Treaty the laws (and thus the legal acts performed under those laws) remain valid in so far as they are compatible with FRG and EU law. Articles 18 and 19 also maintain the validity of GDR judicial decisions and administrative acts respectively, provided that they are compatible with FRG and EU law. In other words, the failure of the GDR legal system to meet the standards of material justice as noted by the judges of the ECHR (e.g. democratic legislative procedures, separation of powers and respect for human rights) did not entail a wholesale legal invalidation. This 'ambiguity' cannot be accounted for by general legal validity. See for the discussion of the GDR border guards cases in the context of relative legal validity Bas Schotel, *Protecting the Alien's Interest in Immigration* (2008), Ph.D. dissertation, at 144–50.

to him directly, if he obeys the law. This is the so-called normal justification thesis. Of course, this is a pretty tough condition to fulfill. Most, if not all, legal systems cannot satisfy the conditions for having legitimate authority. At the very best, they have legitimate authority in *some areas* of the law regarding *some people*. But more often, legal systems have only *de facto authority*, i.e. some individuals regard legal authority as having legitimate authority. Though *de facto* authority should be clearly distinguished from legitimate authority, the former always refers to the latter. While a legal system may not satisfy the conditions of legitimate authority, it must at least have the *capacity* to have legitimate authority (to count as law). It must come close to having legitimate authority, i.e. close to satisfying the normal justification condition. Though a legal directive may be wrong *vis-à-vis* an individual, it must at least reflect the legal authorities' judgment on the reasons that apply to the individual. Even failure to do so need not disqualify the directive as long as reasons to obey the law are provided by other areas of the law. However, if other areas of the law cannot provide a sufficient reflection of the authorities' judgment on the reasons applicable to the individual, the legal directive lacks the capacity to have legitimate authority. It means that an area of the law cannot seriously pretend to claim authority, because it does not even come close to satisfying the normal justification conditions. If an area of the law lacks the capacity to claim authority it cannot have *de facto* authority either. *De facto* authority implies at least that one party seriously claims to have authority. Furthermore, there is a direct connection between the existence of law, *de facto* authority and legal validity. To be in force – to exist – law must have *de facto* authority. Another way of expressing the fact that a rule has legal force is to say it is legally valid. It means that to be legally valid – to have force as law – an area of the law must have *de facto* authority. Consequently, if an area of the law lacks the capacity to have legitimate authority and thus *de facto* authority, its legal validity is compromised. In short, sometimes an area of the law not only fails to have legitimate authority it also lacks *de facto* authority and thus legal validity. To be legally valid the law need not fully satisfy the normal justification conditions. Yet it should come close. The minimum requirement is that the law reflects a judgment on the reasons applicable to the relevant individual. If not it lacks the capacity to have authority and thus, legal validity. Now, the 'applicable reasons' differ per (category of) individuals. This means that an area of the law may come close to satisfying the normal justification conditions with regard to some individuals, but not to others. It follows that an area of the law may be *legally valid* with regard to some individuals but not to all, i.e. *relative* legal validity.

The authority of admission laws

Let us now find out how the authority thesis works out for immigration laws concerning normal migrants. A crucial aspect of law is its capacity to have legitimate authority. It must come close to satisfying the normal justification criterion, i.e. the norm subject is to obey the law if, in general, he does a better job in complying with 'his own' reasons when he obeys the law than when he follows those reasons directly. This then presumes that the law at least accounts for the reasons that apply directly to the individual. The idea is that the law in general makes a better judgment of those reasons than the individual. In the context of admission laws this becomes highly problematic, precisely because of exclusion without justification. At all levels of admission policy (the setting of laws and regulations; individual denial of admission; judicial review) the reasons that apply to normal migrants seeking admission are simply not accounted for (see Chapter 1).[30] It follows that admission laws do not even come close to satisfying the normal justification conditions – due to the absence of justification. As a result, they lack the capacity to have legitimate authority. Does this render those laws legally invalid? Not necessarily. It is probably a bit too much to ask a particular statute to account for every single reason that applies directly to an individual. The fact that reasons change over time makes it practically impossible to have such 'complete' statutes. The same goes for our admission laws. What matters is whether this lack of capacity for the legitimate authority of a particular statute is compensated for by other areas of the law; both procedurally and substantially. It is here that our admission laws fail completely. This failure is provoked by several legal anomalies associated with our admission practices. First, our admission laws operate extra-territorially with regard to normal migrants. Other branches of law are not purely domestic either, but our admission laws are almost exclusively extra-territorial. In fact due to the way they are conceived, our admission laws can only be effective if and when normal migrants seeking admission obey the admission laws outside our territory. This applies, of course, to the normal migrant who does not satisfy the requirements for admission: he is required to obey the admission laws extra-territorially precisely by staying outside the territory. It also applies to the normal migrant who can meet the admission requirements. If he wants to be actually admitted he must show that he has fulfilled all the necessary admission requirements before entering the territory of the host country. In other words, both for purposes of admitting and excluding normal migrants, our admission laws are mainly effective to the extent they are obeyed extra-territorially. Though this extra-territoriality is certainly an anomaly it is not necessarily problematic from a legal perspective. Yet it becomes so as it translates into a second anomaly. The extra-territoriality of our admission laws means that a tiny part of our legal order extends beyond our borders to normal migrants seeking admission. The normal migrants have become relevant individuals for only this part of our law. The purpose and predominant effect of this inclusion of the normal migrant into our admission law are to exclude the normal migrant from the rest of our legal order. The problematic nature of this phenomenon recurs in another legal anomaly associated with our

30 Admission laws may turn out to be favorable for some normal migrants, i.e. those who are admitted. Still the reasons applicable to those (successful) normal migrants have simply not been accounted for.

admission laws. Precisely because the admission laws prevent the normal migrant from becoming a relevant individual of the rest of our legal order, the normal migrant who disobeys or dodges (e.g. by falsely applying for asylum) the admission laws in general improves the scope and effectiveness of his legal position simply by exposing himself to the rest of our legal order. First, the legal conditions and procedure for the expulsion of a normal migrant are more complicated and stricter than for refoulement, i.e. removing a normal migrant from the border. Second, if a normal migrant decides to challenge the decision of immigration authorities his legal defense is in general much more effective while inside than outside. Third, by the simple fact of living in the host territory (and thus disobeying the admission laws) the normal migrant has become a relevant individual of the other areas of the law. For many of these branches of the law, he is just as good a relevant individual as persons living in territory with a legal title of stay (e.g. nationals, legal residents). In effect, there are many areas of the law that facilitate his relations with other relevant individuals and even protect him against their illegal conduct (e.g. criminal law, law of contracts, family law, property law, health care law, laws on the powers of the police and good administration, safety regulations on the workplace,[31] etc.). The admission laws not only fail to account for the reasons that apply directly to the normal migrant, they also prevent the normal migrant from being exposed to other branches of our law that may account for these reasons. In other words, it is practically impossible to see any good reason why normal migrants seeking admission should obey our admission laws. This is exactly the experience of being included for the sake of exclusion.[32]

31 Since illegal workers are often employed in workplaces where legal workers also operate, they can benefit from the incentives for employers (and employees) to respect (parts of) safety regulations.

32 We have not mentioned that Raz leaves a way open for an obligation to generally obey the law: respect for the law (Raz, *The Authority of Law* (1979), at 250–61). This respect is understood as an expression of one's loyalty and commitment to a generally good society (ibid., at 259). We can ask ourselves how this works out for the normal migrant. It is safe to say that many migrants seeking admission to countries with a strong image of liberal values (freedom, equality, pursuit of happiness, rule of law) have a certain commitment to these countries or at least those values. Many may consider those countries to be good societies in terms of justice (and not merely as a more efficient environment to improve their economic situation). If so, some may have loyalties to those societies and as a result have developed attitudes of respect for the law. Accordingly for those migrants it may make sense to obey the admission laws. Raz would probably say that for some of those migrants it may be – morally or normatively – *permissible* to show such respect. However, there is *never an obligation* to adopt such attitude. More *often* than not there are *no good reasons* for such respect. Loyalty to a society is sometimes better expressed by disobeying the law (ibid., at 260–1). In any event, what matters to our case is that – whatever the attitude of the normal migrant – we *cannot require such respect for the law from the normal migrant*. In other words, we simply cannot expect that large numbers of normal migrants seeking admission will feel so committed to our society that it is reasonable for them to take our laws for granted irrespective of their content. Again, what is the point of being loyal to a society if this loyalty is expressed by a respect for the law, which in turn results in a radical disconnection from that same society?

Reform or relative legal invalidity

Our admission laws cannot come close to having legitimate authority *vis-à-vis* normal migrants seeking admission. They lack the capacity for legitimate authority. As a result, the law cannot seriously claim authority over normal migrants. So, in line with our extended reading of Raz's authority thesis, we must conclude that our admission laws do not even have *de facto* authority and consequently fail to count as law *vis-à-vis* the normal migrants seeking admission. What does this mean in practical terms? The authorities can pursue different routes. First, they stop organizing the exclusion of normal migrants through the use of laws directed at normal migrants. In other words, if the normal migrants cease to be relevant individuals all our challenges based on the authority thesis simply disappear. Admission laws are only directed at officials who must take action to the effect of admitting and excluding normal migrants. The normal migrants are not expected to obey or disobey the law;[33] their conduct is simply managed or contained.[34] Like animals cannot obey or violate legislation organizing the presence of animals, normal migrants are incapable of obeying or breaking admission laws. Instead of relevant individuals they become simply objects of the law. This option is in a way logically consistent, but is highly problematic both politically and morally. Fortunately, we find it extremely difficult to treat human beings as objects. After such milestones as the abolition of serfdom and slavery, there is a tendency in law to 'subjectify' human beings rather than objectify. In short, turning normal migrants officially into objects is not an option. The second option is that we change our laws by seriously considering the reasons applicable to the normal migrant. A most adequate starting point for institutional change is the draft directive by immigration law experts, which proposes to apply the proportionality principle to all immigration decisions.[35] Pending such structural reform, there is another route: legal officials can take up their *professional* responsibility. They should reconsider the allegedly unproblematic nature of our admission laws not as a matter of morality, but as a matter of the meaning of law. They should speak up and explain how the law

33 This corresponds with how Thomas Nagel understands immigration laws. In his view, immigration laws do not claim obedience and need not be considered as law by the aliens: 'Immigration policies are simply enforced against nationals of other states; the laws are not imposed in their name, *nor are they asked to accept and uphold those laws*. Since no acceptance is demanded of them, no justification is required that explains why they should accept such discriminatory policies, or why their interests have been given equal consideration' (emphasis added). 'The Problem of Global Justice', *Philosophy & Public Affairs* (2005) 33(2) 130–1. Of course, his account conflicts with the provisions of immigration laws that do contain prohibitions directed at migrants. More importantly, he fails to address what it actually means for an immigration policy if it ceases to treat the migrant as a norm subject.

34 See Bas Schotel, 'EU's Management of Migration Flows and the Rule of Law. From Individual Migrant to Migration Flow', *Journal of Ethnic and Migration Studies* (2011 forthcoming).

35 See Chapter 7.

can claim obedience from normal migrants. They should tell us how such laws can possibly fit other important areas and elements of our legal system. An elusive answer in the sense that it is not their job to do so will not work: lawyers and certainly judges must from time to time tell us why and how the law can claim obedience. These are the instances where the legal profession has to probe into a particular law and see how it relates to other areas of the law up to the point of considering its invalidation. This, though rare, it is an essential part of their job. It is not pure politics or charity. It is legal reasoning.

The outcome should be that our admission laws are declared to be invalid. The legal invalidity is likely to be relative, not general. Relative legal invalidity does justice to the fact that having the capacity for legitimate authority is a matter of degree. With regard to normal migrants seeking admission this capacity is clearly missing. Yet, *vis-à-vis* normal migrants that have been (or will be) successfully admitted on the basis of our admission laws, this lack of capacity for legitimate authority may be less relevant. In any event, absolute invalidation (i.e. with retroactive effect) will adversely affect their legal status. The relative invalidation is of course extremely relevant to the normal migrants that have violated the admission laws (or are planning to do so). They cannot be charged on the basis of those laws, and they cannot be removed from the host territory on the basis of those laws. Of course, this does not mean that invalidation of our admission laws grants legal residence to all normal migrants. The invalidation is more likely to create a kind of stalemate in which the normal migrant is neither illegal, nor a legal resident (see Chapter 7). Yet, this stalemate will allow the normal migrant to gradually improve his legal status by challenging other legal directives that discriminate against him. Again, this is clearly a sub-optimal situation and a more structural reform, as mentioned, above is highly preferable. In terms of what the structure of law requires, relative legal invalidation would be quite an improvement compared to our current situation. As to the officials, it is not fully clear to what extent the admission laws account for the reasons applicable to them. It may well be that there are good overriding reasons for some officials to disobey the admission laws, while others are justified in 'dutifully' executing the admission laws.[36] We can imagine a two-tier treatment of officials. For example, this means that those officials complying with the admission laws cannot be charged (under criminal, administrative or civil law) with illegally holding normal migrants under arrest and depriving them of their liberty (to move). By the same token, officials who disobey admission laws cannot be disciplined.[37]

36 For example, this may depend on the level in the hierarchy and the perceived benefits of non-compliance.

37 In practice this will be an incredibly complicated matter because not all activities of the officials are necessarily 'invalidated', e.g. identity and background checks may still be justified. As a result, to avoid unnecessary chaos, it may be justified for the (junior) officials to continue to execute the flawed admission laws pending a more general replacement.

In short, authorities have the following options. First, they simply do nothing and betray their own legal system. Second, they take out of the admission laws any provisions that are directed at normal migrants. In other words, they make migration laws consistent by treating normal migrants as objects of law (like animals), instead of relevant individuals. However, this compromises the contemporary political culture that has ceased to treat human beings as legal objects. Third, they change their laws to the effect of seriously considering the reasons applicable to the normal migrant. The draft directive introducing the proportionality test for all immigration decisions is a productive starting point. Pending such structural reform we may seriously envisage asking the judiciary to step in and consider the legal invalidation of current admission laws. Whatever is done in the short or long term, it should be clear to the authorities that the current admission laws are fundamentally flawed. Not (only) in an ethical sense, but more importantly, on the basis of the quintessential social institution from which those same authorities derive their competence and agency, i.e. the law.

Chapter 6

The first burden of justification

It follows from the previous chapters that the current policies regarding normal migrants are untenable from a legal perspective because they constitute a form of exclusion without justification. The legal analyses showed that if the authorities deny a normal migrant admission they have a duty to justify the exclusion *vis-à-vis* the excluded migrant. But the claim of this book goes one step further than the duty to justify. It also demands a shift in the *first* burden of justification. The default position or starting point should be that when authorities deny a normal migrant admission, they should carry the first burden of justifying the exclusion. Only when the authorities came up with a serious justification as defined in Chapter 1 (i.e. substantiated by facts and verifiable analyses; balancing the reasons applicable to the normal migrant), is it up to the normal migrant to argue his case for admission. So authorities not only have a duty to justify, they also carry the first burden of justification. While the legal analyses in the previous chapters can account for the former, it cannot explain the latter. The law is all about fixing the default position, burden of justification and burden of proof. Probably the quintessential characteristic of the law is that it organizes these 'normal starting points'. However, when it comes to the *reasons* for fixing a particular default position in a specific way, the law has little to say. Not so much the logic or structure of the law informs the particular default positions laid down in the law. Rather, it seems that predominantly non-legal considerations constitute the ratio behind the default positions.[1] And next to economics and demography, one of the most relevant non-legal considerations in the field of immigration is political theory. In fact over the last decades migration has carved out a place of its own in political theory, i.e. the ethics of migration. This chapter explores how ethics of migration and particularly the different strands of liberalism may help us fix a new default position in migration policy. To be sure, the debate in political theory is not framed in terms of default position or the first burden of justification. It seems

1 Of course, the distinction between legal and non-legal considerations is not always as clean-cut. There are clearly areas of overlap especially when it comes to the so-called legal principles. Yet the distinction still makes sense if we take the perspective of the sources and types of analyses involved.

that the debate is more about arguments in favor or against a particular immigration policy, e.g. should we have (more) open or closed borders? Looming in the background of the discussion is the issue whether states have a right to control migration in the first place. This chapter uses the arguments from the ethics of migration not only to answer these questions, but also as reasons for shifting the burden of justification from the migrant to the migration authorities.

This chapter starts by explaining the mechanism of the default position. It should make clear how this project builds on, but also differs from, the current preoccupations in the ethics of migration. It points out the relevance of the project for legal practice. Furthermore, it spells out how the argument in favor of a new default position is structured. In fact, arguing for a default position is almost like solving a conundrum: Who carries the burden of justification for changing the current burden of justification? In this chapter I assume that it is up to me to carry the burden of proof to change the current default position. As a result the first step involves creating some basic sympathy for considering a new default position in the first place. It should make plausible that there is a value in some form of free movement. Having established the basic sympathy, we can take the argument one step further and consider the dominant reasons for and against restricting immigration. The chapter concludes by showing how we should weight the reasons and why they point to a new default position.

Ethics of migration and fixing a new default position

The current scholarship in the ethics of migration has become increasingly rich in arguments.[2] By the same token these arguments hardly ever make it to the realm of law and actual policy making. Concrete practical impact is not the only measure for the success and value of political theory. But ethics of migration should uphold

2 See for instructive overviews: Veit Bader, 'Ethics of Immigration', 12 *Constellations* (2005), at 331–61; Veit Bader, 'Fairly Open Borders' in Veit Bader (ed.), *Citizenship and Exclusion*, (London: Macmillan Press Ltd, 1997), at 28–60; Rainer Bauboeck, 'Migration and Citizenship: Normative Debates', in Marc Rosenblum and Dan Tichenor (eds), *Oxford Handbook on International Migration*, (Oxford: Oxford University Press, forthcoming 2011); Rainer Bauboeck, 'Global Justice, Freedom of Movement and Democratic Citizenship', *European Journal of Sociology* (2009), 50, 1–31; Michael Blake, 'Immigration', in R.G. Frey and Christopher Heath Wellman (eds), *A Companion to Applied Ethics* (Oxford: Blackwell Publishing, 2003), at 224–37; Phillip Cole, *Philosophies of Exclusion. Liberal Political Theory and Immigration* (Edinburgh: Edinburgh University Press, 2000); Chandran Kukathas, 'Immigration', in Hugh La Follette (ed.), *The Oxford Handbook of Practical Ethics* (Oxford: Oxford University Press, 2003), at 567–90; Antoine Pécoud and Paul de Guchteneire, *Migration Without Borders: An Investigation Into Free Movement of People*, Global Migration Perspectives, 27 (Geneva: Global Commission on International Migration, 2005); Jonathan Seglow, 'The Ethics of Migration', 3 *Political Studies Review* (2005), at 317–34; Berry Tholen, 'The Europeanisation of Migration Policy – The Normative Issues', 6 *European Journal of Migration and Law* (2004), at 323–51.

some reciprocal relationship between theory and practice if it wants to fulfill its critical function. In this respect it may be helpful to better understand the types of questions political theory can adequately deal with. So the question is not so much about the quality of the arguments from ethics of migration but rather an adequate understanding of their normative and practical effect. To put it differently, the question is about the proper domain or task of political theory when it comes to immigration policy. So what should we ask political theorists?[3] First, are restrictive immigration policies to be justified? This question asks whether there is duty to justify the exclusion of migrants seeking admission. Next, who carries the (first) burden of justification: the authorities or the immigrant seeking admission? The first question is obviously the most fundamental and the most radical, and though political theory could say a lot about this issue, the previous chapters have revealed that the salient arguments have to do with the *legal* order and the structure of *law*. In effect, it seems that contemporary political theorists have made up their mind from the start and think it is almost inconceivable to argue that the exclusion of immigrants seeking admission needs no justification. As a result there is not much fundamental or radical disagreement among political theorists. Even the controversy among communitarians and liberal nationalists on the one hand and cosmopolitans on the other is more apparent than really fundamental. For all their emphasis on national identity and communal self-determination, the national liberal and communitarian theses are about what they believe are sound reasons for exclusion. They do not constitute an argument to the effect that exclusion of migrants need not be justified. In other words, the arguments from both liberal nationalism and communitarianism feed into the second task of political theory: setting the first burden of justification.[4] To put it differently,

3 For the purposes of this chapter I mention only two questions. But there is a third question for political theory on how to determine the *effects* of immigration policy. The effects of migration are typically a matter of the empirically oriented scientific disciplines. But the question is *on what* do immigration and immigration policies have an effect. The objects affected by immigration (policy) derive their meaning from normative concepts: social cohesion, public order, economic growth, national identity, etc. So political theory has a great role to play in defining what counts as objects and what counts as a relevant effect on those objects.

4 By contrast, the recent engaging discussion between Abizadeh and Miller on whether immigrants should participate in the democratic processes from which immigration laws result seems situated at the level of the first question as to whether exclusion needs justification. To be more precise, the discussion is about whether a right to democratic participation for all those subjected to coercion follows from the duty to justify coercion. But leaving aside some untenable views from both sides, this inspiring discussion is less controversial than it seems. Both authors answer the first fundamental question affirmatively: the exclusion of migrants seeking admission needs to be justified. Abizadeh adequately refutes Miller's critique regarding the coercive aspects of immigration policy (Arash Abizadeh, 'Democratic Legitimacy and State Coercion: A Reply to David Miller', *Political Theory* (2010), 38, at 121–30; David Miller, 'Why Immigration Controls are not Coercive: A Reply to Arash Abizadeh', *Political Theory* (2010), 38, at 111–20). The real problem with Abizadeh's position (which Miller does not address) is that he derives from the duty to justify coercion (by the state authorities), a right to democratic participation for those subjected to the

liberal political theorists are preoccupied with the question *how* states can justify exclusion of migrants. They are not in the business of justifying that states need not justify the exclusion of migrants. For the sake of clarity and at the risk of being superfluous, we may add some more observations on the proper scope of the current debate. The discussion is not about whether states have a right to control immigration, because they should have this power (just like they have the power to levy taxes or issue a law on mergers and acquisitions). Neither is the question about whether states have an absolute right to control migration, because they have not (no state power is absolute). Similarly, the question is not whether there should be an absolute right to free movement.[5] The question is about the constraints on the right to control migration and the right to free movement. The exercise of both rights needs justification. The problem is finding out where the first burden

coercion (Abizadeh 2010 at 41). Theoretically speaking this may be indeed the purest form of democracy. Yet it puts the bar too high. This is practically impossible. It means that I may disqualify the regulations of the city of Groningen as undemocratic because as a resident of Amsterdam I did not participate in the Groningen city council elections. The same goes for all laws in the Netherlands with respect to foreign visitors. More dramatically, any act of war would be, by definition, undemocratic. For it necessarily involves coercion of foreign nationals who did not participate in the political processes from which the acts of war resulted. We should be careful not to conflate justification and democratic participation. Both have distinct mechanisms and values. Justification has to do with practical reasoning and operates with reference to standards of justification. For centuries both national and international legal norms, i.e. rules and principles, have been quintessential standards of justification. That is not a matter of democracy. A successful justification of immigration policies and laws requires the involvement of those who are directly affected. But the intensity and form of the justification depends largely on the instance of immigration policy under scrutiny (see above: ranging from immigration law to judicial review of individual decision). Democratic participation is quite a different kind of involvement. I follow Bauboeck's model of stakeholders: that it is difficult to see democratic participation granted without any ties other than one's intention to participate (Bauboeck 2009). Furthermore, the discussion reflects a problematic feature not uncommon in the political theory debate of conflating decisions of admission with decision on membership (Arash Abizadeh, 'Democratic Theory and Border Coercion: No right to unilaterally control your own borders', *Political Theory* (2008), 36, at 46). Yet decisions on admission and exclusion of immigrants are not decisions on who is to become a 'member' of the polity. It is much more limited in empirical scope and intentions: it simply means that the person is permitted to stay in the territory and becomes a legal subject of that jurisdiction. Even though that person will necessarily participate in the life of the community, it is quite different from membership in its political normative meaning. We can already find this distinction in Locke when he discusses how a foreigner can obey the laws and enjoy its privileges and protection without becoming a member of the commonwealth (John Locke, *Two Treatises of Government*, [based on text of 1690] (London: Everyman's Library, 1984), Ch. VIII, Book 2, No. 122, at 178–9). It also means that admission policy does not – yet – raise the conundrum 'how and who decides who is a member of the group that decides who is member'. The so-called inconsistencies of self-determination of liberal democracy do not appear (yet). For sure, the fact that somebody who is admitted may make claims of membership as his stay becomes permanent may be taken into consideration when determining the default position. But it bears on a different area of immigration policy, i.e. ethics of incorporation, with different ramifications.

5 The only form of absolute free movement is the right to entry and return to one's own country. But the limitation to one's country in a way defeats the notion of 'free'.

of justification lies. This means that the right to control migration is not tantamount to restrictive immigration policy. Neither does putting the first burden of justification on the authorities equal open borders. Finally, justifying exclusion to excluded immigrants does not amount to granting them membership or democratic participation.[6]

So having spelled out what the debate is not about, let us turn now to my actual claim: shifting the first burden of justification from migrant to authorities. When an immigrant seeks admission, the authorities carry the first burden of proving that the exclusion is justified. If the authorities fail to produce sufficient reasons and evidence for the exclusion, they lack the power to deny the immigrant admission. Putting the first burden of justification on the authorities operates as a kind of justificatory framework for making adequate immigration policy and decisions. It should be understood as the starting point for any actual admission or exclusion of migrants. Yet it does not constitute a policy in itself. Neither does it fully discharge the normal migrant from disproving the reasons for his exclusion. If the authorities come up with a strong case for exclusion, it is up to the migrant to produce overriding reasons (and evidence) to the contrary. What matters is that the ball is first put in the court of the authorities, as the focus shifts from proving admission to disproving exclusion. Rather than showing that there are overriding reasons for his admission, the migrant must only disprove the reasons for his exclusion. At first glance, admission and exclusion seem logical opposites: proving one disproves the other. In contrast, normal migration defeats this logic.[7] Often normal migrants do not have overriding reasons for their admission. Most normal migrants are not fleeing from extreme hardship. They may simply seek admission to improve their economic prospects. Yet their case becomes much stronger if one considers the reasons for their exclusion. Most normal migrants do not pose a threat or a significant net burden to the society of the receiving state. Consequently, authorities may find it difficult to justify the exclusion. In short, it matters what needs to be justified: admission or exclusion. It is one thing to say that authorities must justify migration restrictions. It is quite another to put the first burden of justification on the authorities. What does it take to shift the first burden of justification from the migrant to the authorities? It turns into a conundrum: who has the burden of proving that the first burden of justification should be shifted to the authorities? Perhaps a closer look at the meaning and function of the default position may help us understand how to shift the burden of justification.

The default position constitutes the normal position, i.e. the starting point. It means that those who deviate from the normal position adopt an exceptional position. The 'position' I am talking about is a stance on what we have reason to do,

6 See supra n. 4.

7 See also Chapter 4 for the refutation of 'inclusion implies exclusion'.

i.e. *practical reasoning*.[8] So, in short the default position is what we normally ought to do according to practical reasoning. It is about the reasons we have for doing what we *normally* ought to do. It is hard to ignore the awkwardness of this mechanism. It echoes a kind of chicken or egg problem: is something the default position because it reflects what we have reason to do normally? Or do we have reason to do something normally, because it reflects the default position? More importantly, we may question why we should be interested in what we normally have reason to do. It seems more appropriate to find out what we ought to do, not what we ought to do *normally*. In effect, some argue that when it comes to serious questions about what we owe our fellow human beings and about what we ought to do there is often no place for the presumptions of the burden of proof.[9] Still, sometimes it is either impossible or too costly (or burdensome) to establish with certainty within a given time frame what we have reason to do. In such cases the default position seeks to enhance our *chances* of adopting an adequate practical position knowing that we may *not be certain* about it. The default position assumes that it often constitutes the best bet. Therefore, in our evaluation we are justified in giving it more weight than the alternatives. 'More weight' increases the burden of proving the adequacy of the alternatives. In a sense the default position functions as an efficiency tool. It creates a bias for a particular practical position to the detriment of the alternatives. It presupposes that beforehand we can tell which practical proposition has the stronger (or even strongest) case.

Let me now spell out the generic aspects of the default position in the context of immigration policy: the reasons *for* the admission of immigrants are normally stronger than the reasons for their exclusion. Or rather the reasons for exclusion are normally weaker than the reasons for admission. Only exceptionally do we have stronger reasons not to admit immigrants. To establish that this new position qualifies as normal, we must consider and balance *in advance* the reasons in favor of admission and exclusion. This is precisely what I will do in the next few pages by mobilizing the existing moral and political arguments regarding immigration. The introduction of the new default position will involve two stages. First, it seems that we need some basic sympathy for the case of admission if we are to consider it as a candidate for a new default position in the first place. There must be some initial indications for taking the case seriously. We need a minimum amount of sympathy to get a case off the ground. At first glance this step seems superfluous. Why not directly make the more substantive

8 As opposed to theoretical reasoning, i.e. the reasons we have for adopting particular beliefs.

9 In this respect we may note that in the context of determining the proper moral and normative attitude (e.g. do we have reasons to be a moralist, egoist or an amoralist?) 'no presumptions of burden of proof have a place in philosophical arguments.' Joseph Raz, 'The Amoralist' in Joseph Raz (ed.), *Engaging Reason. On the Theory of Value and Action* (Oxford: Oxford University Press, 1999), at 280 in footnote 17, with reference to Joseph Raz, *The Morality of Freedom* (Oxford: Clarendon Press, 1988), at 8–11.

claims? My central objective is to reconsider the current default position. This means that the current default position is being challenged. The whole point of a successful default position is that it does not require its own defense. It only considers arguments that, in a particular case, there are reasons to make an exception from the normal position. The default position restricts the discussion as to whether or not there is an exception at hand. However, we do not want to argue that there are reasons to make an exception to the normal position. We want to argue for the reverse. There are reasons to consider the current default position as an exception, and, to shift the focus of the debate, we need to make it plausible that there are prima facie reasons for reconsidering the existing default position – even if in the end those reasons may not be conclusive. In other words, the reasons only need to make it plausible that admission is something of value and worthwhile, which makes it prima facie reasonable (in terms of liberal theory) to consider a new default position. An obvious venue seems to be intuition – more particularly, moral intuition. So are there moral intuitions that point to admission?[10] If so, we can move to the next level: considering more generally the practical reasons in favor of admission and exclusion and balancing them against each other.

To be clear and at the risk of stating the obvious, shifting the burden of justification from the migrant to the authorities is not a ticket to a policy of open borders. If the authorities come up with adequate justifications *vis-à-vis* the normal migrant then there is no obstacle to his exclusion. On paper there are many good grounds for exclusion. Yet the question is whether those good reasons obtain in the context of concrete cases. Probably, a lot of today's and past exclusions cannot be properly justified. Consequently, the admission rate under a new immigration policy (where exclusion must be first justified by the authorities) may be significantly higher than under the current regime. However, this is not the same as endorsing an open border policy. The new default position has concrete and practical consequences for the authorities. They must design and organize the different 'instances' of immigration policy (i.e. law making, executive directives and measures, individual decisions and judicial review, including both legal and physical/factual acts) in such a way that they substantiate the reasons for exclusion of normal migrants. This means that immigration policy must provide overriding reasons for exclusion, backed up by sufficient empirical evidence. Furthermore, the level of generalization or individualization of the reasons and evidence should correspond with the level of generalization or individualization of the particular instance of the policy. To make things even more concrete, the new default position paves the way for seriously considering some

10 A positive answer does not preclude the fact that there are equally strong moral intuitions for closure.

of the very concrete policy proposals by migration researchers[11] and experts of immigration law.[12]

Admission, free movement and liberalism

The first step towards shifting the default position is to make plausible that it is worthwhile considering a new default position in the first place. The obvious and most powerful argument is to establish some close or even intrinsic connection between admission and the basic values of liberalism. The connection between admission and the basic values of liberalism is the idea and experience of free movement. Admission is a realization or an instance of free movement. Free movement is directly connected to liberalism. We will now briefly explore how political theory establishes a connection between admission, free movement and liberalism. For most political theorists this is ultimately about finding out whether or not there is a (moral) right to free movement (and a corresponding duty to admission). Yet this is not our task: we only need to establish that free movement and its realization, i.e. admission, is something of great value under liberalism. As a result it is worthwhile considering a change in the default position. Neither do we need to establish that free movement is such a strong value as to shift the first burden of justification. This is something we will do in the next section. For now, we only need to come up with sufficient reasons that allow us to challenge the default position itself.

The most radical argument in favor of free movement is the idea that it is an important value in itself.[13] In other words, free movement is inherently valuable and as such deserves a special status next to other fundamental liberties and rights of man. The most direct way to argue this is to connect free movement to autonomy. So, free movement may simply be one of the fundamental liberties associated with autonomy, i.e. pursuing one's own life project and self-determination: 'I decide for myself where I want to live'. Immigration restrictions constitute a curtailment of this fundamental liberty, thus the denial of admission is a curtailment of one's autonomy. A more dramatic illustration of the connection between free movement and autonomy is to consider the most extreme

11 E.g. contributions of Veenkamp, Düvell, Doomernik in M. Jandl (ed.), *Innovative Concepts for Alternative Migration Policies: Ten Innovative Approaches to the Challenges of Migration in the 21st Century* (Amsterdam: Amsterdam University Press, 2007).

12 Meijers Committee (P. Boeles *et al.*) 'Draft directive on Minimum Guarantees for Individual Freedom, Security and Justice in Relation to Decisions Regarding Movement of Persons', *European Journal of Migration and Law*, 7 (2005), 301–6. See Chapter 7.

13 Joseph H. Carens, 'Migration and morality: A liberal egalitarian perspective', in Brian Barry and Robert E. Goodin (eds), *Free Movement. Ethical Issues in the Transnational Migration of People and Money* (London: Harvester Wheatsheaf, 1992), at 26; Bader (2005) at 338 and endnote 44 at 357.

institutional opposite of personal autonomy, i.e. slavery and serfdom.[14] One of the essential features of serfdom was that the servant was tied to the land and could not move freely to another area. So, in a way, free movement is the value that is liberated when serfdom and slavery was abolished.

One can also argue that moving freely is not in itself an expression of one's autonomy but it may still be instrumental in realizing it. So, realizing one's life project (e.g. starting a business, taking up employment, starting a family, choosing and practising a religion) may require that one can move freely to areas enabling the pursuit of those opportunities.

Equally, but differently connected to autonomy, one may understand the value of free movement from the perspective of consent theory. If people are to leave the state of nature and subject themselves to the authority of the sovereign or the law, what kind of rights would they want to have guaranteed in 'exchange' for their obedience? Would free movement be one of those rights? The classic international law publicists had a very restricted view of free movement. Some argued that, like a property owner, the ruler may exclude foreigners from its territory at will.[15] This is actually a position on the first question for political theory: whether exclusion needs justification. Furthermore, most were of the opinion that there is only a duty to admit exiles, which corresponds with our refugee laws.[16] Yet they seemed to agree that it would be barbarous to deny an alien hospitality (rather a kind of guest right) if he does not mean any harm.[17] It is not entirely clear what

14 According to the well-known observation by Carens: 'Liberals objected to the way feudalism restricted freedom, including freedom of individuals to move from one place to the other. But modern practices of citizenship and state control over borders tie people to the land of their birth almost as effectively. If the feudal practices were wrong, what justifies the modern ones?' Carens, (1992), at 26–7.

15 Christian Wolff, *Jus Gentium Methodo Scientifica Pertractatum*, II, [1764], Publications of the Carnegie Endowment for International Peace, Division of International Law, Washington (Oxford: Clarendon Press, 1934), Ch. III. 'Of ownership of nations and the rights connected therewith', paras 293, 295 and 298; E. De Vattel, *The Law of Nations or the Principles of Natural Law Applied to the Conduct and to the Affairs of Nations and of Sovereigns*, III, [1758] (Washington: Carnegie Institution of Washington, 1916), Bk. II, Ch. VII-VIII, paras 94 and 100.

16 Wolff, Ch. I, paras 148–9; Vattel, Bk. II, Ch. IX, paras. 117, 120, 121, 123 and 125.

17 '. . . those who keep foreigners out of their city are by no means worthy of approval.' H. Grotius, *De Juri Belli ac Pacis Libri Tres*, [1646], Publications of the Carnegie Endowment for International Peace, Division of International Law, Washington (Oxford: Clarendon Press, 1913), Bk. II, Ch. II, para xvi, at 202 (page). Only Pufendorf can be said to hold that there is a duty to admit aliens: 'Among the duties of humanity there is included the further one of admitting strangers, as well as of kindly providing travelers with shelter and hospitality.' Samuel Pufendorf, *De Jure Naturae et Gentium Libri Octo*, II, [1688], Publications of the Carnegie Endowment for International Peace, Division of International Law, Washington (Oxford: Clarendon Press, 1934), Bk. III, Ch. III – *On the General Duties of Humanity*, at 363 (page). But this duty needs considerable qualification. If the alien does not come out of necessity or does not deserve our sympathy, the state may exclude at will. Ibid., at 363 (page). In effect, even Pufendorf seems to accept that there is no general duty to admit aliens from the legal perspective: 'Most writers feel that the safest reply to make is this: Every state may reach a decision, according to its own usage, on the admission of foreigners who

their position is with regard to those seeking admission for an indefinite stay. What matters for our purposes is that though the classic theorists certainly did not argue in favor of a right to free movement, it seems safe to say that they considered it an important value which, depending on the foreigner, is virtuous to honor. Still, in terms of consent these classic theorists had a rather one-sided view of consent. Consent was important to establish that a ruler had authority over foreigners that entered into their territory: the entrance constituted a tacit consent or subjection to the authority of the ruler.[18] When it comes to the exclusion of the foreigner, there is simply no mention of his explicit or tacit consent. At first glance we find a similar one-sidedness with the modern[19] contract or consent theorists. They are focused solely on the consent of those who are already member of a particular community. Consent is necessary to justify the authority to be exercised over those members. As a result emigration is of importance since it allegedly expresses the withdrawal of consent by a subject/emigrant.[20] But *im*migration is not interesting.[21] Worse, according to a contemporary interpretation of Hobbes, the authorities can exclude aliens at will.[22] As explained above, this is

come to it for other reasons that are necessary and deserving of sympathy. Only no one can question the barbarity of showing an indiscriminate hostility to those come on a peaceful mission.' Ibid., at 365 (page).

18 Pufendorf, Bk. III, Ch. IV 'On the consent required in promises and pacts', at 403 (page); Wolff, *Jus Gentium*, Ch. III, para. 300, at 151–2 (pages); De Vattel, *The Law of Nations*, Bk. II, Ch. VIII, para. 101, at 144 (page).

19 Of course, I consider Hobbes and especially Locke modern, not in a chronological, but more an ideological sense.

20 Jeremy Waldron, 'Theoretical Foundations of Liberalism', 37 *The Philosophical Quarterly* 127 (1987), at 138.

21 Bader (2005), at 333.

22 A contemporary interpretation of the mainly Hobbesian perspective by Whelan pushes this one-sidedness even further. (Frederick G. Whelan, 'Citizenship and Freedom of Movement: An Open Admission Policy?', in Mark Gibney (ed.), *Open Borders? Closed Societies? The Ethical and Political Issues* (Westport (CT)/London: Greenwood Press, 1988). I have adopted Phillip Cole's interpretation of Whelan's view (Cole (2000).) According to Whelan's Hobbesian account the world external to liberal communities is one of (hostile) nature, and as a result, liberal communities can do whatever they want to protect their liberal interests, including excluding aliens at will (Whelan, 21). Also as a matter of democracy a division must be made among insiders and outsiders: '. . . democracy requires that *people* be divided into *peoples* . . . with each unit distinguishing between its own citizens . . . and others, who are regarded as aliens *here* . . .' (Whelan (1988), at 28). The idea that the relationship between a liberal community and the non-liberal world is one of a hostile state of nature is obviously highly problematic from an empirical perspective. International law and morality produce actual standards (not necessarily liberal) which organize an environment that hardly qualifies as a hostile state of nature. As to consent, Whelan's view presupposes that communities are voluntary associations, which is only plausible if one accepts an extremely hypothetical notion of consent. In addition, if consent is taken seriously it must be explained why the consent of the excluded alien does not matter. As Philip Cole points out: 'On the one hand, all members that are included freely consented to their inclusion; but on the other hand, those who applied for membership but are excluded did not freely consent to their exclusion. . . . [T]here has been no free and voluntary consent to the laws which control this body of people.' (Cole (2000), at 186–7.)

not so much an answer to the second question of political philosophy, i.e. who has the first burden of justification. Rather this is an answer to the first question: does exclusion need to be justified in the first place? Accordingly we will not further address this account.[23] Still, there may be more in the works of the first modern consent theorists than meets the eye. In particular Locke's picture of the state of nature paves the way for establishing the value of free movement. According to Locke the conditions in the state of nature are not such that it is rational for men to subject *all* their rights and liberties to the sovereign to establish peace and order.[24] One way of understanding this position is to argue that it means that we can conceive of the existence of rights and liberties independently from a *particular* and *institutionalized* political and legal order. Though the *institution* of a society and government is needed to realize the full potential of these rights and liberties, their existence does not depend on the institutions. Furthermore, the rights and liberties have a universal character as their existence does depend on a *particular* society and government. So imagine Mr. A being a member of Society B. The existence of Mr. A's rights and liberties does not depend on him being a member of that particular society. These simple observations have two direct and indirect consequences for free movement. First, as the existence of rights and liberties does not depend on a particular society, there is no prima facie reason for having people tied to a particular community. People may have good reasons to move to other societies if this enables them to better realize their rights and liberties. It does not follow that the other societies have a duty to admit. But it shows that admission would be a realization of this possibility to move freely, which in turn indicates that free movement is an important value. The second, indirect, consequence for free movement is more philosophical. The Hobbesian state of nature almost makes it rational to subject

23 Still there is the contention that depriving a democratic community from its power to determine who counts as its own citizen implies that new members may be imposed on the community *without the consent* of the community or its citizens. This goes against the core feature of democracy, i.e. self-determination (Whelan (1988), at 28–9). Of course this is again a conflation of the decision on admission and the decision on membership (see n. 4). Furthermore, taking into account the interests of others and practical reasons in general do not amount to being deprived of a power. In any event, to the extent Whelan's point is not be understood as an ontological and existential claim – and hence concern the first question of political theory about the need to justify exclusion – it may be construed as an communitarian argument for setting the first burden of justification.

24 Locke identifies a limited set of particular inconveniences of the state of nature which justifies the creation of a commonwealth and government: irrational interpretation and application of the law of nature (due to bias and ignorance), absence of independent judges, lack of power to enforce judgments (Locke, Ch. IX 'of the ends of political society and government', Bk. 2, nos. 124–6, at 180). As a result, people will (and only need to) subject their rights and liberties under the law of nature to government *in so far* as necessary for government to address those inconveniences (Ch. IX, Bk. 2, No. 131, at 181–2). This limitation is also informed by Locke's doubt about whether the monarch – who is only a man after all – will always do much better than the state of nature (Ch. II, Bk. 2, No. 13, at 123).

to the authority of the sovereign, whatever the conditions, as long as it provides order and civil peace. By contrast, Locke's version makes it rational to really envisage what rights and liberties one would like to see guaranteed in exchange for one's consent to government. Furthermore, as the existence of rights and liberties are detached from a particular institutionalized government, this exercise becomes relevant for every man, irrespective of his membership of a particular society. By the same token, it also paves the way for considering the rights and liberties of all other men, including those beyond our particular polity. This offers opportunities for universalizing in the Kantian sense. It is now a small step to envisage the categorical imperatives that will make the realization of a Kingdom of Ends possible.[25] More importantly what would be the role of free movement in realizing the Kingdom of Ends? Though Kant's own take on (normal) immigration was restrictive – every stranger has the right (not a favor)[26] 'of not being treated as an enemy in the country in which he arrives'.[27] But states are free to refuse him 'if it can be done without endangering his existence . . .'[28] A general duty to admit aliens requires 'particular conventions' and is not a matter of a universal rule.[29] By contrast, Kant's approach and substantive claims about people being ends in themselves led contemporary political theorists to different conclusions. Joseph Carens and others mobilize the neo-Kantian approach of John Rawls and apply it to immigration. They add to the model concerns of distributive justice by stressing both the arbitrary nature and distributive relevance of place of birth and nationality. They conclude that behind the veil of ignorance people would chose free movement (across states) as one of the basic liberties which they would

25 Mary A. McCloskey, 'Kant's Kingdom of Ends', *Philosophy* (1976) vol. 51, no. 198, at 331–9.

26 Immanuel Kant, *Perpetual Peace* (New York: Columbia University Press, 1939), at 23.

27 Ibid., at 23–4.

28 Ibid., at 24

29 Ibid. Still, even on the terms in Perpetual Peace, Kant's position seems untenable, if we read the following passages: 'But the man, or the nation, that lives in the state of nature, deprives me of that security, and attacks me without being an aggressor, *by the mere circumstance of living contiguous to me*, in a state of anarchy and without laws; . . . menaced perpetually by him with hostilities, against which I have no protection, I have the right to compel him, either to associate with me under the dominion of common laws . . . All men, who have a mutual influence over one another, ought to have a civil constitution' (emphasis added) ibid. at 11 (footnote). Perhaps the mutual influence over on the one hand immigrant and on the other the host state and its nationals was limited in Kant's times. Yet today this mutual influence is difficult to deny. As a result there is a duty ('ought') for both immigrant and the host state to enter into a civil constitution. This simply follows from Kant's own emphatic notion of the 'state of nature' between the nation and the foreigner seeking admission. Kukathas seems to make a similar extended reading of Kant as I have done. He argues that the Kantian commitment to lawfulness should urge states to admit aliens fleeing conditions of lawlessness (Kukathas (2003), at 586). However my point is a bit different. It is not so much that only the alien is living in a condition of lawlessness, rather the *relationship* between on the one hand the receiving community and its members and on the other hand the alien is one of lawlessness, i.e. a state of war. So in a sense by entering into a civil constitution both the host community and the alien are fleeing conditions of lawlessness.

expect authorities to guarantee.[30] For our purposes it is not necessary to actually further investigate whether one would come up with a basic *right* to free movement. What really matters is that this exercise again shows that free movement is something of great value, which clearly fits our liberal political intuitions.

Apart from deriving the value of free movement from autonomy (either as an instance of autonomy or through consent theory), one can also understand the value of free movement as a corollary of other rights. So, some argue that free movement is the corollary of the right to exit,[31] because the latter will remain ineffective if the former is not guaranteed.[32] Of course, this does not follow because for an effective right to exit it suffices to have 'entry options in *some* states'.[33] I may add that the entry option need not even be legally protected. For the right to exit to be effective, it suffices that a person can physically leave his country and physically enter another country. The fact that the legal status of the emigrant in the new country is precarious need not affect the effectiveness of the right to exit. Strictly speaking, what matters for an effective right to exit is that leaving is a better option than staying. Another right on which free movement may piggy-back is property. According to the libertarian argument, the state's exclusion of immigrants deprives national property owners of the potential to enter into contracts with immigrants seeking admission.[34] This is, of course, not

30 Joseph H. Carens, 'Aliens and Citizens: The Case for Open Borders', 49 *Review of Politics* (1987), at 258. Equally interesting are the other applications of Rawls' theory on immigration. For example James L. Hudson and Timothy King focus on the Difference Principle. But rather than arguing that free movement follows from the difference principle, they hold that nevertheless immigration restrictions violate the difference principle: immigration restrictions constitute an unequal treatment of persons while they do not tend to improve the worse off. Hudson also mobilizes Rawls' contractarian instrument but remains extremely brief: he believes that when placed behind a veil of ignorance he would certainly chose free movement as an immigration policy. James L. Hudson, 'The Philosophy of Immigration', 3 *The Journal of Libertarian Studies* (1986), at 53 with reference to Timothy King, 'Immigration from Developing Countries: Some Philosophical Issues', 93 *Ethics* 525 (1983).

31 Some have also argued in favor of free movement as an *analogy* of internal free movement. Carens (1992), at 27; Robert E. Goodin, 'Commentary: The political realism of free movement' in Brian Barry and Robert E. Goodin (eds), (1992), at 12; Ann Dummet, 'The Transmigration of People seen from within a Natural Law Tradition', in Brian Barry and Robert E. Goodin (eds), (1992), at 173. The most important objection against this argument is nicely summarized by Bader: 'it either neglects moral principles of democratic self-determination completely, or it neglects the importance of democratic states among other units in emerging democratic multi-level polities. . . . If it is accepted that states still are important *loci* of democratic self-determination, it cannot show why limited "sovereignty" should be regularly overruled: the prudential and realistic reasons limiting internal freedom may be much stronger in the case of free entry.' Bader (2005), at 339–40.

32 Dowty almost builds his entire case for free movement on the right to exit. Alan Dowty, *Closed Borders: the Contemporary Assault on Freedom of Movement* (New Haven (Conn.): Yale University Press, 1987).

33 Bauboeck (forthcoming 2011).

34 Hillel Steiner, 'Libertarianism and the Transnational Migration of People', in Brian Barry and Robert E. Goodin (eds), (1992); Hudson (1986), endnote 5 at 61.

an argument for free movement, but simply an argument against the state, as nothing under the libertarian argument prevents private property owners from coming up with their own exclusionary scheme (e.g. gated communities). In a recent contribution Blake and Risse reiterated the classical property argument in the sense that the earthly resources are in common property to all men. Depending on the state's rate of resource utilization in relation to its population, immigrants may have a claim to admission depending on the resource utilization/population rate of their source country.[35] Though I find their account engaging, intelligent and well intended, I am not convinced that such a strategy is ultimately productive.[36] However, for our purposes, it is a welcome reminder of the well-known fact that most liberal accounts of men's claims to goods started from a notion of common property.[37] It follows that only by moving freely across the commons

35 Michael Blake and Matthias Risse, 'Is there a Human Right to Free Movement? Immigration and Original Ownership of the Earth', (2006). Faculty research working paper series, Kennedy School of Government, Harvard University, at SSRN.

36 As Bauboeck notes, the parameters seem outdated as they focus on resources and population pressure, which do not correspond with the reality of densely populated urban areas being pockets of economic growth and opportunity. Bauboeck (forthcoming 2011). But Blake and Risse may address this objection. They might produce a new and more complex ratio that renders the opportunities in such pockets of economic growth susceptible to a form of common property. This brings me to my more fundamental objection. Why do we need to understand our use of resources in terms of possession or property in the first place? Why should we accept that originally this possession was in common? Furthermore, it is unclear in what respect these objects are in common: are resources in common as a function of our needs, merits, desires, etc.? Furthermore the argument from property seems just as problematic as the thesis that the state's title to its territory is to be understood as one of (international) property. International experts have replaced this thesis with the competence theory (see Chapter 2). The point is that the material and intangible goods from which migrants are excluded hardly coincide with the goods that are susceptible to any meaningful theory of property. In a sense, it will inflate the notion of property and at the same time do injustice to the complexity of exclusion. Finally, there is a concern – I am not sure it is an objection – that Blake and Risse may unintentionally drive the debate into a logic which is difficult to stop once entered into. The use of the ratio's really expresses a notion of the pressure of population on the territory and resources. Hence their reference to Cavallero. (Eric Cavallero, 'An Immigration-Pressure Model of Global Distributive Justice', *Politics, Philosophy & Economics*, (2006), vol. 5, at 97–127.) By the same token, these pressures are easily understood as fluxes, which are to be controlled or rather managed. This drives the debate to the logic of population control and management as described by Foucault. (Michel Foucault, *Sécurité, Territoire, Population: Cours au Collège de France, 1977–1978* (Paris: Gallimard, 2004.) One concern is of course that migration becomes a purely technical matter that is framed in such a way that it defies scrutiny from standard liberal and legal theory. See Art. 79 of the Lisbon Treaty, which speaks only of 'a common immigration *policy* aimed at ensuring, at all stages, the efficient *management* of *migration flows*' (emphases added). 'Policy', 'management', 'flows' these are all terms that are difficult to capture in standard liberal theory. In any event, the notions are really foreigners in the theory and philosophy of law. See Bas Schotel, 'EU's Management of Migration Flows and the Rule of Law. From Individual Migrant to Migration Flow', *Journal of Ethnic and Migration Studies* (forthcoming 2011).

37 Locke, Ch. V, Bk. 2, No. 26, at 129; Wolff and de Vattel *supra* n. 15; Kant, at 24.

one can fully enjoy this property. Again, no duty to admission is established, but it does show the value of free movement for those committed to certain notions of property.

Finally, rather than just referring to the idea of free movement as advanced in the different approaches of liberal theory, we may also concentrate on the experience of free movement to establish its great value for liberal democracies. There are countless examples. It seems that any form of political and legal union or close cooperation typically involves the creation of a right to free movement for the citizens of the area to which that union applies (city and nation states, diplomatic cooperation, advanced custom unions, supra national union, etc.).[38] This is true to the extent that if an area is identified as sufficiently unified from a legal and political perspective (irrespective of the size of the actual territory/space involved) residents have a right to internal free movement under international and national law. Now, this does not show that free movement across national borders is a right. But it does demonstrate that moving freely in an area – no matter the size – is considered to be of great value.

In short, it seems clear that both the ideas and experience of liberal tradition all point to the value of free movement. The admission of migrants obviously constitutes a realization of this important value. The strategy of our discussion so far has not been to look for overriding reasons to establish a fundamental right to free movement, or to set a new default position. We just want to establish the value of admission and its connection to liberal theory so we can *start* to challenge the current default position.

Shifting the burden of justification

The previous section merely constitutes the first step towards considering a reversal of the default position. It made plausible that admission as a realization of free movement is an important value and experience for liberal political theory. Focusing primarily on the value of free movement, we did not make any argument for actually shifting the first burden of justification. This requires a balancing exercise of the relevant reasons *ex ante* and in general. To this end we cannot restrict ourselves only to moral reasons. We must take into account different types of practical reasons: moral, political, prudential and realistic.

> Moral philosophy may solely specialize in moral reasons and arguments, but political philosophy has to deal with the complexity of practical reason and judgment. Normative arguments include not only moral *oughts* (what we owe to humanity), ethical/political *oughts* (what we should do as members of specific communities, e.g. 'nationstates'), prudential *oughts* (requiring us to

38 J.A.R. Nafziger, 'The General Admission of Aliens under International Law', 77 *American Journal of International Law* (1983), at 833–7.

> do what is in our well-informed, rational, longterm interests), and realist *oughts* ('ought implies can'). Evidently, these requirements conflict with each other and it is increasingly recognized that there is no clear, context-independent formula for weighing and balancing them, even if one agrees on a lexical ordering, e.g. that – all things considered – moral arguments should trump ethical–political and prudential ones.[39]

We will start by spelling out the central tenets of the moral and ethico-political objections against general admission. We will provide two types of counter-arguments. First, the objections may be largely accommodated by taking a minimal moral and contextual perspective. Second, the remainder of the ethico-political objection will be refuted by an argument to the effect that migration restrictions do not build a political community. So our discussion starts with and focuses largely on the moral and ethico-political reasons against admission. The underlying idea is that though political theory must consider prudential and realistic arguments, their impact on the default position is less stable. By their – empirical – nature, prudential and realistic arguments are more oriented to an *ex post* and particular perspective, while the moral and political reasons have a more *ex ante* and general character. This also means that the most important part of the balancing exercise for the purposes of determining the default position takes place at the moral and political level. We will focus on refuting the assumptions underlying the prudential and realistic objections.

Moral and communitarian objections to admission

The strongest argument against admission from the moral perspective is to debunk the intuition from distributive justice. Or to put it differently, the moral argument for the value of free movement seems weakest when based on distributive justice. The problem is that the connection between general admission and equal distribution is not so direct. In fact, the worse off, who are the primary concern for Rawlsian theorists, hardly ever benefit from freedom of movement, simply because they don't have the resources (financial and physical) to move to another country.[40] In addition, major geo-political and economic factors driving the distributive inequalities remain unaffected by general admission, turning it not into a second-best solution, but a third- or a fifth-best solution.[41] In other words, unequal distribution of resources among humanity is a

39 Veit Bader, *Secularism or Democracy? Associational Governance of Religious Diversity* (Amsterdam: Amsterdam University Press, 2007), at 90.

40 James Woodward, 'Commentary: Liberalism and migration', in Brian Barry and Robert E. Goodin (eds) (1992), at 67.

41 Bader (2005), at 341 (with reference to Mark Tushnet).

legitimate and sound moral concern, but general admission is simply not the thing that can address it.

The objections from the ethical/political perspective, in particular the communitarian critique on general admission, are probably the ones taken most seriously by contemporary (liberal) political theorists, proponents and opponents of general admission alike.[42] The critique has two closely related but distinct sets of arguments: conceptual and moral; and prudential and realistic. We concentrate on the first set, which is pointedly captured by this passage from Walzer cited earlier in Chapter 3:

> Admission and exclusion are at the core of communal independence. They suggest the deepest meaning of self-determination. Without them, there could not be communities of character, historically ongoing associations of men and women with some special commitment to one another and some special sense of their common life.[43]

According to the conceptual and moral critique, general admission denies the centrality of the community as the basis for meaningful and worthwhile human life. First, the distinctive character of a community is one of the things which makes human life so meaningful. General admission renders it impossible to create and maintain communities of distinctive character, because the existing members of a community can no longer decide on new membership. This means that the community ultimately loses its self-determination. Second, in line with the concern for self-determination, it is only through the possibility of closure that people can undertake special commitments; if it was not for closure our commitments would stretch out to all, rendering them universal not special. One of those commitments is internal free movement. According to the communitarian view, internal free movement is only possible if communities can close their external borders.[44] The arguments are conceptual because they assume that as a matter of concept, meaningful communities have a distinct character and as a matter of concept, the power to include and exclude is constitutive to this distinctiveness.[45] The arguments are moral because the closure and thus immigration restrictions are a *conditio sine qua non* for autonomy and thus moral agency.

42 I relied heavily on the discussion of Michael Walzer's position by Cole (2000), at 60–85; Bader (2005); Seglow (2005), at 319–21; Hudson (1986), at 55–7; Blake (2003), at 231–3.

43 Michael Walzer, *Spheres of Justice: A Defence of Pluralism and Equality* (New York: Basic Books, 1983), at 62.

44 Walzer (1983), at 38–9.

45 This conceptual argument, when construed in a more radical way, becomes an ontological and existential thesis on the role of exclusion for the constitution and continuity of any political and legal order. If so, then the argument is in fact an attempt to answer the first question of ethics of migration: Is exclusion to be justified? However, I believe that Walzer is still trying to argue why exclusion can be justified. So I take that the argument is not about whether authorities should justify exclusion of immigrants in the first place.

The communitarian critique is important because it takes us beyond abstract and idealized moral reasons. It urges us to think about what makes our political communities and their members so special. In a sense the communitarian critique is a first step to a more contextualized approach to political philosophy. Yet, as we will see, a closer examination of our own political community will reveal the mythical and idealized assumptions underlying the communitarian critique.

Counter-arguments from minimal morality and contextual pluralism

Unequal distribution based on arbitrary facts supposedly provides us with the moral intuition to favor free movement. However, critics have argued that while arbitrary unequal distribution is a legitimate moral concern, general admission is simply not the thing that can address it. A minimal moral argument accommodates this pertinent critique by proposing an *oblique* connection between distributive justice and general admission. The moral argument under a contextual approach boils down to the contention that we have basic minimal obligations *vis-à-vis* other human beings. Those obligations do not stop at the borders of our communities but have a global reach.

The argument that mobilizes Thomas Pogge's argument for a system of global resource dividend goes as follows.[46] First, we can recognize that there are some needs or necessities that we perceive to be so basic to the effect that they become relevant, important, and to a large extent essential to all persons irrespective of their cultural background.[47] Second, we can also recognize that there are today large numbers of persons whose basic needs are not satisfied. Prospective immigrants often count as being part of those persons in need. In other words, the fact that a large part of the world population misses out on the satisfaction of basic needs constitutes a structural inequality. Third, we can recognize that we, affluent communities, are in a material position to address those inequalities. Fourth, we can recognize that we, affluent communities, are partially responsible for causing and maintaining these inequalities due to the establishment and maintenance of political, financial and commercial structures that constitute an obstacle to mitigating these inequalities (e.g. unfair trade arrangements for natural resources and agricultural products). In addition, even if affluent countries were not responsible for the inequalities, this still does not entail the absence of an obligation.[48] For

46 The following restatement is drawn from Bader (2005), at 343–4 and Bader (1997).

47 In this respect we should think of the basic needs as identified and substantiated by Shue. Henry Shue, *Basic Rights: Subsistence, Affluence and US Foreign Policy* (Princeton: Princeton University Press, 1980).

48 This is precisely the point liberal nationalists fail to appreciate. See Seglow's discussion of David Miller, Seglow (2005), at 323.

example, in the context of political refugees the receiving countries have no responsibility for the unjust treatment of the refugee by the authorities of the source state. Nevertheless they have an obligation to admit the refugee.

It follows from these four considerations that we have an obligation – if not strong reasons – to address those needs. Moreover, it is a global concern in the sense that those affected are all persons whose basic needs are not fully satisfied. The connection with general admission is then not direct but oblique, because we do not have reasons to advance general admission as the best or a very good solution to address poverty, but rather *we have no good reasons to keep the borders closed as long as we have not addressed poverty*.

The argument is productive because it prevents the 'worse-off' argument from hijacking the discourse. It means that immigration restrictions should be relaxed not only for the worse-off, but with regard to all who seek to legitimately improve their living conditions. If places are limited and selection becomes inevitable, the worse-off have a better case (all things being equal, which is rarely the case in reality). It is up to the affluent countries to show that the limitations are justified in the first place. In other words, as long as the global moral obligations are not fulfilled, general admission also extends to the normal migrants – who are as a matter of empirical fact rarely worse off.

A second connection with general admission is that though it may not address poverty in general it certainly alleviates the hardship of particular immigrants. In connection with the first argument, while there are no better, effective solutions, there are no reasons to prevent individual immigrants from achieving a better outlook.

The moral considerations of the contextual approach have considerable merit compared to the previous universalistic arguments. The former can claim universal or global application without relying on unacceptable counterfactual constructs. The global obligations are not derived from some hypothetical state of nature. Nor does the obligation seek to establish some future ideal state of affairs, e.g. highest utility, wealth maximization, socialism, the greatest equal liberty to all, etc.[49] Instead it simply starts from current needs that are easily ascertainable and substantiated. Similarly, the establishment of basic needs neither requires an inquiry into, nor agreement about, the concept of 'the good life'. Neither does it presuppose a commitment to particular political arrangements or aspirations (e.g. liberal egalitarianism). An important aspect of the contextual argument is precisely the observation that liberal-egalitarians and communitarians alike recognize these needs and obligations.[50] Finally, the fulfillment of the global

49 Bader (2005), at 343.

50 'States, whether nation-states or not, have to fulfill their Global Moral Obligations (GMO's). This rules out any unconditional priority to compatriots ('my country right or wrong'). All reasonable defenders of moderate patriotism, liberal nationalism or communitarianism acknowledge this limitation (Walzer, Miller, Tamir, Nathanson, Scheffler)'. Id., at 346.

moral obligation does not demand that we make sacrifices or adopt attitudes of heroic proportions. On the contrary, proportional changes in international trade and development schemes may already address some of the problems without turning members of affluent countries into martyrs of distributive justice. In effect, the minimal obligations do not focus on *equal* concern or respect, but on *minimal* respect.[51]

The pluralist and contextual approach can also address many of the communitarian objections. The contextual approach recognizes the existence, importance and legitimacy of the community and the special commitments that arise out of political communities.[52] In this respect, it accepts that priority be given to compatriots. Yet the contextual argument subjects this priority to the proviso that states meet their global moral obligations as well as their minimal domestic duties. It is here that the contextual approach valorizes the current system of particular political communities, i.e. nation states. In fact, nation states still constitute a central vehicle for allocating and enforcing our minimal moral obligations, both globally and domestically.[53] In addition, some communities entertain values that actually require its members to undertake special obligations with regard to non-members; these correspond with and go beyond minimal moral obligations. Irrespective of their soundness, these values can be held against the members. It is here that the arguments for general admission in terms of our moral intuition kick in again. Whatever the value of autonomy, ownership and consent, those who take these notions seriously may find themselves in a special relationship with normal migrants who appeal to these values. Similarly, increasingly confessional and non-confessional politicians are emphasizing the Christian origin and nature of Western states and societies (sometimes even to the point of having this contention laid down in constitutional documents).[54] Yet with that same eagerness they marginalize every concrete initiative that endorses precisely the Christian values with regard to migrants (e.g. charity, hospitality, tolerance and using one's

51 Bader (2007), at 85. This approach should take the sting out of the so-called universal-particular paradox, which allegedly renders liberalism so incoherent when it comes to immigration. See for the argument from incoherence Cole (2000) and Blake (2003).

52 Bader explicitly recognizes that not only intimate interactions give rise to special relations. In fact, non-thick cultural practices such a common political history and practices can create special ties and obligations. And thicker ethno-national common cultures may – depending on the culture – create special ties with members and non-members (cf. *infra* my reference to Christian values). Finally, the pluralistic approach recognizes that even in political communities that profess a value and ethno neutral political culture there is still need to rely on particular civic virtues. Bader (2005), at 346.

53 Ibid., at 347.

54 Cf. suggestions to incorporate reference to Christian origins and nature into the Treaty for the European Constitution. Also, opponents of Turkish membership of the EU often invoked the EU's Christian roots as incompatible with the Islamic nature of Turkish society. See also reference to the German people's 'responsibility before God and men' in the preamble of the FRG Constitution.

talents).[55] Their professed commitment to Christian values does not justify the distance they seek to create between their community and migrants.

The contextual approach also recognizes and endorses the distinctiveness of particular political communities. Since there are no preset or fixed models to organize the fulfillment of their global and domestic obligations, each community is encouraged to build the institutional arrangements it deems fit. This may lead to substantive differences between communities in their treatment of migrants and compatriots. As long as the minimal requirements are met, these differences are fully compatible with and sometimes endorsed by the contextual approach. Yet, the advantage of the contextual approach is that it acknowledges and values distinctiveness without resorting to implausible claims about the homogeneity of the – original – communities.[56]

55 See for example police raids on Catholic churches sheltering illegal aliens in France during the presidency of Jacques Chirac, who professes state neutrality while underscoring the Christian character of Western society. See also initiatives by local officials to provide basic help to illegal aliens against the instructions of the Christian-Democrat-led national government in the Netherlands. See also proposals by Belgian Minister of Interior Affairs, Patrick De Wael to prosecute those giving shelter to illegal aliens (*Gazet van Antwerpen*, 7 January 2006). (However, I am not sure whether De Wael, a liberal democrat, likes to underscore the Christian origins and nature of Western societies.) See also the situation in the USA where self-professed Christian politicians from both the Democrat and Republican parties seeking to penalize the provision of basic help (e.g. water tanks, First Aid services) to illegal immigrants crossing the Mexican–US border. See how US civil society is at the same time trying to circumvent these restrictions.

56 The homogeneity and originality of the community are of course the weakest point of the communitarian critique. It has been adequately refuted in various ways, e.g. cultures change over time and a lot of states are self-professed as multi-cultural (Seglow (2005), at 321–2; Peter C. Meilaender, *Towards a Theory of Immigration* (Basingstoke: Palgrave, 2001) at 163); if cultural homogeneity and continuity were so important then exit restrictions should be imposed (Cole (2000), at 75); if nations were homogenous no immigration restrictions would be needed for 'no immigrant could gain foothold in a community where no one would have anything to do with him' (Hudson (1986), at 55–6).

Still, it seems that communitarians may resist the mandatory introduction of the moral proviso if they become emphatic about the importance of exclusion as a constitutive aspect of the community. It follows from Phillip Cole's interpretation of Walzer's reasonable and unreasonable self-conceptions of the community and immigration controls that the legitimacy of a community's identity and immigration control is a matter of brute facts (Cole (2000), at 77–8). The immigration controls are reasonable (and thus legitimate) if they correspond with the identity or self-conception of the community. The identity of the community is reasonable if it corresponds with the social realities and intentions behind its creation. However, there are no constraints from reasonableness on the selection of the social realities and the intentions. So racist and oppressive social realities and intentions may constitute an adequate basis for the self-conception of a community and accordingly its immigration policy; what matters is that there are facts that constitute a distinctive community. According to the communitarian view, this distinctive character necessarily involves closure in the sense of exclusion. It means that in a lot of cases the moral proviso may not correspond with the exclusionary facts that grounded the community. If so, it would be unreasonable and thus illegitimate for a community to adopt the moral proviso. This position corresponds with the exclusion thesis. See Chapters 3 and 4.

Immigration restrictions do not build a community

Though the contextual approach is capable of accommodating most of the relevant objections advanced by communitarians, the latter can still argue that *in fact* exclusion for particular types of political communities is constitutive, namely for nation states. The contention is that the actual immigration policies of actual nation states were instrumental to their construction. So the power to exclude migrants and immigration restrictions are constitutive for a community not as a matter of concept or structure, rather they happened to be constitutive for nation states as a matter of empirical or historical fact.

Yet, John Torpey's excellent study into the genesis of the contemporary passport systems points in quite a different direction.[57] First, the permanent and comprehensive immigration restrictions supported by the elaborate passport system is relatively recent. It is only from the end of the nineteenth century to the First World War that liberal immigration policies[58] were abandoned by both US and Western European countries.[59] By the end of the Second World War, an elaborate and internationally standardized passport system had been put in place.[60] If systematic and comprehensive immigration restrictions are so recent, how can they have been so crucial for nation and state building? Either no serious nation and state building took place prior to the two World Wars, or the power to control migration and immigration restrictions are not so instrumental after all. It seems that the latter hypothesis is more plausible than the former.

Second, the main historical reasons behind immigration restrictions have little to do with building the community or the nation state. The dominant reason behind immigration restrictions from the eighteenth to the twenty-first centuries has been public order and security, rather than building the community. So the primary concerns of the authorities have to do with preventing military invasions, (counter-) revolutions, coups d'état, riots, strikes, epidemics, etc. In times of (imminent) public unrest foreigners are suspect, so entry restrictions are seen to be justified. The exclusionary measures against foreigners themselves are not aimed at creating any stronger ties among citizens and nationals; far from it. Great numbers of non-foreign subjects are equally suspect and are excluded accordingly (e.g. vagabonds, peasants, intellectuals, religious officials, proletarians, etc.). It is just that foreigners are *in any event suspect.*

Now, one may argue that the authorities maintain public order in the interests of the community members and that as such they contribute to building the community. However, the motives behind maintaining the public order may be less community oriented than some would hope for. The authorities, or rather the

57 John Torpey, *The Invention of the Passport. Surveillance, Citizenship and the State* (Cambridge: Cambridge University Press, 2000).

58 Ibid., Chapter 3.

59 Ibid., Chapter 4

60 Ibid., Chapter 5.

persons acting as the authorities (and those dependent on them), have a clear prudential interest of their own to secure public order: it is the least they have to do if they want to remain in power. In addition, we must avoid being too emphatic about the notion of public order and security. Again, maintaining order is primarily a matter of preventing chaos and violent power struggles. This notion of public order hardly fits the much thicker concept of a political community defended by communitarians. They have in mind a society where a particular culture and particular positive rights and duties attributed to the members of a community, *create special ties among the members*. It is clear that keeping others out does not create such culture; it certainly does not establish such rights and duties.

By contrast, restrictions on *e*migration are much more closely connected to building the community or nation. The dominant rationale behind emigration restrictions was to make sure that subjects fulfilled their 'communal' duties (or privileges), particularly military service and paying taxes. So, the French Kings and Revolutionary authorities had already issued exit restrictions to their subjects in the seventeenth and eighteenth centuries to prevent them from dodging conscription.[61] Similar motives were behind German (nineteenth century)[62] and Italian (early twentieth century) exit restrictions.[63] To the extent one accepts the characterization of military service as one of the quintessential instruments for community and nation building, the exit restrictions clearly aim to contribute to the building of a community. Apart from safeguarding communal duties, from time to time exit restrictions were motivated by economic (mercantile) reasons and fears of dissident émigrés mounting resistance/a revolution from abroad. Yet more often than not authorities did not hesitate to exile undesirable elements (e.g. by banishment), rather than keeping them within the country. With the rise of totalitarian regimes, which were relatively successful in *effectively* controlling their subjects, exit restrictions became a useful tool for control and oppression.[64] However, communitarians do not argue against the freedom to leave one's country; their argument is against the freedom to move into the country 'of someone else'.

What about the protectionist rationale behind twentieth-century immigration restrictions? It seems difficult to deny that immigration restrictions that aimed to protect national economic resources (e.g. jobs, welfare benefits) and national culture/ethnicity contributed to community and nation state building. The protective measures allegedly were a condition or prerequisite for having the resources and culture in the first place. By the same token, the protective measures establish and render explicit that these resources and culture belong to a particular group

61 Torpey (2000), at 19 and 21.

62 Ibid., at 64.

63 Ibid., at 105.

64 Cf. Dowty (1987); Torpey (2000), at 104.

only. Though intuitively attractive, this picture is not correct. A closer look at the measures reveals that even immigration restrictions for (economic) protective purposes have little to do with community and nation state building and those protective measures that are directly connected with nation building are too morally suspect to do the communitarian position any good.

First, the connection between immigration restrictions and the protection of economic resources (welfare arrangements included) is very weak. For instance, one of the first important state-sponsored welfare initiatives, i.e. the German Socialist or Anti-Socialist Laws of 1878, was passed when the German states were still under the liberal migration and passport regime of the North German Passport Law of 1867.[65] So welfare arrangements need not coincide with immigration restrictions.[66] But even if they do, the restrictions themselves do not establish any welfare arrangements. In addition, the welfare arrangements were initially directed at one class – the poor, the needy – rather than a particular type of member (citizen, national). It is also highly questionable whether the economic protectionist measures depict (or even aim to do so) a unified community. It rather seems that the measures single out particular groups within a country (e.g. farmers, blue collar workers, medical staff, etc.). The measures are often called upon to protect a social and professional *class* rather than nationality. For instance, labor organizations demand the protection of minimal labor standards not only for those working in their own country but also for those working in developing countries.[67] So the focus is on ensuring minimal labor standards, rather than minimal labor standards *for national workers only*.

Finally, although the exclusion of non-members from the 'national' or 'communal' resources is taking place on a large scale, by the same token the operational mechanics behind the distribution of economic resources have proved to be extremely resistant to exclusionary measures based on nationality. The failure to eliminate the employment of illegal immigrants in the 'national' labor market is a clear case in point. But typical socio-economic arrangements are equally resistant. For instance, in some Western countries, illegal minors can receive primary and secondary schooling. Similarly, most countries – though under pressure – provide basic health care to illegal minors and adults alike. Crucial protective schemes such as workplace safety standards apply – legally – to both legal and illegal employment. More generally, to the extent that immigration

65 Torpey (2000), at 75–92.

66 See also Will Kymlicka and Keith Banting, 'Immigration, Multiculturalism, and the Welfare State', *Ethics & International Affairs* (2006), vol. 20, issue 3, 281–304. Their empirical analyses suggest that immigration and the subsequent multicultural policies need not compromise the social cohesion required to sustain a social welfare system.

67 This is fully compatible with the often hostile attitude of the national labor movement with regard to new arrivals. See for a discussion of the *apparently* ambiguous position of the labor movement with regard to immigration Chris Brown, 'Marxism and the Transnational Migration of People: Ethical issues', in Brian Barry and Robert E. Goodin (eds) (1992), at 137–41.

restrictions are imposed to avoid too much pressure on the labor market and welfare system, it seems that the concern has been more about maintaining the system and providing the basic services rather than reserving it for the nationals. In short, immigration restrictions for the purposes of 'national' economic resources have little to do with building an exclusive community or nation state.

Conversely, the immigration restrictions for the sake of protecting a particular culture or ethnicity are directly connected to building a community and nation state. For it is possible to phrase the exclusion standards in such a way that it simultaneously indicates who is included (see Chapter 4). The problem, however, is that most of these policies turn out to be racist.[68] Though the notion of a homogenous community or nation is a myth, it can nevertheless be argued that these immigration restrictions at the very least reflect an awareness of a community or nation: an 'us' as opposed to 'them'. But even if in fact these measures were intended to build a community or nation and were successful in doing so, the question remains what does this mean for the normative position communitarians must adopt? The communitarian position is not a racist one. Yet anything that makes a direct link between immigration restrictions and community building is highly suspect from a moral perspective.

In fact, if there is a connection between immigration control and nation state building it is rather *oblique* and *accidental*. Torpey nicely reveals this connection.[69] The passport system was invented as a tool to enforce the control and restriction of migration and travel. From the end of the nineteenth century, nationality increasingly gained importance as a marker for all kind of state policies (in terms of both benefits and control). As a result, establishing the nationality of a person became crucial. However, contrary to the other markers that had previously been used (e.g. gender and social status) nationality was not easily read from a person's appearance or acquaintances. So a new instrument was needed to establish a person's nationality. The passport system turned out to be such a

68 Cf. Saudi-Arabia: Jews and atheists not allowed; Israel: Jews preferred. Also past policies in the US: Chinese Exclusion Acts, quota system based on origin; UK: restrictions on subjects of the Commonwealth countries; Australia: White Australia Policy. Michael Dummett, for one, contends that all immigration restrictions have been racist in essence. Michael Dummett, *On Immigration and Refugees* (London: Routledge, 2001).

69 Torpey also contends that there is an *intrinsic* connection (next to an *oblique*) between migration control and nation building. Under the intrinsic connection '. . . state's monopolization of the right to authorize and regulate movement has been intrinsic to the very construction of states since the rise of absolutism in early modern Europe'. Torpey (2000), at 6. I believe that Torpey successfully shows that authorities sought to legally and physically control the movement of people. As I have argued above, the evidence does not show that this is constitutive for building the state, let alone building the *nation* state. State authorities, like any authorities, display a tendency to penetrate and embrace all aspects of life (for the notions of 'embrace' and 'penetrate' see ibid., at 10–12). Movement of persons is no exception. But this does not render it more intrinsic to the construction of the state than say environmental legislation or birth control. In other words, Torpey's own evidence does not substantiate the intrinsic connection.

comprehensive system and was already available. The passport system – and thus *obliquely* and *accidentally* immigration restrictions – contributed to the roll out of the 'nation' state.

Still, it is commonly argued, by scholars[70] and politicians[71] alike, that our immigration policies reflect our national identity. In other words, who we let in reflects who we think we are ourselves. So, immigration policies must contribute to the construction and maintenance of communal identity. However, we must avoid being too emphatic about this kind of connection. The preceding analysis showed that the drivers and stated reasons for immigration restrictions have been primarily tactical in the sense of public security and safety. Public security and safety do not give a community its distinctive character. Even when political scientists have identified the invocation of stronger values (e.g. equality, free enterprise, anti-communism) the actual changes in immigration policies were driven by external events that tended to correspond with the circumstances typically associated with tactical reasons (e.g. for the US the two World Wars, the Cold War, foreign economic competition).[72] Second, one seems to confuse causes and effects. Surely, immigration policies may *reflect* the interests and values of the community, but that does not mean that those immigration policies are prior and constitutive to those interests and values. Rather values are (or at least should be – if a reason for exclusion) in place prior to the immigration policies. Third, even if immigration law were to shape the communal identity, it is not doing this any more (probably less) than other branches of the law (e.g. criminal, family and torts law). So why grant it special status? In fact, if we look at the admission criteria in

70 For instance Peter Schuck frames in his view the essence of the immigration debate: 'U.S. immigration policy . . . determine[s] – in a tautological sense – the answers to the kinds of political identity questions that arise in any democratic polity: Who are we?' P. Schuck, 'Immigration at the Turn of the New Century', 33 *Case Western Journal of International Law* 1 (2001).

71 For example in 1982 US Senator Edward Kennedy contended that 'what we do on the issue of immigration says a great deal about *the kind of society that we are* and that we want to become'. His colleague George Huddleston stated that 'immigration, without question, is one of those rare policies which ultimately impacts upon almost every aspect of our society and economy, and to a large degree *determines what kind of country we are*'. Both quoted from US Congress materials in Cheryl Shanks, *Immigration and the Policy of American Sovereignty 1890–1990* (Ann Arbor: Michigan University Press, 2001), at 227 and 229 (in both emphasis added).

72 I am thinking particularly of the excellent study conducted by Cheryl Shanks, ibid. She showed that external events constituted the impetus for changes in immigration policies (as opposed to the changes in the enforcement of immigration policies). At the same time, she analyzed the actual debates and arguments of legislators and found that the arguments invoked shaped the actual outcomes of particular immigration policies. So the particular interests and values of the community do matter. Yet it does not follow from her analysis that those distinctive interests and values are the result of immigration policies. In fact, her point is rather that because arguments, discourses and negotiations shape actual immigration policies, the outcomes are unpredictable. So we cannot explain and predict particular immigration policies purely in terms of structural theories. In other words, she is mainly concerned – as a political scientist – with finding sound theoretical methods to explain immigration policies, while I am concerned with finding sound theories for evaluating actual immigration policies.

the actual and enforceable legal texts few people would think that those criteria adequately cover the aspects typically associated with the identity of a particular community or nation. If there is an American, French or German identity it is certainly not reflected in the admission criteria laid down in the admission laws. It follows that either the meaning of communal identity is rather empty, or immigration criteria have little to do with communal identity. In both cases communal identity makes a poor ground for justifying immigration policies. Finally, the actual immigration laws do not mention 'membership'. The same goes for other legal texts of public law addressing the current members of the community or nation. Yet when publicists argue and theorize about immigration policy, it seems appropriate to think in terms of membership. As soon as it comes to drafting actual immigration laws, however, the metaphor of membership and identity disappears. I believe this is not purely a matter of labels or historical legacy, but rather an indication that admission laws are not properly understood in terms of membership and maintaining a distinctive community.

Having discussed the main moral and ethical/political arguments against admission as well as the refutation or accommodation of those concerns, it seems that *ex ante* and in general, the reasons for exclusion are weaker than the reasons for admission. It also became clear that often both the moral but especially the ethical/political arguments against admission are based on false empirical assumptions about the history, sociology and practical functioning of political and legal communities. In a sense – as noted earlier – the more we question the assumptions behind the moral and political arguments against admission, the more we get into the realm of the empirical, which either contradicts the assumptions or is too particular to operate as a basis for general and *ex ante* claims. Still, it may be the case that some insights from prudence and realism – based for example on a long and shared experience – indicate that it simply happens to be the case that under certain conditions which often obtain, general admission is not reasonable. Let us briefly discuss the most important of potential concerns from prudence and realism.

Prudential and realistic arguments against general admission

A part of the communitarian critique was not discussed earlier because rather than moral or ethical/political it actually comprises prudent and realistic objections to admission. Immigration restrictions are necessary not only to construct and construe the community, but also to protect the goods it produces: liberty and welfare; political and civil commitments; common life.[73] Opening up the borders will provoke an incoming wave of needy migrants with illiberal political habits who will ultimately destroy the very goods that made the particular community so

73 Walzer (1983), at 39.

valuable for its members (and arguably for the newcomers).[74] So as a matter of their long-term self-interest and as a matter of material incapacity, communities must exclude migrants seeking admission. It is probably at the level of special commitments or obligations that this realistic critique coincides with the moral objections in the communitarian critique. The 'forced' admission of the migrants by the community (under a regime of general admission) creates insufficient social capital and solidarity to back up the fulfillment of the special obligation.[75]

To the prudent and realistic arguments from communitarianism (protection of liberty and welfare; political and civil commitments; common life) we can add the (other) arguments that typically support current and past immigration restrictions. According to the standard view general admission of migrants poses a threat to:[76]

- public order and national security;
- public health;
- national economy.

Moreover, a general duty to admit migrants is simply an unrealistic option, because it is too expensive and lacks public support. Like the communitarian critique these objections urge us to consider the contextual and real effects of general admission, notwithstanding its possible moral and political merits. Some have especially valued the concern for the short-term economic effects of migration on resident workers. Though various studies are by and large positive about the economic effects of migration on residents and migrants alike,[77] in the real world, the worse off laborers may need protection. First, they are the most likely to suffer from competition from cheaper and better-skilled newcomers. Second, in the real world capital tends to move faster than people (even in the absence of legal restrictions) and the worse-off move the slowest (if they move at all). This

74 Some have even argued for closure on the basis of the argument that too much migration will be harmful for the prospective migrant self because it may take away the distinct character of the particular community; this was the very reason for the migrant to migrate in the first place. Raffaele Marchetti, 'Right to Universal Mobility: A Consequentialist Cosmopolitan Reading', 4 *Éthique et économique/Ethics and Economics* 1 (2006).

75 The strongest version of this social capital argument is probably advanced by liberal nationalists like David Miller. See David Miller, *On Nationality* (1999), at 18, cited in Kukathas (2003), at 576.

76 See for the list of typical items: *Ibid.*, at 573; Seglow (2005), at 319 with reference to Meilaender (2001) and N. Harris, *Thinking the Unthinkable: The Immigration Myth Exposed*, (2002); Hudson (1986), at 58.

77 Howard F. Chang, 'Liberalized Immigration as Free Trade: Economic Welfare and the Optimal Immigration Policy', 145 *University of Pennsylvania Law Review* 1147 (1997); Pécoud and de Guchteneire (2005), at 9–12 with references to, inter alia, George Borjas, *Heaven's Door. Immigration Policy and the American Economy* (1999); Cole (2000), at 168–9 with reference to, inter alia, D. Held *et al., Global Transformation: Politics, Economics and Culture* (1999) and A. Inchino, 'The Economic Impact of Immigration on the Host Country' in G. Luciani (ed.), *Migration Policies in Europe and the United States* (1999); Kukathas (2003) at 574 with references to work of Kenneth Galbraith and Julian L. Simon; Bader (2005), at 337.

means that they are the least likely to benefit from the new market equilibrium that is supposed to be established through the movement of 'fresh labor'.[78]

A contextual and pluralistic approach can also accommodate these prudential and realistic objections to general admission. I will concentrate on the main objections:

- threat to safety and security;
- threat to political institutions and lack of public support;
- threat to the welfare system and harm for the worse off;
- excessive levels of expenditure.

I believe a productive way to accommodate and refute the objections is to address the underlying problematic assumptions. The objections share the following assumptions:

- general admission entails a huge wave of migrants;[79]
- the newcomers are dangerous, illiberal, economically net beneficiaries rather than net contributors;
- states will have no control over who enters;
- states will have no control over what happens in the country after they enter.

These assumptions have a clear realistic aura around them. But it is precisely a realist look at the assumptions that considerably attenuates their persuasive force.

The first assumption predicts that general admission entails huge waves of new migrants. However, the most plausible defenders of this assumption cannot do better than stating that it is just a possibility, that if realized, poses a serious threat and must therefore be taken very seriously. However, if there is any empirical evidence in this respect it rather points in the opposite direction.[80] The second assumption, that newcomers have more criminal or subversive tendencies than the residents, lacks any serious evidence. The difference in political culture may be important, but we must be cautious not to impose high liberal standards that only correspond with our idealization of the liberal polity and its citizens, but do not obtain in reality.[81] Also, there seems to be sufficient empirical evidence available for the fact that the particular political culture of most migrants has not prevented most of them from adopting a new political culture. As to the economic

78 Bader (2005), at 337–8.

79 It is important to note that ultimately all objections (including moral and ethico-political ones) rely on the empirical truth of the size and quality of the expected immigration. See also Bader (2005), at 341.

80 See Cole's refutation of the first assumption under *Section 2: The Catastrophe Prediction* in Cole (2000), at 167–71 by criticizing James Woodward's views in Woodward (1992). Bader (2005), at 348.

81 Bader (2005), at 349; Cole (2000), at 173.

burden posed by waves of migrants, the same lack of empirical evidence applies. The third assumption – states will lose control over entrance – is not self-evident either. This assumption is informed by the commonly held view of both proponents and opponents of general admission, that states have already been losing control over immigration as evidenced by the huge numbers of illegal immigrants. The claim that current immigration controls are ineffective presupposes a criterion or ratio for effectiveness. The ratio must set the desired effects against the actual effects obtained. It also presupposes that there is a baseline or benchmark against which the actual obtained ratio can be measured. Most, if not all, commentators invoking the ineffectiveness argument fail to mention their criterion and baseline for measuring the ineffectiveness of immigration controls. A possible ratio may be the total number of new illegal entrants (actual effect) divided by the total number of admission refusals (desired effect). Though it lies far beyond my competency to come up with an adequate analysis of the effectiveness of immigration policies, a very rough evaluation on the basis of this sketchy ratio is likely to suggest that a lot of people are effectively prevented from migrating due to immigration policies. Depending on the baseline there may be a strong indication that states still have effective control over immigration. If so, the question then arises as to whether general admission renders control ineffective. This depends on the particular policy that will be adopted. The fact of generally admitting migrants does not mean that states must give up control over this process. In addition, if indeed general admission would entail huge waves of migrants turning the 'free movement project' into a big failure, there are no indications that states will be unable to reintroduce effective immigration restrictions. Historical analysis of immigration policies has shown the states' capacity to switch back and forth from relaxed to restrictive immigration policies. A similar refutation applies to the fourth assumption – states have no control over what happens after entrance. The fact that migration – like all complex phenomena – will have some adverse effects does not mean that the state cannot do anything about it. There are no indications that states become totally ineffective when dealing with issues affecting immigrants. The question is rather whether states are ready to make the extra effort. The fourth assumption supports the realistic objection that general admission is not possible because it is too expensive. Rather than being a question of impossibility and ineffectiveness, it becomes an evaluative matter of whether it is reasonable for a state to bear those costs.[82] The contextual and pluralistic approach would respond in two ways. First, the contextual approach will urge policy makers to examine the costs on an on-going and concrete basis. This means that policymakers do not ignore the possible important costs associated with general admission, but at the same time, can prevent them from remaining inert on the basis of abstract, general and hypothetical cost assumptions. Second, the pluralistic approach will urge policymakers to give appropriate weight to what social and

82 Goodin (1992), at 253; Cole (2000), at 175.

political justice requires from us. Justice is not and need not always be a win-win situation; it may justify substantial costs.[83]

Refuting these four assumptions should largely debunk the main prudential and realistic reasons against general admission. In addition, we may consider two more counter-arguments. A serious realistic objection against general admission is, of course, lack of public support. However, public opinion can be influenced by the adequacy of the mitigation policies and the way they are communicated.[84] In other words, those responsible for the design, execution and communication of policies can do something. All those 'mitigations' do have a price and sometimes the costs may not be offset fully against the benefits associated with migration. Again, according to the pluralistic argument, general admission is also a matter of distributive justice and the requirements of justice have a price. This also hints at another argument for attenuating the prudential and realistic reasons against general admission that is rarely put forward.[85] The prudential and realistic arguments all start from the idea that migration has some kind of negative effect. These negative effects allegedly do not or cannot outweigh the positive effects associated with general admission. The mere notion of 'effects' presupposes a set of highly political questions:[86] What are relevant effects? Who are the relevant persons affected by the effects?[87] What is the relevant period of time needed to measure the effects? What are the relevant measurement criteria? What are the proper measurement tools/sources? Who is to measure them? Most importantly, who is to decide (and participate in decisions) on the answers to these questions? So even if we concede to all of the objections, I cannot see how prudence and realism can answer those questions. It is difficult to find arguments that make it legitimate to exclude the alien from participating and answering those questions. In other words, there may be room for the view that even the most extreme

83 Bader (1997).

84 See Dora Kostakopoulou and Robert Thomas, 'Unweaving the Threads: Territoriality, Asylum Policy and National Ownership of Land', 6 *European Journal of Migration and Law* 5 (2004), at 25. In this respect it is very surprising how (to my knowledge) relatively calmly the principle of family reunification has been received in Western Europe. Yet, it has the potential to double, triple or quadruple the number of foreign-born people in a country within less than a decade.

85 See Kukathas (2003), at 574–5 for some comments on the technical problems associated with cost measurement.

86 So while we must welcome Seglow's suggestions to establish a kind of global migration quota system based on objective criteria such as GDP and population density, it would be naïve to rely too heavily on the objective nature of these criteria. To mitigate these concerns we must at the same time come up with mechanisms that allow affected actors to challenge the criteria. Seglow (2005).

87 As Ugur rightly points out: the effects of migration policy differ among national residents. Some find immigration control necessary, whereas others resent it (and both may do so for economic purposes). Mehmet Ugur, 'A Reinterpretation of the "Insider"–"Outsider" Divide in the European Union', xxix *International Migration Review* 964 (1995), at 993.

versions of prudent and realistic arguments must be sensitive to the perspective of the immigrant.[88]

Conclusion

We have considered *ex ante* the general reasons against general admission of immigrants. The objections against general admission raised important issues: general admission does not address directly our moral concerns of social justice; general admission may compromise the centrality of the community and its self-determination; general admission will produce a wide set of adverse effects in terms of safety, the welfare system, the economy and political institutions. However, a closer examination of the objections showed that they could be either refuted or accommodated. Though the objections against general admission have the aura of being contextual ('our liberal polity') and realistic ('it is simply not feasible') they often turned out to be relying on abstract and idealized assumptions that were flawed either conceptually or empirically. Still, some of the objections pointed to real matters of concern. But those concerns did not produce reasons for rejecting general admission; rather they urge the responsible agents to design measures to mitigate the adverse effects associated with general admission. In short, *ex ante* and *in general* the reasons against admission do not hold. By the same token, it was shown that – though not a fundamental right, free movement and its realization are a central value under liberalism. As the arguments against realizing this value do not hold *ex ante* and in *general*, it seems that we have succeeded in putting the first burden of justification on the authorities, who intend to exclude normal migrants seeking admission.

Still, there is something really tricky here. On the one hand I adopt the pluralistic and contextual approach, which reminds us that 'there is no clear, context-independent formula for weighing and balancing [the different practical reasons]'.[89] On the other hand, that is precisely what I have been doing: weighing and balancing. In the absence of a clear formula, how can one find comfort in my conclusions? Perhaps there is an additional argument that has tipped the balance in favor of putting the first burden of justification on the authorities. It has to do with the level and nature of the (dis)agreement among theorists as to the reasons for relaxing or restricting immigration. Bauboeck reports that when it comes to restricting immigration there is 'considerable agreement among liberal theorists

88 A way out for these prudential and realistic objections is to redirect these questions to the level of moral and political reasons. At these levels then, one may hold that the questions are simply a matter for the community or nation to decide, i.e. a position that may fit both the modern consent theories and communitarianism. But this means that the validity of the prudential and realistic arguments ultimately depends on the soundness of the consent theories or communitarianism, which is highly questionable.

89 See reference to Bader (2007), n. 40.

concerning unacceptable reasons but much disagreement about acceptable ones'.[90] From an argumentative perspective, this observation alone constitutes a reason for putting the first burden of justification on the authorities. Apparently we are all on the same page as to when exclusion is not acceptable. The only question remaining is under what conditions the exclusion becomes acceptable. It seems that the authorities are the parties most interested in coming up with arguments and evidence in this respect.[91] Perhaps we overstated the level of disagreement about the acceptable reasons for exclusion. In fact, Bauboeck mentions only one category of contested reasons for exclusion, i.e. cultural criteria. For the rest, there seems to be a consensus about a set of categories of acceptable reasons for exclusion: public order, democratic autonomy or self-governance, domestic arrangements of social justice. Also, theorists agree about the criteria giving preference to particular immigrants over others: domestic economic demand, family ties and humanitarian needs. The key here is of course the level of abstraction or generality of the reasons. If we remain at the level of categories it is difficult for any liberal theorist to deny the potential plausibility of these reasons for exclusion. Hence the agreement. By contrast, if we probe further and ask *how* and to *what extent* these categories constitute reasons for restricting immigration, things get more complicated.[92] It boils down to the very difficult question as to how exactly the admission of immigrants affects the valued aspects of a (liberal) political community, e.g. public order, democratic self-governance, arrangements of social justice. Political theorists may play a vital role in answering this question. If we want to understand how the admission of migrants affects public order, democratic self-governance, the arrangements of social justice, we first need to know what these notions are supposed to mean. This requires an inquiry into political and legal history, philosophy and practice, which is largely the domain of political theorists. Especially on the matter of democratic self-governance and social justice, political theorists have been extremely prolific.[93] And although many participants in the debate agree on the basic ideas and features, it is clear that there is no comprehensive agreement on these matters. For example, if authorities restrict migration for reasons of public order, one needs to know what *version* of

90 Bauboeck (forthcoming 2011). They agree about what are in any event inacceptable reasons for exclusion (e.g. restrictions based on race, gender, religion, or sexual orientation).

91 The reverse supposes that the immigrant must produce a kind of *a contrario* argument. He should first list the potential reasons for exclusion and then show that they do not obtain. This is of course an unproductive and inefficient way of structuring the first burden of justification, as the immigrant has a vested interest to come up with clearly unsound reasons for his exclusion, or with reasons that do not obtain in the case at hand.

92 For example, the contextual approach is not necessarily opposed to introducing immigration ceilings, but immediately asks for the proper thresholds. Bader (2005), at 352.

93 Public order is a less prominent matter. I expect the soaring attention in the literature for the state of exception and emergency will also direct scholars to a most needed investigation into the concept of public order.

public order the authorities have in mind.[94] Again it seems that the authorities are most interested in showing that their version is adequate and sound. Finally, as we have seen, most of the arguments against admission boil down to assumptions about empirical reality. This was obviously the case not only for the prudent and realistic arguments, but also the ethical/political. Most of these empirical data primarily relate to the situation in the receiving country: economy, social cohesion, the welfare system, housing potential, security, the current 'stock' of immigration, etc. It seems clear that the authorities have more knowledge of these matters and access to evidence than individual or even groups of migrants. So as a matter of mitigating the effects of a structural information asymmetry, the authorities should carry the first burden of justification. In short, all things considered that can be considered beforehand and in general, political theory tells us that authorities must adopt a new default position when it comes to normal migrants seeking admission. They must design and organize the different 'instances' of immigration policy[95] in such a way that the immigration authorities carry the first burden of justification *vis-à-vis* the migrant seeking admission.

94 Cf. M.-J. Redor (ed.), *L'ordre public: Ordre public ou ordres publics? Ordre public et droits fondamentaux*, Actes du colloque de Caen des jeudi 11 et 12 mai 2000, (Brussels: Bruylant, 2001).

95 I.e. law making, executive directives and measures, individual decisions and judicial review, see Chapter 1.

Chapter 7

Institutional proposal

Testing the proportionality of exclusion

This book started by labeling current immigration policy as a legal problem. The authorities exclude normal migrants without giving them proper justification. Next we tried to show that this practice is untenable from a legal perspective. Instead, the authorities have a duty to justify, and this is not only a moral duty but also a legal one. Moreover, arguments from ethics of migration showed that the authorities should carry the first burden of justification. If our arguments in the previous chapters are sound it seems that we have accomplished our mission stated in the beginning of this book: challenging the current situation (illegality of admission laws) and calling for a change (fixing a new default position). Yet, these arguments from positive law, legal theory and political philosophy all have practical pretensions in the sense that they are reasons for action. But 'ought' implies 'can'. If at the outset the suggestions for change have no chance of success, they may cease to constitute solid reasons for action. In other words, one way or another the feasibility of the call for change must be made plausible. One aspect of feasibility is institutional fit. So we should be looking for a realistic institutional arrangement that organizes the justification of exclusion and puts the first burden of justification on the authorities. To this end we will consider a Draft directive proposed by experts of European immigration law. The strength of the proposal is that it organizes a new default position while remaining faithful to the existing form and content of European legal tradition and practice. The only weakness of the proposal is its legal foundation. The drafters located the legal basis in the fundamental liberty of everyone to move, i.e. the right to free movement. The problem, of course, is that under positive law this right does not exist. This means that the directive – if adopted – would introduce a *new* basic right for everyone. From the perspective of EU institutional law, such a new right would probably require an amendment to the EU Treaties, which from an electoral–political perspective is unfeasible. So this chapter mainly concentrates on finding an adequate legal basis for the directive without the need to amend the Treaties. The thrust of the argument is that (contrary to free movement) the principle of proportionality is already a core element of the rule of law and legal practice. The Draft directive is 'just' rendering explicit that the test of proportionality is to be applied to all cases where authorities directly affect the legitimate interests of individuals. Again the challenge is to make legal change, not legal revolution.

The chapter begins by briefly stating the central tenets of the Draft that are relevant for the new default position. Next, we will examine the stated legal basis for the Draft and its inadequacy from the perspective of EU institutional law. The remainder of the chapter explores whether the proportionality principle can constitute a more apt legal basis. This exploration involves a brief inquiry into the nature and history of the proportionality principle. The chapter closes with some suggestions on how to accommodate potential interpretational issues, which may affect the effectiveness of the Draft.[1]

Central tenets of the Draft

In 2003 the Meijers Committee presented a proposal to improve the legal protection of third-country nationals seeking admission.[2] The committee is not an official body or agency of the EU, but an independent academic think tank of experts in criminal and migration law. Still, it laid down the proposal in a format that makes it extremely concrete and tangible for policymakers in the EU, namely a (draft) directive.[3] The Draft is structured like a real EU directive including a preamble and explanatory report. This approach makes it look and feel very realistic. It also reflects how the proposal may fit the existing body and practice of law in the EU, which in turn contributes to removing the utopian character typically associated with any important call for change.

The Draft provides for two types of legal protection: procedural and substantive. The procedural protection operates at two levels. First competent authorities must justify their decisions of exclusion.[4] It follows that the authorities must put their decisions in writing and state the reasons, facts and legal provisions that substantiate their decision.[5] Second, the alien can file an appeal against the decision with an independent court.[6] The court may annul a decision if it is found to be arbitrary, disproportionate or unlawful.[7] As a matter of general procedural law the courts must also motivate their decisions. The legal protection is also substantive. Not any kind of justification by the competent authorities will do. There are substantive conditions that must be satisfied. In fact, the Draft only allows two

1 The following discussion will be rather juridical. As a result we will often use the term 'alien' rather than normal migrant.

2 Reprinted in Meijers Committee (P. Boeles *et al.*) 'Draft directive on Minimum Guarantees for Individual Freedom, Security and Justice in Relation to Decisions Regarding Movement of Persons', *European Journal of Migration and Law*, 7 (2005), at 301–6. (hereafter: Draft).

3 Article 288 TFEU (ex Art. 249 TEC).

4 Article 3(1) Draft.

5 Ibid.

6 Article 6(1) Draft.

7 Article 6(5) Draft.

types of justifications for refusal of admission: the alien poses a risk to public policy or national security;[8] or there are overriding reasons of general interest to refuse admission, provided that the refusal is proportionate.[9] An example of the first type of justification may be the alien who has a criminal record or has merely been signaled by the law enforcement agencies (cf. Schengen Information System). Such a person allegedly poses a threat to the security of a receiving state. An example of the second type of justification may be an alien seeking employment in an industry where there is already a high rate of unemployment among residents. The admission of this alien allegedly may go against general social–economic interests because the alien does not satisfy the need for labor in areas where there are shortages, while increasing unemployment in an area where there is a surplus.

The fact that the authorities have to consider public policy, national security or the general interest when excluding aliens is nothing new. The novelty of the Draft is that these considerations must now be contextualized and balanced against the interests pertaining to the alien. So the exclusion for reasons of public policy and security is not justified on the basis of a mere *potential* of risk related to the alien's *profile*. The Draft mobilizes the criteria of the so-called 'Family Directive'.[10] and applies it to all aliens. This means that the actual *conduct* of the aliens must pose a specific and actual risk: a genuine test of 'clear and present danger'.[11] It is obvious that this regime offers the alien greater opportunities to challenge refusals based on public policy and national security.

Where the clear and present danger test focuses primarily on establishing the actuality and level of the risk, in the case of general interest the emphasis lies on a balancing of reasons and interests. Pursuant to Article 3(4) of the Draft, there must be overriding reasons of general interest to refuse admission and the refusal must be proportionate. This twofold requirement corresponds with the three elements of the proportionality test under European law: suitability, necessity and proportionality *sensu stricto*.[12] Suitability and necessity are captured by

8 Article 3(3) Draft.

9 Article 3(4) Draft.

10 Directive 2004/38/EC of the European Parliament and of the Council of 29 April 2004 on the right of citizens of the Union and their family members to move and reside freely within the territory of the Member States, repealing Council Directive 64/221/EEC of 25 February 1964.

11 See for a recent application of the Directive 64/221/EEC in connection with the Schengen Information System, see *Commission of the European Communities v Kingdom of Spain*, ECJ, Case-C-503/03, 31 January 2006. *Available at* http://curia.europa.eu.

12 Walter Van Gerven, 'The Effect of Proportionality on the Actions of Member States of the European Community: National Viewpoints from Continental Europe', in Evelyn Ellis (ed.), *The Principle of Proportionality in the Laws of Europe*, (Oxford: Hart Publishing, 1999), at 37–9. See Lothar Hirschberg, *Der Grundsatz der Verhältnismäßigkeit*, (Göttingen: Verlag Otto Schwartz & Co, 1981) for a comprehensive study of the three elements of the proportionality principle as developed under German law.

overriding reasons of general interest.[13] Suitability means that the refusal must serve a legitimate objective ('general interest'). The necessity criterion checks whether the refusal is the only way to attain this objective. If so there are 'overriding' reasons to refuse the admission. If there are less burdensome ways to obtain the objective, the refusal is not necessary (at best the refusal will be 'useful'). In this case there are reasons of general interest to refuse the alien, but the reasons are not 'overriding'. The requirement of proportionality *sensu stricto* acknowledges the suitability and necessity of the refusal, but checks whether the disadvantages caused by the refusal are not disproportionate to the aims pursued. In fact, this test contextualizes the costs that the alien must bear to promote the general interest. If the costs are too high compared to the benefits then the refusal is not proportionate *sensu stricto*.[14]

Another novelty of the Draft is its broad scope. To date EU immigration law has been a patchwork of specific arrangements for special categories of third–country nationals. The problem for the normal migrant is that he does not fall under any of these special regimes (see Chapter 1). By contrast, the Draft organizes a truly basic scheme that applies to all migrants seeking admission. According to the general formulation of Article 1, the provisions of the Draft, i.e. the legal protection scheme, applies to *all* decisions regarding the admission of aliens. In other words, both privileged and unprivileged third-country nationals are covered by the protection of the proportionality principle. The Draft's scope is not only broad in terms of the persons to which it applies, but also regarding the types of refusals it covers. Under European and domestic law, legal regimes differ depending on the type of application for admission: applications for short-term entry, long-term entry, residence permits, renewal of permits, admission applications at the border, applications abroad (e.g. consulates), etc. The Draft does not distinguish between the different types as far as the minimal legal protection is concerned: the refusal by authorities of any form of demand for admission is covered by the Draft. Also, the legal format of the refusal decision is equally irrelevant. Pursuant to Article 1(2), the Draft extends its application not only to admission refusals incorporated in a *legal* and *documented* decision, but also to 'any act or measure taken by or attributable to an authority'. The drafters are very clear about the rationale of this paragraph:

> In order to prevent that acts and measures that *de facto* have the same effects would be excluded from the applicability of this Directive,

13 There may be some overlapping: the necessity requirement may also be covered by 'proportionality'.

14 The difference between proportionality *sensu stricto* on the one hand and 'overriding reasons' or necessity on the other, can be illustrated by the requirement under domestic administrative law of some Member States (e.g. the Netherlands) to compensate for disproportionate measures. If the measure is not necessary, then there is simply no ground for taking it. However if the measure is necessary but disproportionate *sensu stricto*, it may be carried out provided that the affected person is compensated for the excess in disadvantages.

paragraph 2 explicitly includes *de facto acts and measures* in the concept of 'decision'.[15]

It is clear that the Draft would constitute a major improvement of the legal position of the alien seeking admission. The clear and present danger test – if taken seriously – really puts the burden of proof on the authorities. In contrast, to date, the burden of proof in public policy and security cases lies *de facto* with the migrant. Today, the unfavorable profiling of the alien is the starting point and the alien must then prove that there are no reasons to believe (contrary to his profile) that in the future he will not pose a risk. It is clear that producing such negative proof is an uphill battle, if not one already lost. The introduction of the clear and present danger test may indeed change the default position. Perhaps even more important is the proportionality test. First, it will mean that authorities must produce contextualized and concrete evidence to the effect that a measure is really necessary. As a consequence, authorities have a duty to seriously consider alternatives in lieu of an outright refusal. For example, today a misfit in labor skills constitutes sufficient grounds for excluding an alien, while there are less burdensome measures available (e.g. intensive short-term training programmes).[16] More generally, the necessity criterion allows challenging the basic assumption underlying the exclusion of an alien workforce: the exclusion of aliens is *necessary* to combat domestic unemployment. It will be up to the authorities to prove this contention rather than simply assume it. Second, even if the refusal is necessary, the authorities must also prove that the actual benefits of the refusal outweigh the concrete disadvantages caused to the alien, i.e. proportionality *sensu stricto*. If applied seriously, the proportionality test *sensu stricto* should radically enhance the chances of success for aliens seeking employment. However, I will argue at the end of this chapter that we better concentrate on the necessity test and drop the emphasis on the proportionality *sensu stricto* because the latter is likely to provoke insurmountable complications and controversies.

The substantive legal protection provided by the Draft changes the current default position. While today the authorities may simply refer to the particular pieces of legislation and regulations to substantiate the refusals, under the Draft simple legality is not enough. The actual context must justify a decision to refuse admission. Of course, it is up to the courts to decide what counts as evidence and how to weigh the evidence.[17] It may well be that in practice, the courts will easily conclude that there are overriding reasons and that the refusal is proportionate.

15 Meijers Committee, 'Explanatory Report', *European Journal of Migration and Law* (2005), at 310 (emphasis added).

16 See the peripheral arrangements, such as educational programs and job placement schemes, proposed by Theo Veenkamp *et al.*, *People Flow. Managing Migration in a New European Commonwealth* (London: Demos, 2003).

17 J.H. Jans, 'Evenredigheid Revisited', *Sociaal-Economische Wetgeving. Tijdschrift voor Europees en Economisch Recht* (2000), 279–80, with reference to L. Krämer.

This means that *de facto* the burden of proof will still lie with the alien seeking admission. In any event, the drafters have done their best to reverse the default position – as they have opted for the proportionality test that puts the heaviest burden of proof on the authorities. Pursuant to Article 3(4) the refusal must be 'proportionate', instead of 'not disproportionate'. The judicial review is more intensive when the authorities have to prove the existence of proportionality than where they are required to show the absence of disproportionality.[18]

Inadequacy of the Draft's legal basis

The central tenets of the Draft tie in perfectly with the arguments from legal and political theory in the previous chapters of this book. In a way, these arguments may operate as the theoretical support for the Draft: hence, my concerns have little to do with its content and format. In contrast, there seems to be a serious obstacle in terms of the legal basis proposed by the drafters. In their effort to make their proposal as plausible as possible, the drafters have suggested that the Draft is in line with current European law. More precisely the drafters sought support in the notions of *procedural rights* and the *liberty to move*. However, under current European law, these two legal institutes do not apply to normal migrants seeking admission. So rather than being supported by these institutes, the Draft introduces afresh the two legal arrangements in the field of migration. This raises a question of European institutional law: can a simple directive introduce a liberty to move for all? In what follows I will argue that from the perspective of institutional law the Draft lacks legal basis if it seeks to rely on procedural rights and liberty to move. The challenge is to find a legal basis that allows current European law to change, but within the framework of European institutional law. Later on I will suggest that an extension of the proportionality principle may produce such legal basis. If sound, my critical observations hardly affect the wording of the Draft. Only the preamble and the explanatory report (which is not a part of the Draft) must be adapted to the effect of not making reference to the liberty to move and procedural rights as such. The texts should mention how extending the scope of the proportionality principle to legitimate interests fits the *ratio legis* of the European proportionality principle and the legal practices of Member States. In addition, the texts may indicate that the notion of Justice under the Area of Freedom, Security and Justice refers, inter alia, to the concept of law. As a matter of its structure, the law may require the extension of the proportionality principle to legitimate interests.

If the upshot of my observations (if sound) is so minor in terms of actual wording, why bother getting into this legal nitty-gritty? First, the fact that discussing the legal basis of a directive 'degenerates' into subtle (or if you want

18 J.H. Jans (2000), at 280. See for the same point in more detail, Hirschberg (1981), at 92–7 and especially at 96.

futile) legalistic reasoning cannot be held against these critical observations. This is simply an aspect of our general practice of law setting and applying the law: this is what we do. Second, institutional law happens to have an incredible capacity to dominate the legal discourse on migration to the effect of distracting lawyers from the legal (de)merits of our admission laws. In other words, it is important to try to get the institutional picture straight so that full attention can be given to the merits of the Draft.[19]

Procedural rights instead of a material right to admission

Under European law the admission of aliens is a matter of particular subjective *rights* (or liberties) explicitly guaranteed by European Treaties, the Convention or the laws of the Member States. So, to challenge a refusal of admission an alien must invoke the infringement of a particular subjective right. This is clearly reflected in the dominant channel of legal immigration in Europe, i.e. family reunification. To bring his case to court, an alien seeking admission must invoke the infringement of a subjective right. This right or liberty must be either applicable to him, or applicable to a person closely related to him. In effect, early EC law allowed the admission of third-country nationals who were family members of a Member State national, not on the basis of a right applicable to the alien, but in virtue of the right of his family members. Restricting the free movement of the alien may *de facto* infringe the right to free movement of his family member.[20] The European Convention then offered the alien another possibility: namely to invoke the infringement of a right applicable to everyone, i.e. the right to family life.[21] Today this right applicable to everyone is also recognized under EU law.[22]

19 See the example of such institutional controversies in Chapter 1, n. 5.

20 *Commission of the European Communities v Kingdom of Spain*, ECJ, Case-C-503/03, 31 January 2006, par. 41, emphasis added, *available at* http://curia.europa.eu

> 'Recognising the importance of ensuring the protection of the family life of nationals *in order to* eliminate obstacles to the exercise of the fundamental freedoms guaranteed by the EC Treaty . . . the Community legislature has considerably expanded . . . the application of Community law on entry . . . to nationals of third countries who are the spouses of Member State nationals.'

21 See for a detailed analysis of what actually counts as family life according to the Court's case law, Pierre-François Docquir, 'Droit à la vie privée et familiale des ressortissants étrangers: vers la mise au point d'une protection floue du droit de séjour', *Revue Trimestrielle des Droits de l'Homme*, (2004), at 921–49.

22 *Commission of the European Communities v Kingdom of Spain*, ECJ, Case-C-503/03, 31 January 2006, par. 47, emphasis added, *available at* http://curia.europa.eu.

> 'In the case of a national of a third country who is the spouse of a Member State national a strict interpretation of the concept of public policy [as provided for in Art. 6 Council Directive 64/221 of 25 February 1964. BS] also serves to protect the latter's right to respect for his or her family life under Article 8 of the European Convention for the Protection of Human Rights and Fundamental Freedoms . . . [reference to *Carpenter* and *Akrich*]'.

However, apart from the right to family life, under European law there are no rights which would allow the alien to challenge the refusal of admission. Under European law there is no such thing as a right to admission: states are free to determine who may enter their territory (subject to international obligations).[23] The drafters seemed to have acknowledged this current state of European law. Hence, rather than concentrating on the distinction between rights applicable to everyone (including aliens) and rights applicable to citizens only, they relied on another typical legal distinction, i.e. the distinction between material rights and procedural rights.

A material right establishes a particular normative position that pertains to a particular condition of a person (e.g. material, physical, emotional). Procedural rights are instruments for challenging actions by others (in this case the state) that may compromise one's normative and material condition. The procedural rights allow the recognition of this particular condition and organize the way in which this condition should be maintained or repaired. Some material rights apply to everyone and others are reserved for citizens only. In our case the right to family life is a material right applicable to everyone, while the liberty to move is restricted to citizens only. In contrast, in principle, most procedural rights are applicable to all persons, the idea being that procedural rights do not establish a particular normative position. So no harm is done by giving procedural rights to everyone. In fact, the whole point of procedural rights is to find out what the normative position of a person is and what kind of protection it deserves. That is why typically the state's obligation to justify, proportionality of national measures and judicial review are not reserved to citizens only.

This is precisely how the drafters have tried to extend legal protection beyond the limited scope of the material right to free movement under European law. The preamble of the Draft refers to the 'right to good administration' laid down in Article 41 of the Charter of Fundamental Rights of the European Union. This right applies to every person and includes 'the obligation of the administration to give reasons for its decisions'. In other words, the competent authorities also have an obligation (under EU law) to give reasons for excluding an alien. Failure to give a reason will trigger the alien's right to go to court pursuant to (inter alia) Article 47 of the Charter: '*Everyone* whose rights and freedoms guaranteed by the law of the Union are violated *has the right to an effective remedy* before a tribunal . . .' (emphasis added). So by the simple fact that the right to judicial review is applicable to 'everyone' and that 'every person' has the right to good administration, the alien may challenge an exclusion decision that is inadequately justified. In addition, the drafters recall with reference to the ECJ's *Haim* judgment that the proportionality principle also applies in the case of free movement.[24] More

23 See Chapter 1.

24 Meijers Committee, 'Explanatory Report', *European Journal of Migration and Law* (2005), at 319.

generally the drafters have concluded after an insightful analysis of the current state of European case law:

> The overall picture arising from this case law is that individuals are, according to the rule of law, entitled to effective safeguards against arbitrariness provided by law. . . . The drafters of the text of the provisions have let themselves be guided by the wording of relevant legal texts and judicial rulings.[25]

Procedural rights only triggered when material rights are at stake

Though procedural rights are in a sense applicable to everyone, there is an important qualification. Under European law the procedural rights are only triggered to the extent that a material right is at stake. Now, normally this qualification does not pose any problems because material rights are often at stake. Yet when it comes to the admission of aliens, the qualification turns out to be decisive, since in most cases an alien cannot invoke the infringement of a material right. And if the alien cannot connect his claim to a material right his claim simply fails. The regime of due process is probably the clearest case of the *rights*-based logic of procedural protection under European law. It is at least the most explicit case of the failure to provide legal protection to an alien seeking admission because he cannot invoke the infringement of a material right:

> The Court [ECHR] concludes that decisions regarding the entry, stay and deportation of aliens do not concern the determination of an applicant's civil rights or obligations or of a criminal charge against him, within the meaning of Article 6 § 1 of the Convention.[26]

The drafters have indicated correctly that this gap is covered by the coming into force of the Charter, especially Article 47.[27] But even under Article 47, to benefit from procedural rights specific rights and freedoms must be at stake: 'Everyone whose *rights and freedoms guaranteed by the law of the Union* are violated has the right to an effective remedy before a tribunal . . .' (emphasis added). This is precisely the problem when it comes to the normal migrant seeking admission: he cannot invoke a particular right or freedom guaranteed by the law of the Union.

The same logic applies to the proportionality principle. Under current EU law the proportionality principle is only triggered to the extent that material rights are

25 Meijers Committee 'Explanatory Report'.

26 *Maaouia v France*, 5 Oct. 2000, ECtHR. para. 40. *Available at* http://www.echr.coe.int/Eng/Judgments.htm.

27 Meijers Committee, 'Explanatory Report', *European Journal of Migration and Law* (2005), at 311.

at stake. The ECJ[28] has not explicitly stated that aliens seeking admission are excluded from the protection of the proportionality principle, but the Court has always referred to the application of the proportionality principle in connection with the infringement of (fundamental) rights guaranteed by the Treaties, the Convention and the constitutional traditions common to the Member States.[29] As already mentioned, the Charter remains fully in line with ECJ's (and ECHR's) case law on the proportionality principle: it only applies to 'the rights and freedoms recognized by the Charter'.[30]

Now, it may be argued that the Court not only refers to rights, but also considers interests, i.e. legitimate interests. But these are not so much the legitimate interests of individuals as we will discuss below. Rather they correspond with the legitimate interests pursued by the European institutions and the Member States: economic stability, national security etc.[31] Legitimate interests are best

28 In this paragraph I only refer to ECJ rulings. Yet, the ECtHR and the Commission for Human Rights display the same exclusive focus on (fundamental) rights when applying the proportionality principle. See for instance, Jürgen Schwarze, *European Administrative Law* (London/Luxemburg: Office for Official Publications of the European Communities/Sweet and Maxwell, 2006), at 704–7. See in general Sébastien Van Drooghenbroeck, *La proportionnalité dans le droit de la Convention européenne des Droits de l'homme: prendre l'idée simple au sérieux* (Brussels: Bruylant, 2001).

29 Cf. *Stauder* case (1969): '. . . prejudicing the fundamental human rights enshrined in the general principles of community law and protected by the Court.' Case 29/69, *Erich Stauder v Stadt Ulm, Sozial Amt*, 12 November 1969, [1969], ECR 419, para. 7, text from Eur-Lex. At stake were the right to human dignity and equality before the law. *Internationale Handelsgesellschaft* case (1970): '. . . respect for fundamental rights . . . infringed rights of a fundamental nature, respect for which must be ensured in the community legal system.' Case 11/70, *Internationale Handelsgesellschaft mbH v Einfuhr- und Vorratsstelle für Getreide und Futtermittel*, ECJ 17 December 1970, para. 4., text from Eur-Lex. At stake were the freedoms of action and disposition and the right to property. *Nold* case (1974): '. . . it cannot therefore uphold measures which are incompatible with fundamental rights recognized and protected by the constitutions of those states.' The right at stake was the right to property. Case 4/73, J. *Nold, Kohlen- und Baustoffgroßhandlung v Commission of the European Communities*, 14 May 1974, [1974] ECR 491, para. 13–14, text from Eur-Lex. At stake were the right to non-discrimination and property. *Haim* case (2000): 'According to the Court's case-law, national measures which restrict the exercise of fundamental freedoms guaranteed by the Treaty can be justified only if they fulfill four conditions: they must be applied in a non-discriminatory manner; they must be justified by overriding reasons based on the general interest; they must be suitable for securing the attainment of the objective which they pursue; and they must not go beyond what is necessary in order to attain that objective.' Case C-424/97, *Salomone Haim v Kassenzahnärztliche Vereinigung Nordrhein*, ECJ, 4 July 2000, para. 57. *Available at* http://curia.europa.eu.

30 Article 52(1) Charter.

31 See also the observation by Emiliou when discussing particular ECJ case law on proportionality, Nicholas Emiliou, *The Principle of Proportionality in European Law. A Comparative Study*, European Monographs (London: Kluwer Law International, 1996), at 198:

> 'The Court ruled, in both cases, that there was no violation of the basic rights invoked by the applicants. It is quite remarkable that the Court examined whether a violation of the principle of proportionality had occurred in the course of the examination of a complaint against Community legislation based on subjective rights, and did not do so where the applicants invoked legitimate interests covered by national constitutional law.'

understood as legitimate *public* interests under German public law.[32] In effect, it is precisely its link with German public law – or rather its German origin – that explains why the European proportionality principle concentrates exclusively on (fundamental) rights.

The only protection that seems to survive is the right to good administration. The state's obligation to give reasons also applies to aliens, irrespective of the limited scope of any material rights. So, after all existing European law offers aliens real grounds for challenging exclusion decisions. Yet, it is clear that the authorities' obligation to give reasons easily turns into an empty gesture. The authorities must give reasons and those reasons must be sufficient in light of the decision taken; but since the decision is about an interest that is not protected by European law there is little that will prevent the authorities from not fulfilling the obligation. For example, reasons that only include the interests of the receiving state and that do not consider the alien's interests and reasons to admission (other than interests and reasons protected by European law, e.g. family life) already count as sufficient reasons. There is simply no evaluative criterion available that takes into account the alien's perspective. Of course, the proportionality principle may produce such a criterion, but as argued above, it does not apply because there is no protected freedom at stake (other than the right to good administration). Even if the proportionality principle applied to exclusion decisions, under its current construction it is hard to see how the principle will operate without any recognition of the alien's legitimate interest in free movement. For example, the Draft's requirement whereby the decision must be justified by *overriding* reasons of general interest is easily satisfied in the absence of any notion of *what is to be overridden.* It will be extremely difficult to establish that a measure *goes beyond what is necessary in order to obtain the objective* if there is no external interest that can be balanced against 'what is necessary'.

Liberty to move for everyone

How then can the drafters argue that the Draft is in line with existing European law? The drafters seemed to be aware of the problem and have sought to justify the extension of the proportionality principle by reiterating the liberty to move. In their explanatory report they suggest that the liberty to move exists and that any refusal decisions simply interfere with the liberty to move.

> This draft Directive provides for a coherent set of rules offering minimum protection in immigration matters against unjustified interference in *anyone's liberty to move . . .*

32 Emiliou (1996), at 58–9.

> The decisions enumerated in the first paragraph of this Article [1 of the draft] have in common that they interfere in *the liberty to move*. . . .[33]

But, of course, the whole problem with the lack of legal protection for aliens seeking admission is that under current European law there is *no* liberty to move. So, these so-called exclusion decisions do not 'interfere in the liberty to move' and they cannot constitute 'unjustified interference in anyone's liberty to move', because there is no such thing as a liberty to move (other than the one restricted to EU citizens and privileged third-country nationals). According to the drafters the problem seems to be that the current legal regime is lagging behind in its ability to protect the alien's liberty to move. In fact, things are the other way around: the legal protection is lagging because there is no liberty to move. Due to the way the European legal institutions have been reasoning there can be no genuine protection – not even a procedural one – of the alien's interests without the *introduction* of an autonomous legally recognized and protected *counter*-interest: a liberty to move that applies to everyone.

In short, the drafters are faced with a twofold gap between the Draft and existing European law: the proportionality principle only applies to (fundamental) rights and the liberty to move is not a fundamental right applicable to all aliens. There are two ways to bridge this gap. Either we introduce a fundamental liberty to move applicable to everyone and the infringement of this fundamental right or liberty triggers the protection of the proportionality principle. Or we adapt current European legal reasoning to the effect that the proportionality principle is triggered not only when rights are at stake but also when legitimate interests are infringed. It must be noted that the differences between the two options is a matter of European institutional and public law. The upshot of both options is the same if they are equally successful. But this is precisely my concern. The introduction of a universal liberty to move is less likely to be successful than the adaptation of the European proportionality principle. Both options will require important changes to existing European law, but the changes required by the latter are less radical than those necessary for the former. I explore the two options in the following paragraphs.

Let us assume that the Draft introduces a new fundamental right or liberty to move.[34] This proposition, then, immediately raises a question of European institutional law: What should be the legal basis for the introduction of a new fundamental right? The drafters were aware of the problem and decided to play it safe:

33 Meijers Committee, 'Explanatory Report', *European Journal of Migration and Law* (2005), at 309, emphasis added.

34 Of course one may argue that the draft does not introduce a new right, but simply reminds us of the fact that such right has always existed under European law: it just happened to have been overlooked by the courts. I believe that it is difficult and probably undesirable to maintain that the courts have been in error for more than 50 years. So, it seems more plausible to assume that the draft actually introduces a new right.

> To avoid confusion, and to avoid discussion about the question as to whether Articles 18 and 61 effectively offer a sufficient legal fundament at all, the legal basis for this Directive has been sought in Article 308 TEC [Art. 352 TFEU].[35]

Understandably the drafters sought recourse with the so-called catch-all provision of Article 308 TEC (Art. 352 TFEU):

> If action by the Community should prove *necessary* to attain, *in the course of the operation of the common market*, one of the *objectives of the Community*, and this Treaty has *not provided the necessary powers*, the Council shall, acting unanimously on a proposal from the Commission and after consulting the European Parliament, take the appropriate measures.

The passages in italics capture the conditions for the application of Article 308 TEC (Art. 352 TFEU) which are relevant for our purposes:[36]

- attain *one of the objectives of the Community*;
- actions must be *necessary*; and
- the Treaty has not provided for the necessary *powers*.

So, the article seeks to fill out the gaps in the system of *powers* that have been granted to the EC and its institutions but it leaves the objectives untouched. In other words, if the Draft creates a new right to free movement it must do so to attain the existing objectives of the Treaty. The question that then arises is does a universal liberty to move fits the objectives of the Treaty? The preamble of the Draft refers to the objective mentioned in *ex* Article 2 of TEU:[37] The Union shall set itself the following objectives: . . . to maintain and develop the Union as an area of freedom, security and justice [hereafter: AFSJ], in which the free movement of persons is assured in conjunction with appropriate measures with respect to external border controls, asylum, immigration and the prevention and combating of crime'.[38] The real question is then what freedom of movement and the AFSJ can possibly mean in light of Article 308 TEC (Art. 352 TFEU). To put it

35 Meijers Committee, 'Explanatory Report', *European Journal of Migration and Law* (2005), at 309.

36 For my analysis of the applicability of Art. 308 TEC I primarily relied on R.H. Lauwaars, 'De Institutionele Structuur', in P.J.G. Kapteyn and P. VerLoren van Themaat (eds), *Het Recht van de Europese Unie en van de Europese Gemeenschappen* (Deventer: Kluwer, 2003), at 184–7.

37 Now Art. 3 TEU; different in structure and wording, but not in substance.

38 Now *ex* Art. 308 only speaks of 'objectives of the Community' and this does not necessarily include the Union. But since *ex* Art. 61 of the TEC also incorporates a similar objective: 'In order to establish progressively an area of freedom, security and justice, the Council shall adopt: . . .', there is no doubt that the AFSJ is one of the objectives of the Community.

differently: are freedom of movement and the AFSJ the objectives that justify the creation of a fundamental right to move? I am afraid that the answer to this question is negative. Freedom of movement as an objective of the Community has an inherently restrictive scope. This is caused by the particular way in which freedom of movement has been conceived. The founders of the EC and EU could have confined themselves to simply stating the particular rights and duties of individuals and states regarding freedom of movement. Among those rights could figure the right to move into the territory of another Member State. Instead the founders pursued a two-step conception of free movement. Step one established the Community and the Union in terms of two *common areas*: the internal market ('the internal market shall comprise an area') and a Union ('to maintain and develop the Union as an area'). Step two then introduced freedom of movement. As there are already two areas that cover the territories of the respective Member States, there is no need to frame free movement as movement *into another* territory, it suffices to stick to the more familiar institute of domestic and international law: movement *within* the territory. Hence, *ex* Article 14 TEC[39] refers to 'an area without internal frontiers *in which* the free movement of . . . persons . . . is ensured'. *Ex* Article 18(1) speaks of 'the right to move and reside freely *within* the *territory* of the Member States'.[40] *Ex* Article 2 TEU[41] also speaks of 'an area of freedom, security and justice, *in which* free movement of persons is assured'. In other words, due to the way the founders have conceived free movement it is very difficult to construe it as an objective that requires the creation of a right to move *into* the area of the EC/EU.[42] In other words, it seems that there is an insufficient connection between the objective of 'freedom of movement' under the Treaty and the liberty to move as envisaged by the Draft.

What about the objective of the AFSJ; can it serve as an objective that requires the introduction of a fundamental liberty to move? Its wording is rather vague and broad. Even though lately the emphasis has been on security and justice for EU citizens, the AFSJ holds the promise of 'guarantees for those who seek protection in, but also for those seeking access to the European Union'.[43] Now, most political theorists will agree that freedom to move (indirectly) may promote justice.[44]

39 Emphasis added. Now Art. 26 TFEU.

40 Emphasis added. Now Art. 21 TFEU. One may also note the use of 'the territory' in the singular in conjunction with the plural 'the Member States', instead of 'the territory of another Member State' or 'the territories of the respective Member States'. This combination of singular and plural suggests that there is already one territory that belongs to the Member States as a whole.

41 Now Art. 3 TEU.

42 Again, I am not saying that the way in which the founders have framed the freedom of movement is a matter of conceptual, logical or historical necessity. On the contrary, it is of course perfectly possible to establish free movement without the prior (or even subsequent) creation of a common area.

43 Evelien Brouwer, 'Effective Remedies for Third Country Nationals in EU Law: Justice Accessible to All?', 7 *European Journal of Migration and Law* (2005), at 219 and also her analysis of the current move 'From "Justice Accessible to All" to an "Area of Justice for EU Citizens" ', at 220–1.

44 See Chapter 6.

However, they have in mind a particular form of distributive justice and I am not sure whether the notion of distributive justice corresponds with the central meaning of justice under the AFSJ. Moreover, the creation of a new fundamental liberty ceases to be necessary, if the same objective – i.e. justice for aliens – may be attained through less radical means. In effect, I will argue below that adapting the proportionality principle as developed by the ECJ may constitute such a less radical mean.

The inadequacy of *ex* Article 308 TEC for purposes of introducing a universal liberty to move reflects the fundamental nature of this initiative. The establishment of free movement for *EU citizens* involved amending the Treaties. It would be awkward if free movement for *everyone* could be introduced by a mere directive. In effect, it is difficult to deny that the introduction of the freedom to move for everyone implies an amendment of the Treaties. Accordingly, the amendment procedure of Article 48 TEU must be observed. But this is an extremely heavy procedure which directly involves the national institutions of the Member States and which may ultimately trigger national referenda. This route introduces a major political obstacle. Obtaining an electoral buy-in for treaty amendments that are allegedly in the interest of EU citizens has proven to be extremely difficult (see e.g. the French and Dutch 'no' vote in the referenda on the treaty for the introduction of a European Constitution). Imagine how difficult it will be to get sufficient electoral support for amendments that are *not* aimed directly at promoting the interests of the EU citizens.[45]

Alternative legal basis: extending the proportionality principle to legitimate interests

The previous paragraph showed that there is insufficient legal basis for the introduction of the liberty to move for everyone through a directive. Moreover, a fully fledged amendment procedure pursuant to Article 48 TEU is unlikely to be successful. By contrast, it lies within the reach of the Draft to adapt the European proportionality principle. For sure, such adaptation requires a change in current legal reasoning of the European Courts. However this change is

45 Whereas the right to move for everyone is *not necessarily against the interests of EU citizens*, it would be false to hold that the Draft's right to move purports to promote the interests of EU citizens. Of course, on some accounts a right to move for everyone is in the self-interest of host countries, but this is clearly (and rightly so) not the rationale behind the legal regime provided for by the Draft. Still, more relaxed immigration policies are expected to boost economic growth, and as such serve the interest of the host country. But when asked to make the trade-off between immigration restrictions and economic growth, it is not unlikely that voters will opt for restricted immigration. See for example in the Netherlands, the outcome of the comprehensive policy poll conducted by McKinsey Company *et al.*, 21minuten.nl (2005), at 26–9. On top of this tactical objection, from the perspective of the ethics of migration it is far from certain that free movement really deserves such a fundamental status (see Chapter 6).

less radical and controversial than the introduction of a universal liberty to move. The current European proportionality principle must be adapted to the effect that not only the infringement of rights will trigger its application but also the infringements of legitimate interests. In the following paragraphs I will discuss some arguments that support this extension of the proportionality principle. The arguments are general in the sense that they make the case for including legitimate interests in general and not only the interests of aliens seeking admission. The arguments are based on the *ratio 'legis'* of the German/European proportionality principle and the developments in administrative law of some other Member States.

Ratio 'legis' of the proportionality principle in Europe

The European proportionality principle is a clear product of German public law.[46] The main reason is that 'it was especially the German administrative courts which referred cases to the ECJ in which disproportionality of measures was raised'.[47] The German roots of the European proportionality principle did not prevent the ECJ from pursuing its own roll-out of the principle.[48] Yet in practice, the ECJ's interpretation of the proportionality principle has remained very much in line with the German original. In fact, it is precisely the German element that explains the exclusive focus on basic rights: 'The proportionality principle occupies a similar position in [European] Community law as that taken up by the basic rights under German law.'[49] But if basic rights are so characteristic for the German and – by implication – the European proportionality principle, can we go beyond basic rights without going beyond the proportionality principle? A brief look at the *ratio legis* of the German proportionality principle may provide us with a better understanding of the proper role of basic rights.

The starting point for the necessity criterion and thus the principle of proportionality is that the law must have a purpose.[50] In the second half of the nineteenth century the Prussian supreme administrative court issued one of the first explicit rulings establishing the necessity criterion: it examined 'whether the measures taken by the police did not exceed in intensity that which was required by the pursued objective'.[51] And these early rulings have been further developed into a more detailed necessity criterion applicable to both the law of policing and administrative law in general.[52] This necessity criterion is largely based on the simple

46 Francis G. Jacobs, 'Recent Developments in the Principle of Proportionality in European Community Law', in Evelyn Ellis (ed.) (1999), at 1; Schwarze (2006), at 855.
47 Schwarze (2006), at 855 in fn. 560.
48 Ibid., at 855.
49 Ibid., at 864.
50 See in general the introductions in Hirschberg (1981) and Van Drooghenbroeck (2001).
51 Schwarze (2006), at 686.
52 Ibid.

notion that the law must serve a purpose for (human) individuals or human society.[53] Though this notion goes back to Greek, Roman and Byzantine law, it became a dominant movement among nineteenth-century German legal scholars through the likes of Jhering.[54] The important aspect of this so-called purpose rationality (Zweck Rationalität) is that it established a relation between the means of government and its purposes. From this relation the necessity criterion follows automatically, because the ends only justify the necessary and appropriate means.[55]

Though the necessity criterion as developed by the German courts up to the demise of the Weimar Republic constitutes a central element of the legal protection of citizens against state action, the Nazi-regime also showed its shortcomings. The purpose rationality not only operates as a constraint on state action, it also easily degenerates into a pretext for the annihilation of individuals: 'Recht ist was dem Volke nützt'.[56] Furthermore, the Nazi regime revealed that not only the executive but also the legislator can threaten the position of citizens.[57] What vehicle could provide protection beyond the necessity criterion against both the executive and the legislative branch of government? In the aftermath of the Second World War basic rights seemed the most adequate legal vehicle available. First, the notion of basic rights respects the German positivistic legal tradition of the hierarchy of norms.[58] The legislator must also respect basic rights from a *legal* perspective. Second, the notion of basic rights nicely fits the emergence of the human rights discourse (cf. Universal Declaration of Human Rights). Third, basic rights were the most solid way to ensure that the purpose rationality does not fully discard the *individual* impact of measures that are, in principle, necessary. The fundamental nature of this protection scheme was guaranteed by incorporating the scope of the judicial review into the constitution: access to the courts of law is open to any person whose rights are adversely affected by *any* public authority (including the legislator) (Article 19(4) Basic Law). The actual intensity of the substantial review was developed by the courts and resulted in the proportionality test. In a sense the proportionality test allowed the substance of state actions to be checked while still respecting the separation of powers, since the actual expediency of executive and legislative acts is still determined by the executive

53 Franz Wieacker, 'Geschichtlige Wurzeln des Prinzips de verhältnismäßigen Rechtsanwendung', in Marcus Lutter, Walter Stimpel and Herbert Wiedemann (eds), *Festschrift für Robert Fischer* (Berlin/New York: Walter de Gruyter, 1979), at 878.

54 Ibid.

55 Ibid., at 879: 'auch der Zweck heiligt *nur* die notwendigen und tauglichen Mittel' (emphasis added).

56 Ibid., at 880.

57 In effect, it was only after the Second World War that the concern for protection against all state actions, including the legislator was seriously developed. Schwarze (2006), at 686.

58 See for its reflection in the current German legal system, Meinhard Schröder, 'Administrative Law in Germany', in René Seerden and Frits Stroink (eds), *Administrative Law of the European Union, its Member States and the United States* (Antwerpen: Intersentia, 2002), at 92–7.

and legislative branch respectively. This very brief historical overview shows us that the starting point of the proportionality principle is the need for the protection of persons against excessive and inappropriate state actions. At its conception the proportionality principle relied on the legal vehicle that could at that time provide the surest and most intensive restrictions on such excessive and inappropriate state actions, i.e. basic rights. Basic rights were 'the best legal technique available' for purposes of providing the most comprehensive legal protection against state actions. The intended role of basic rights is to operate as an impetus for legal protection, not as a constraint on legal protection.[59] In other words, extending the protection of the proportionality principle to legitimate interests (and thus to all aliens seeking admission) is more than compatible with the *ratio legis* of the German and by implication the European proportionality principle.

While domestic public law of Germany produced the European proportionality principle, the European proportionality principle in its turn influenced administrative law in the Member States. Initially, the judicial review of state acts organized under French ('*légalité externe*') and UK law ('*ultra vires*') has been rather restricted and legalistic. Under the influence of the European proportionality principle the review has been gradually intensifying.[60] At the same time, while the German proportionality principle has always been the most advanced, today its exclusive focus on basic rights is starting to become problematic.[61] By contrast

59 German administrative law is quite specific about the criterion for standing: 'A suit for invalidity and a suit for a mandatory injunction can only be filed by a person whose legal rights have been violated by an administrative action or omission. Section 42(2) of the Law on Administrative Courts.' Ibid., at 136. Yet, there is a tendency to relax the requirement when it comes to some injunction procedures: '[I]n the case of a suit for a mandatory injunction the requirement of standing is not as important. A declaratory suit can be filed if the plaintiff has a legitimate interest in a prompt declaration, but this need not be a legal interest. Every interest, which can be justified on rational considerations, i.e. economic, political, cultural and religious interests, is admissible.' Ibid., at 136.

60 Though the underlying rationale behind the two regimes is different (separation of powers and supremacy of the executive in France, and supremacy of Parliament in the UK. See Van Gerven (1999), at 60) the upshot has been similar: a restricted legalistic review. See for the development of the French proportionality principle, Emiliou (1996). For the influence of the European proportionality principle on UK law, see Brian Jones and Katharine Thompson, 'Administrative Law in the United Kingdom', in René Seerden and Frits Stroink (eds) (2002), at 244–5; David Feldman, 'Proportionality and the Human Rights Act 1988', in Evelyn Ellis (ed.) (1999), at 143–4; Schwarze (2006), at 696. *Contra* Rt. Hon. Lord Hoffmann, 'The Influence of the European Principle of Proportionality upon UK law', in Evelyn Ellis (ed.) (1999), at 114–15 who argues that UK law already contains all the features of the proportionality principle, but that the institute is just named differently.

61 According to some the focus on (fundamental) rights has restrictive effects on current German legal practice: important interests are excluded from administrative decision making, and the judicial protection of procedural participation has become of secondary importance. See Karl-Heinz Ladeur and Rebecca Prelle, 'Judicial Control of Administrative Procedural Mistakes in Germany: A Comparative European View of Environmental Impact Assessments', in Karl-Heinz Ladeur (ed.), *The Europeanisation of Administrative Law. Transforming National Decision-Making Procedures* (Aldershot: Dartmouth, 2002), at 93–4.

and quite unexpectedly, it is precisely the rather conservative focus on legality typical of the French and UK systems that now operates as a potential impetus for extending the proportionality principle to legitimate interests. UK and especially French law have built the legal protection against state action around the notion of legality or competence. The authorities must always act within the confines of the competence granted to them by the law. If not they simply lack the power to lawfully perform the act. It follows that the challenges against such acts ('*ultra vires*') are in a sense 'objective' and do not depend on the legal position of the person challenging them. In other words, one need not invoke the infringement of a subjective basic right to challenge such state actions; legitimate interests suffice.[62]

If we combine this 'objective' aspect with the earlier described intensification of the judicial review as a result of the European proportionality principle described earlier, it should become clear that, as has been argued by leading scholars of European law,[63] extending the proportionality test to legitimate interests lies within the reach of administrative law. A concrete case in point for such an extension is the proportionality principle under the Dutch General Administrative Law Code.[64] We can only second Van Gerven's

62 See Jones and Thompson (2002), at 230–2 and Jean-Bernard Auby, 'Administrative Law in France', in Karl-Heinz Ladeur (ed.) (2002), at 81 for standings under UK and French law respectively.

63 See Paul Craig: 'The central issue is therefore whether a proportionality type-test should be applied in cases other than fundamental rights. There is a normative justification for the use of proportionality even where ... there are no fundamental rights at stake.' Paul Craig, 'Unreasonableness and Proportionality in UK Law', in Evelyn Ellis (ed.), (1999), at 100–1. David Feldman: 'How will all this affect proportionality as it operates, or may come to operate, in proceedings which do not directly involve the Human Rights Act 1988 and the Convention rights? ... It seems to me likely that the growing frequency with which courts will have to grapple with issues of proportionality will lead them to be more open about using proportionality-based reasoning in other circumstances.' Feldman (1992), at 142.

In effect, the position of these authors is in line with the more theoretical observation – but still positivistic – that the similarities, differences and relationship between rights and interests can be understood as a *continuum* (illegitimate interests, indifferent interests, legitimate interests, subjective rights). See in general the comprehensive thematic treatment of the relationship between rights and interests, Philippe Gérard *et al.* (eds), *Droit et Intérêt*, (Brussels: Facultés Universitaires Saint-Louis, 1990). See for the continuum François Ost, *Entre droit et non-droit: l'intérêt. Essai sure les functions qu'exerce la notion d'intérêt en droit privé*, 2 (Brussels: Facultés Universitaires Saint-Louis, 1990), at 35–41.

64 According to Art. 3:4 Awb:

1 When making a decision the administrative authority shall weight the interests directly involved in so far as no limitation on this duty derives from a statutory regulation of the nature of the power being exercised.

2. The adverse consequences of a decision for one or more interested parties may not be disproportionate to the purposes to be served by the decision.

English translation from René Seerden and Frits Stroink, 'Administrative Law in the Netherlands', in René Seerden and Frits Stroink (2002), at 194.

suggestion that it could serve as a model for adapting the European proportionality principle, because it requires the authorities to consider *all interests* and the impact of measures on *interested parties*, rather than only the interests of those able to invoke the infringement of a basic right. In short, whereas once German domestic law produced the European proportionality principle and the European proportionality principle influenced the domestic law of other Member States, it is now time to initiate another cross-fertilization: from the proportionality principle of Dutch administrative law to the European proportionality principle.

I have argued that a directive cannot amend the Treaties – in the case at point, introduce a new fundamental liberty to move. The question arises as to whether a directive can extend the proportionality principle to the effect of including legitimate interests. I believe it can and the legal basis is the same as proposed by the drafters: Article 308 TEC (Art. 352 TFEU). In effect, the AFSJ is one of the objectives to be attained by the European institutions and its Member States. Something that falls within the objectives of justice is not a right to free movement for aliens, but the adequate administration of the law. Today proportionality is one of the quintessential principles governing the administration of the law. So it seems difficult to argue that the meaning of the proportionality principle is something that falls beyond the scope of justice as meant by the AFSJ. By the same token, the European institution that developed and rolled out the proportionality principle was not the Council of the European Union or the Commission, but the ECJ. Yet it is not because proportionality is a principle used by the courts to guide their judicial review that the legislative branch cannot codify and determine its meaning and scope. Furthermore, by extending the scope of the proportionality principle to legitimate interests the directive in no way affects the rights and liberties already guaranteed by the Treaties. In short, it is safe to say that Article 308 can serve as the legal basis for a directive that extends the proportionality principle to the effect of including legitimate interests (of aliens).

Interpretational issues

Like any legal norm, the effect of a directive lies in its application. The application of a directive is in the first place a matter for the Member States who must make the necessary arrangements to implement the directive. The directive can also have direct application if individuals bring their case to court, invoking a violation by the national authorities of standards provided for in the directive. The application of a directive always involves interpretation. The challenge for legal practice is to come up with interpretations of a legal norm that are as stable as possible. Yet depending on the legal provisions and the facts of concrete cases, diverging interpretations are possible. This is not, as such, a problem so long as the so-called 'hard' cases remain marginal relative to the 'easy' cases. Yet when legal controversy becomes the norm, the effectiveness of the norm is at risk. If one takes a first glance at the Draft directive this risk is far from theoretical. The

Draft contains notions that may fuel legal controversy. If at the outset this risk seems material, it raises serious concerns about the feasibility of the proposal. Consequently, we should consider some of the interpretational issues potentially associated with the Draft. We restrict our discussion to three issues: the scope of the proportionality test, scope of judicial review, and the legal status of migrants after judicial annulment of exclusion decisions. We conclude with an observation on the (relative) importance of distinguishing the proportionality test from the *right* to free movement. The purpose of the following discussion is not to fully address these interpretational issues beforehand. The issues are too complex to deal with comprehensively. In any event, addressing the issues beforehand is impossible because application – and thus interpretation – is always a matter of the concrete case. The purpose is just to remove the *prima facie* concerns to prevent the Draft from being disqualified at the outset.

Scope of proportionality test

The principle of proportionality hardly needs any explanation. It seems to correspond perfectly with our intuitions about what justice and law require. Yet the clarity of the principle can turn into an interpretational nightmare when confronted with the concrete cases of migration decisions. When is the exclusion of an individual normal migrant proportionate? How can a court ever be in a position to properly judge such a complex issue? Without denying the essence of the problem, it seems that the challenge is not so massive in every case. We can easily imagine that there may be many cases where the exclusion is *obviously* proportionate and cases where the exclusion is *obviously not* proportionate. The question is, of course, how the number of these so-called 'easy' cases relate to the number of 'hard' cases. It will take another study to make any serious estimates and guesses about the distribution of actual and future cases. In any event, at the outset there are no clear indications that the 'hard' cases outnumber the 'easy' cases. Furthermore, courts[65] may alleviate their task by concentrating on the *necessity* aspect of the proportionality test rather than on proportionality *sensu stricto*. The latter is of course more difficult to establish than the former. Imagine a denial of admission of a normal migrant on economic grounds. Testing the necessity of the exclusion primarily involves checking whether there are alternative measures available that equally serve the economic objectives but are less burdensome for the normal migrant than outright exclusion. Though this test is not without its complications, at least the notion of 'a less burdensome alternative' suggests that a large part of the test involves a measurable and verifiable inquiry into the alternatives. By contrast, what is there to measure or verify when checking whether the burden placed on the excluded migrant has been disproportionate in

65 We concentrate on the task of the court. Of course, it is first up to the other branches of government to ensure that the exclusion is proportionate.

light of the benefits, i.e. proportionality *stricto sensu*? If one takes the impact of exclusion seriously, it seems that an incredibly heavy burden is put on a single individual to service the public at large. Moreover, there is hardly any burden sharing between the individual migrant and others (authorities, public). This suggests that the exclusion of an individual migrant for economic reasons is virtually never proportionate *sensu stricto*. Of course, this is not a feasible position. It would mean that if authorities were to respect the proportionality *stricto sensu* they could never deny a migrant admission on economic grounds. Hence, our suggestion to drop – for the time being – the proportionality test *sensu stricto*.

Still, even if one concentrates only on the necessity criterion, the proportionality test is exceptionally complicated in the context of migration. The central question is of course whether or not harming the interests of an individual migrant is necessary for the benefit of the public interests. There is nothing special about the opposition between individual and public interests. It is the central problem of all areas of public policy and especially administrative law. Equally common is the idea that one way or another, honoring the interests of the individual – in our case the admission of the migrant – adversely affects the public interest. Also, more often than not, the problem is not so much the particular individual – his impact on the public interest is in most cases insignificant, especially when it comes to economic and social policies.[66] Rather the individual is considered to be an element of a larger set of individuals whose aggregated actions and presence do have an effect on the public interest. To prevent this, the authorities will have to anticipate and intervene at an individual level at an early stage, thus deterring other members of the 'group' from following suit. This strategy inevitably entails harming the interests of the individual whose own isolated actions and presence do not significantly affect the public interest. This is a very common logic in public policy and it clearly applies to migration. Yet, the position of the migrant differs in two ways from an individual in other areas of public policy. First, the 'group' of individuals whose aggregated actions and presence may adversely affect the public interest is, in the case of migration, virtually unlimited. A migrant is allegedly part of a migration flux (cf. Art. 79 TFEU).[67] However, policy makers and legal practice have little experience in grasping the quantity and quality of this flux. This means that, potentially, an individual migrant is part of a massive migration flux whose aggregated impact on the public interest may have catastrophic proportions. As a result, the necessity to exclude elements of such a massive flux becomes self-evident. Against this background the exclusion of normal migrants on socio-economic grounds will always be necessary, which

66 By contrast, sometimes in health, environmental and security areas, one individual person or legal entity can have a material impact on the public interest.

67 For a critical analysis of management of migration flows from legal theory, Bas Schotel, 'EU's Management of Migration Flows and the Rule of Law. From Individual Migrant to Migration Flow', *Journal of Ethnic and Migration Studies* (forthcoming 2011).

would turn the necessity test into an empty gesture. Second, in most areas of public policy, the balancing of individual and public interests has a particular reasonableness to it, based on a kind of reciprocity. The individual facing the public interest has, in theory, an interest in the public interest being served. By the same token the public has an interest in the respect for individual interests as each member of the public may one day find himself in the same position against the public. This logic does not apply to the migrant. He does not have much to gain from the public interest being served by his exclusion.[68] This makes the necessity test an extremely difficult exercise. The central question is whether there are less burdensome alternatives to exclusion. However, an alternative that is less burdensome for the migrant may be more costly for the public. How can the acceptable cost level of the alternative be appreciated, bearing in mind that the migrant stands to gain nothing from the cheaper option, i.e. exclusion? Unfortunately, I do not have any suggestions for how to address these two peculiarities associated with the proportionality test in the context of migration. More research is needed into how, today, we are to understand *in legal terms* migration and migration policy, especially the notion of necessity and migration flux. However, this current lack of knowledge should not affect the feasibility of the Draft. In a way the Draft – probably unintentionally – anticipated these complications and placed the responsibility with the most informed and, in a way, the most interested party, the authorities. The burden of proof lies with the migration authorities who have to show that their decision is proportionate. So they must first produce evidence to the effect that the denial of admission is necessary. And this should inevitably involve a substantiated position on the proper criteria for establishing necessity, cause and effects, migration flux, etc. In a way, the Draft is a great opportunity for the authorities to show that they take their own policies seriously.

Scope of judicial review

The Draft provides for the review and annulment of 'decisions' (see Arts 1 and 6(1–5)). From the perspective of constitutional and administrative law the notion of decision typically contains two elements: a legal act taken by the administrative authorities and individual scope of application. Yet, the exclusive reference to 'decisions' does not mean that the review and annulment only affect individual decisions taken by the administrative authorities. The review also pertains to the underlying general measures taken by the executive and even the statutory provisions issued by the legislator. The whole point of the European/German proportionality principle, as discussed earlier, is that Member States cannot hide behind a formal separation of powers to dodge the application of the proportionality principle. In other words, although the Draft may not give the national courts the power to strike down legislation, it does give them

68 See Chapter 5.

the power to render legislation ineffective.[69] For if the statutory provisions are found to be disproportionate then, by implication, the measures and decisions of the administrative authorities that are taken in virtue of these provisions will also be disproportionate. This is extremely relevant for immigration cases, because, to date, the actual admission criteria for a long-term stay are still a matter of domestic statutory immigration law.[70] As to the individual application of the 'decision' we must not be too strict. As noted above, the Draft deliberately includes *de facto* measures. Now, some measures are not directed at a particular individual alien, yet they directly affect individual aliens and constitute a form of *de facto* exclusion.

According to Article 6(5) Draft the court *shall have the power to annul* a decision when it finds the decision arbitrary, disproportionate or unlawful. Now, the wording of this provision may suggest that there is some room for judicial discretion: the national courts only have the power to annul disproportionate decisions, there is no obligation to do so. This is obviously not the intention of the Draft. In any event, disproportionate exclusions will violate the directive. And since the directive has direct effect in the Member States a disproportionate decision violates the law of the Member States. When a court has the power to annul unlawful decisions and when it finds a particular decision unlawful, failure to annul will ultimately constitute a denial of justice.[71]

Legal status of migrants after annulment of exclusion decision

Imagine the alien obtains the annulment of a disproportionate exclusion decision. What is his legal status? What is he allowed to do? The answers to these questions are far from obvious. Since no liberty to move is applicable to the alien, the alien is not allowed to enter and to stay in the territory without a legal permit (e.g. visa and permit to stay). By the same token the authorities are not entitled to keep the alien out because that would equal an exclusion, which is disproportionate. It seems that this stalemate drives the alien into a legal limbo. Different 'solutions' have tobe envisaged.

Rather than a stalemate we may characterize the situation as an instance of an official non-enforcement policy ('*gedogen*' in Dutch). And if we follow van Dijck's thesis, official non-enforcement need not always create a legal limbo

69 Indeed, the Draft directive grants this power directly to the national courts: pursuant to Art. 10 Draft, the directive is directly binding and applicable *in* the Member States.

70 If the Council adopts measures that establish conditions for entry and long-term stay in virtue of *ex* Art. 63(3)(a) TEC, national statutory admission criteria may become irrelevant. However, in this case the proportionality principle should apply to the legislative branch of the European institutions, as it already does.

71 This emphasis on the centrality of judicial review in migration matters is in line with the recent amendments in the Lisbon Treaty abolishing ex Art. 68 TEC, see Chapter 1.

(i.e. non-law) but should be perceived – depending on the case – as law enforcement.[72] In effect, the authorities may be upholding the law ('*het recht*') by refraining from enforcing the immigration statutes ('*de wet*'). Still, the drawback of this solution is that outside the Netherlands, an official policy of non-enforcement is arguably less widespread. In addition, the situation may not be satisfactory to the alien because the absence of any legal status will deny him access to a whole set of resources, most importantly the (legal) labor market.

So another solution must be considered. According to Article 6(6) Draft the national courts are competent to order any appropriate measure against the authorities repairing or compensating the damages caused by the disproportionate decision. Now, the alien seeking admission is typically not claiming damages. Yet the fact of being excluded clearly causes damage. And as the Draft puts it, the court may order compensation or *repair*. In fact, under the general principles of contractual and extra-contractual liability, one must first seek to make the victim whole in kind, before offering compensation. In the case of the alien who has been denied admission, repairing the damages may actually equate to admitting the alien: admission will extinguish the disproportionality.[73] Alternatively, if the authorities still want to push through the exclusion, they may do so in principle, provided that they compensate the alien for the damages associated with the disproportionality. So, while the Draft may provoke a stalemate between the alien and the authorities, it also offers the tools to solve it.

Proportionality principle versus right to move: what's in a name

The previous paragraph predicted a stalemate further to the annulment of a disproportionate decision. To break the stalemate I suggested that the court should order the authorities to grant admission if there are no reasons and evidence to withhold it. However, it seems that this 'solution' spills over into establishing a *de facto* liberty to move. So rather than merely accounting for the alien's legitimate interest to admission, the Draft introduces a new fundamental liberty to move. This takes

72 Maarten van Dijck, *Gedogen. Over vermogen en onvermogen tot handhaving van wet en recht* (Nijmegen: Wolf Legal Publishers, 2003).

73 It must be noted that, strictly speaking, full admission is not the only alternative to an annulment of a disproportionate decision. Sometimes neither full exclusion nor full admission is proportionate. This may occur in the case of serious security and public policy considerations that are insufficient to justify an exclusion decision, but may justify restricted and supervised access. This may be illustrated by the distinct but analogous situation of the indefinite detention of illegal aliens who cannot be deported to country of origin as addressed by the US Supreme Court ruling in *Zadvydas v Davis*: 'The choice, however, is not between imprisonment and the alien "living at large". It is between imprisonment and supervision under release conditions that may not be violated. . . . [W]e believe that an alien's liberty interest is, at the least, strong enough to raise a serious question as to whether, irrespective of the procedures used, the Constitution permits detention that is indefinite and potentially permanent.' 121 S.Ct. 2491, (2001), at 2502.

us back to square one: the directive lacks the legal basis for introducing a new fundamental liberty in EC/EU law.

Yet this objection is misconceived. It assumes that the difference between the protection of fundamental rights/liberties, plain rights and legitimate interests is a matter of the *de facto effectiveness of the protection*. The real difference lies in the *way* the *legal* protection is organized. The legal protection of fundamental rights and liberties typically covers two levels: protection of objective right and protection of subjective right.

The legal institute in itself, i.e. the *objective* fundamental right, enjoys a special protection from the whims of electoral opinion and forces: in most legal systems a special and qualified majority is required to make laws that abolish fundamental rights. When laid down in international law instruments, abolition is rendered even more difficult. Yet the fact that a fundamental right cannot be abolished by a simple law does not exclude the legality of its occasional infringements. The reason is that fundamental rights are not absolute.[74] They must be balanced against other fundamental rights, plain rights, public interests and even legitimate private interests.

If the fundamental rights can be balanced against other legally protected interests what then guarantees their special status? It is here that the second level of protection kicks in: protection of subjective rights. First, though the authorities may infringe the exercise of an individual's fundamental right, they can only do so pursuant to or in virtue of a special law that grants them the power. Typically, in the case of the infringement of legitimate interests no such special law is needed.[75] Second, in terms of judicial review, when balancing fundamental rights against other legally protected interests, the court must give special weight to fundamental rights. Legitimate interests are not granted such special weight. In other words, fundamental rights are synonymous with special legal protection. Of course, this is no guarantee for the *de facto* effectiveness of the protection.

Two aspects attenuate the difference in *de facto* effectiveness between fundamental rights and legitimate interests. First, the actual extent and content of the special weight granted to fundamental rights is not something that can be determined in the abstract. This is a matter of particular courts deciding concrete cases. In practice some legitimate interests may benefit from the same weight that has been granted to fundamental rights in other cases. Second, the special weight is clearer when in a particular case fundamental rights are to be balanced against plain rights or legitimate interests. This is typically what happens when balancing

74 With the right to enter the country of one's nationality being precisely one of the rare exceptions. See discussion below.

75 This does not mean that the authorities have the *liberty* to infringe legitimate interests. Again, the application of the proportionality principle (including the necessity criterion) to legitimate interests means that the state may only act within its purpose. Yet this purpose may be more generic than the specific objectives laid down in special laws to which the authorities must refer when infringing fundamental rights.

conflicting private interests (horizontal dimension). However, in the case in point the conflict is between the private interests of the alien against the *public* interest defended by the state (vertical dimension). Though the public interest is probably more than a mere legitimate interest it cannot be understood as a fundamental right; the state has no fundamental rights *vis-à-vis* its norm subjects.

A fundamental right can place more weight against the public interest than a legitimate private interest. But the question of *de facto* effectiveness is whether in fact the public interest will prevail over the private legitimate interest, or vice versa. Again, the outcome cannot be determined in the abstract, but instead depends on the court's assessment of the particular case. This means that a legitimate interest may, in fact, be just as effective as a fundamental right.

The objection that legitimate interests are put on an equal footing as fundamental rights also points to another misconception. It suggests that interests protected by fundamental rights deserve more effective protection than legitimate interests, because the former are more valuable or important than the latter. Though the status of a fundamental right may express in a symbolic way that an interest is of more value than others, this need not be the case. The fact that an interest is not protected by a right or a fundamental right does not mean that it is valued less than interests that are protected by a right. Similarly, the fact that an interest is protected by a 'plain' right does not mean that it is valued less than an interest protected by a fundamental right. The reason for granting one interest more legal protection than another is that the former is more likely to be discarded without special protection than the latter.[76] Still, interests are often constantly infringed irrespective of their special legal protection. In other words, we must examine whether people can practically pursue a particular interest that is considered to be valuable. If not, it is worthwhile to consider the interest for special legal protection. This is not a matter of the interest being fundamentally valuable, but rather a matter of a valuable interest being effective. In short, seeking effective protection for legitimate interests does not turn legitimate interests into fundamental rights.

There is another – more tactical – reason for maintaining the formal distinction between a human right to free movement and a legitimate interest protected by the proportionality principle. It has to do with the suggestion that the principle of

76 This may be illustrated by the following observation. In contemporary Western European society religion plays probably an equally (if not less) important role in the personal lives of most people as sports. Both religious and non-religious individuals can and do acknowledge that religion and sports are objects of value. The interest in the free exercise of one's religion is protected by a special fundamental right. This is not the case for sports. Does this mean that playing sport is of less value than going to church? No, of course not. So, why don't we introduce a fundamental right to play sport? The answer is simple: it happens to be the case that the interest to play sport is already effectively guaranteed without such special protection. In contrast, it also happens to be the case that in Western society, practicing a different religion has been a much more current pretext for oppressing people than playing a different sport.

proportionality may be introduced in immigration law via the principle of non-discrimination and equality.[77] In principle, states are not allowed to discriminate on the basis of nationality. They may only do so subject to very strict criteria, including proportionality. As the European Court of Human Rights puts it:

> According to the Court's case-law, a distinction is discriminatory, for the purposes of Article 14, if it 'has no objective and reasonable justification', that is if it does not pursue a 'legitimate aim' or if there is not a '*reasonable relationship of proportionality* between the means employed and the aim sought to be realised'. Moreover the Contracting States enjoy a certain margin of appreciation in assessing whether and to what extent differences in otherwise similar situations justify a different treatment . . . However, *very weighty reasons* would have to be put forward before the Court could regard a difference of treatment based exclusively on the ground of nationality as compatible with the Convention. (emphasis added)[78]

It seems that admission laws are a clear case where the difference of treatment is based exclusively on the ground of nationality.[79] Accordingly they should trigger the 'very weighty reasons' and proportionality test. A closer look at the case law suggests that the Court considered cases that are clearly to be distinguished from the situation of normal migrants seeking admission. In the ECHR case law the foreign national could either invoke a fundamental human right, especially right to family life, or had a legal title to stay in the host country which allowed him or her to participate in social/economic life of the host country very much like a national. These situations do not apply to the normal migrant seeking admission. Moreover, applying the non-discrimination principle may lead to a very odd and ultimately undesirable situation. The current difference in treatment between nationals and foreign nationals may be understood in connection with the national's unqualified or absolute right to admission to his own country: 'No one shall be deprived of the right to enter the territory of the State of which he is a national.'[80] Not discriminating between nationals and non-nationals would mean that foreign

77 See, inter alia, Sylvie Saroléa, 'La souveraineté en droit belge: mythe *et* réalite', in Jean-Yves Carlier (ed.), *L'étranger face au droit. XXes Journées d'etudes juridiques Jean Dabin* (Brussels: Bruylant, 2010), at 110–11; Tim Eicke, 'Paradise Lost? Exclusion and Expulsion from the EU' in Kees Groenendijk, Elspeth Guild and Paul Minderhoud (eds), *In Search of Europe's Borders* (The Hague/London/New York: Kluwer Law International, 2003), at 167–8.

78 ECHR, 30 Sept. 2003 – *Koua Poirrez v France* (No. 40892/98), para. 46, with reference to *Gaygusuz*, p. 1142, para. 42; *Larkos v Cyprus* [GC], No. 29515/95, para. 29, ECHR 1999-I; and *Thlimmenos v Greece* [GC], No. 34369/97, para. 40, ECHR 2000-IV).

79 See Chapter 6, fn. 69 for reference to Michael Dummett's contention that all immigration restrictions have been racist in essence.

80 Article 3(2) of Protocol No. 4 Convention for the Protection of Human Rights and Fundamental Freedoms.

nationals have an equally absolute right to admission, which boils down to a universal *unqualified* right to free movement. This is of course not feasible. It would mean that states could never refuse the admission of foreigners. The only alternative is a *qualified* right to admission. But the non-discrimination principle requires that this qualified right applies to both foreigners and nationals. The ultimate consequence is that nationals may be refused admission to the territory of their own state. In other words, applying the non-discrimination principle may lead to equality, but at a very high price – it denies the absolute right to enter the territory of the state of which one is a national. For most people this would mean denying them the absolute right to enter their homeland.

This last discussion is clearly a warning against over-asking the law. Not only might we do injustice to the structure and technique of the law if we establish a fundamental right to free movement, but it may also compromise dearly held existing fundamental rights. In a way, this discussion reflects what has been the central approach of this book. It was an attempt to find out what the law actually requires when it comes to normal migrants seeking admission. In other words, what to do if we want to respect the law? It certainly meant that when trying to improve the position of migrants seeking admission we cannot over-ask the law. So, from a legal perspective it does not demand full equality between nationals and normal migrants when it comes to admission. But without downplaying the consequences of over-asking the law, the real problem with admission policies today seems to be a structural under-asking of the law. The official stance is that from the legal perspective there is not much that can be done to improve the position of normal migrants seeking admission. By contrast, this chapter was an attempt to show that the law can do better. The concrete proposal by the Meijers Committtee is not so much plausible and feasible because it relies on a fundamental right to free movement. Rather the proposal is feasible because it is based on the principle of proportionality, which is probably one of the most fundamental principles of our legal thought and, more importantly, our legal practice. It is an indication that it is institutionally possible to change the default position. In other words, we already have the basis for the institutional arrangements that can put the first burden of justification on the immigration authorities rather than on the excluded migrant seeking admission. While the previous chapters tried to show that current admission practices are legally untenable and that a change in the default position is ethically justified, the final chapter suggested that it is also institutionally possible. So, we pursued a three-pronged argument. First, authorities do not have the legal backing for today's admission policies; it goes against the structure of law to exclude without justification. Second, not only must authorities justify exclusion, political theory suggests that they should carry the first burden of justification. Third, it is also institutionally possible for the authorities to carry this first burden of justification. Have we come full circle? Obviously not. Much more can be said about the exclusion thesis, the authority of admission laws and testing the proportionality of exclusion. Extending the application of the proportionality principle may raise many challenges. This will be primarily a matter of context and experience that should be addressed by legal practitioners in real cases. Of course, this implies that cases become *real*. In other words: launch and learn. It is not just legal practitioners who have a lot of work to hand. Legal theorists have a really long way to go. This book is one of the few attempts to look at immigration policy from the perspective of the structure of law. Undoubtedly there are many more ways in which legal theory can help us to grasp the peculiarities of our immigration policies. We are only starting to see the possibilities. Clearly, we have not come full circle. In fact, any actual change to our admission policies will prove to be an incredibly complex and long-term effort. Still, we may have accomplished at least one thing. We have put the ball in the court of those who still believe that, from a legal perspective, there is nothing wrong with current admission policies. The current default position of immigration laws and policies is no longer self-evident. Policy makers cannot keep hiding behind the (formal) law. In a sense, the book may already have achieved its goal: the burden of justification has been reversed.

Annexes

Annex 1 Estimation of yearly exclusion of normal migrants seeking admission in the EU

Items	*Number of migrants seeking admission (x1,000)*
1. Refusals	
Border*	1,437
diplomatic posts**	700
Total	2,137
2. Illegal aliens***	
High estimate	500
Low estimate	120
Median	310
3. Estimated exclusions	
Zero double counting	2,447
Full double counting	2,137
Median	2,292

* Average Y2000–2001 for 25 Member States, European Commission/Eurostat, *Europa-Justice and Home Affairs-Refused Aliens 1997–2001*, 2003 consulted at Eurostat website November 2004, documents on file with BS.

** Data for Y2003 Council of the EU, *7496/04 Exchange of Statistical Information on the Issuing of Uniform Visas*, 1, (2004). Ryszard Cholewenski, 'The Need for Effective Individual Legal Protection in Immigration Matters', 7 *European Journal of Migration and Law*, 237 (2005).

*** Based on data from before Y2003, International Organization for Migration, 'Facts and Figures on International Migration', *Migration Policy Issues* 1 (2003), at 2.

We reach this estimate by counting the number of migrants who have been refused entry by border officials and diplomatic posts. We must add to this the estimated annual increase in illegal aliens (and adjust for double counting), because it seems reasonable to assume illegal immigrants would have been denied entry or admission if they had observed the official procedure (if not they would have opted for official immigration, which is much safer and cheaper). Therefore those illegal immigrants can be counted as excluded aliens.

A modest estimate?

Recent estimates of the *stock* of illegal immigrants suggest that the yearly flow of illegal immigrants must be higher than the official estimates for the EU. Assume that indeed the stock of illegal immigrants amounts to 6 Mio. and that it does not decrease (Vogel and Cyrus, 2008). It follows that with the current flows of illegal migrants the attrition rate of illegal migrants is 8% (500k/6,000k). This rate suggests that on average illegal migrants stay 12 years in the EU. If, on average, illegal migrants are staying for a shorter period than 12 years in the EU and if the stock of migrants does not decrease, then indeed the inflow is higher. As a consequence the number of normal migrants that are *de facto* denied admission should much higher than our estimation.

Annex 1b Exclusion of normal migrants in the US

In 2008, of the 1,107k immigrants that received a permanent residence permit only 166k were what we may call normal migrants (15%). The rest was largely based on some kind of family reunification (65%, this includes the categories 'Family-sponsored preferences' and 'Immediate relatives of U.S. citizens'). The 15% employment migrants are composed of 9% highly skilled (1st and 2nd preference employment). More than half of these highly skilled workers were actually family members of other highly skilled workers already having legal residence. The remaining 6% of employment migrants consists of lower skilled workers of which again half comprises of family members of highly skilled workers holding already legal permanent residence permits. These numbers are based on resident permits granted to those arriving from outside the US (new arrivals) to which are added the permits granted to those who were already present in the US territory, legally or illegally (adjustments to immigration status). The absolute number (16k) and percentage (4%) of normal migrants are significantly lower if one only looks at the new arrivals. Other years give a similar picture.

Source: US Department of Homeland Security, *Yearbook of Immigration Statistics, issues 2002–2009*. For editions 2004–2009 especially table 7 'Persons obtaining legal permanent resident status by type and detailed class of admission'. For editions 2002–2003, especially table 5 'Immigrants admitted by type and class of admission' (available at official website http://www.dhs.gov/files/statistics/publications, last consulted on 5 May, 2010).

Bibliography

Abizadeh, Arash, 'Democratic Theory and Border Coercion: No right to unilaterally control your own borders', *Political Theory* (2008), 36, 37–65.

——, 'Democratic Legitimacy and State Coercion: A Reply to David Miller', *Political Theory* (2010), 38, 121–30.

Adam, Christine and Devillard, Alexandre (eds), *A comparative study of the laws in the 27 EU Member States for legal immigration including an assessment of the conditions and formalities imposed by each Member State for newcomers* (Geneva: IOM, 2008).

Agamben, Giorgio, *Homo Sacer. Sovereign Power and Bare Life* (trans. Daniel Heller-Roazen) [1995] (Stanford: Stanford University Press, 1998).

——, *State of Exception* (trans. Kevin Attell) [2003] (Chicago: The University of Chicago Press, 2005).

Aleinikoff, Alexander T., 'International Legal Norms and Migration: A Report' in Alexander T. Aleinikoff and Vincent Chetail (eds), *Migration and International Legal Norms* (The Hague: TCM Asser Press, 2003), 1–27.

Aleinikoff, Alexander and Chetail, Vincent (eds), *Migration and International Legal Norms* (The Hague: TCM Asser Press, 2003).

D'Amato, Anthony, 'The Concept of Human Rights in International Law', 82 *Columbia Law Review* (1982), 1110–59.

Angenendt, S. (ed.), *Asylum and Migration Policies in the European Union* (Berlin: Research Institute of the German Society for Foreign Affairs, 1999).

Arendt, Hanna, *Eichmann in Jerusalem: A Report on the Banality of Evi* (New York: Penguin Books, 1994).

Auby, Jean-Bernard, 'Administrative Law in France', in Karl-Heinz Ladeur (ed.), *The Europeanisation of Administrative Law. Transforming National Decision-making Procedures* (Aldershot: Dartmouth, 2002), 59–88.

Bader, Veit, 'Fairly Open Borders' in Veit Bader (ed.), *Citizenship and Exclusion* (London: Macmillan Press Ltd, 1997), 28–60.

——, 'Ethics of Immigration', 12 Constellations (2005), 331–61.

——, *Secularism or Democracy? Associational Governance of Religious Diversity* (Amsterdam: Amsterdam University Press, 2007).

Bartelson, Jens, 'The Concept of Sovereignty Revisited', 17 *European Journal of International Law* (2006), 463–74.

Bauboeck, Rainer, 'Global Justice, Freedom of Movement and Democratic Citizenship', 50 *European Journal of Sociology* (2009), 1–31.

——, 'Migration and Citizenship: Normative Debates', in Marc Rosenblum and Dan Tichenor (eds), *Oxford Handbook on International Migration* (Oxford: Oxford University Press, forthcoming 2011).

Beaulac, Stéphane, *The Power of Language in the Making of International Law. The Word Sovereignty in Bodin and Vattel and the Myth of Westphalia* (Leyden/Boston: Martinus Nijhoff Publishers, 2004).

Van Bellingen, Jozef, *De Rechtsfilosofie van Carl Schmitt* (Brussels: PhD thesis VUB, 1988), Faculty of Arts and Philosophy.

Bhabha, Jacqueline, 'Children, Migration and International Norms' in *Migration and International Legal Norms* (The Hague: TCM Asser Press, 2003), 204–23.

Blake, Michael, 'Immigration', in R.G. Frey and Christopher Heath Wellman (eds), *A Companion to Applied Ethics* (Oxford: Blackwell Publishing, 2003), at 224–37.

Blake, Michael, and Risse, Matthias, 'Is there a human right to free movement? Immigration and original ownership of the earth' (2006), Faculty research working paper series, Kennedy School of Government, Harvard University, at SSRN.

Blum, Carolyn Patty *et al.*, *Brief of Law Professors as Amici Curiae Supporting Affirmance. US Supreme Court Janet Reno V. Kim Ho Ma*, 1 (2000).

Brochman, G. and Hammar, T., *Mechanisms of Immigration Control. A Comparative Analysis of European Regulation Policies* (Oxford: Berg, 1999).

Brouwer, Evelien, 'Effective Remedies for Third Country Nationals in EU Law: Justice Accessible to All?' 7 *European Journal of Migration and Law* (2005), 219–36.

Brown, Chris, 'Marxism and the transnational migration of people: Ethical issues', in Brian Barry and Robert E. Goodin (eds), *Free Movement. Ethical Issues in the Transnational Migration of People and Money* (London: Harvester Wheatsheaf, 1992), 127–54.

Brownlie, Ian, *Principles of Public International Law* (Oxford: Clarendon Press, 1998).

De Bruycker, Philippe, 'L'émergence d'une politique Européenne d'immigration' in Jean-Yves Carlier (ed.) *L'étranger face au droit. XXes Journées d'etudes juridiques Jean Dabin* (Brussels: Bruylant, 2010), 351–63.

Campbell, Tom D., *The Legal Theory of Ethical Positivism* (Aldershot: Dartmouth Publishing, 1996).

Carens, Joseph H., 'Aliens and Citizens: The Case for Open Borders', 49 *Review of Politics* (1987), 250–73.

——, 'Migration and morality: A liberal egalitarian perspective', in Brian Barry and Robert E. Goodin (eds), *Free Movement. Ethical issues in the Transnational Migration of People and Money* (London: Harvester Wheatsheaf, 1992), 25–47.

Cassese, Antonio, *International Law* (Oxford: Oxford University Press, 2001).

Cavallero, Eric, 'An immigration-pressure model of global distributive justice', *Politics, Philosophy & Economics* (2006), vol. 5, 97–127.

Chang, Howard F., 'Liberalized Immigration as Free Trade: Economic Welfare and the Optimal Immigration Policy', 145 *University of Pennsylvania Law Review* (1997) 1147.

Chetail, Vincent, 'Freedom of Movement and Transnational Migrations: A Human Rights Perspective' in Alexander Aleinikoff and Vincent Chetail (eds), *Migration and International Legal Norms* (The Hague: TCM Asser Press, 2003), 47–60.

Chimi, B.S., 'Development and Migration', in Alexander Aleinikoff and Vincent Chetail (eds), *Migration and International Legal Norms* (The Hague: TCM Asser Press, 2003), 255–68.

Cholewenski, Ryszard, 'No Right of Entry: The Legal Regime on Crossing the EU External Border' in Kees Groenendijk, Elspeth Guild and Paul Minderhoud (eds), *In Search of*

Europe's Borders (The Hague/London/New York: Kluwer Law International, 2003), 105–30.

——, 'The Need for Effective Individual Legal Protection in Immigration Matters', 7 *European Journal of Migration and Law* (2005), 237–62.

Cole, Phillip, *Philosophies of Exclusion. Liberal Political Theory and Immigration* (Edinburgh: Edinburgh University Press, 2000).

Craig, Paul, 'Unreasonableness and Proportionality in UK Law', in Evelyn Ellis (ed.), *The Principle of Proportionality in the Laws of Europe* (Oxford: Hart Publishing, 1999), 85–106.

—— and De Búrca, Grainne, *EU Law: Text, Cases, and Materials* (Oxford: Oxford University Press, 2003).

Crépeau, François and Atak, Idil, 'Les politiques migratoires au Canada et en Europe: des convergences', in Jean-Yves Carlier (ed.) *L'étranger face au droit. XXes Journées d'etudes juridiques Jean Dabin* (Brussels: Bruylant, 2010), 319–49.

Crowley, John, 'Locating Europe', in Kees Groenendijk, Elspeth Guild and Paul Minderhoud (eds), *In Search of Europe's Borders* (The Hague/London/New York: Kluwer Law International, 2003), 27–44.

Derrida, Jacques, *Cosmopolitanism and Forgiveness* (London: Routledge, 2003).

Derrida, Jacques and Dufourmantelle, Anne, *Of Hospitality. Anne Dufourmantelle invites Jacques Derrida* (trans. Rachel Bowlby) (Stanford: Stanford University Press, 2000).

Van Dijck, Maarten, *Gedogen. Over vermogen en onvermogen tot handhaving van wet en recht* (Nijmegen: Wolf Legal Publishers, 2003).

Docquir, Pierre-François, 'Droit à la vie privée et familiale des ressortissants étrangers: vers la mise au point d'une protection floue du droit de séjour', *Revue Trimestrielle des Droits de l'Homme* (2004), 921–49.

Doehring, Karl, 'Aliens, Admission', in Rudolph Berhardt (ed.), *Encyclopedia of Public International Law* (Amsterdam/New York/Oxford: North Holland, 1985), vol. 8, 6–11.

Donnelly, Jack, 'State Sovereignty and Human Rights', *Human Rights & Human Welfare*, working paper no. 21 (2004), available at www.du.edu/korbel/hrhw/workingpapers/2004/21-donnelly-2004.pdf.

Dowty, Alan, *Closed Borders: The Contemporary Assault on Freedom of Movement* (New Haven (Conn.): Yale University Press, 1987).

Van Drooghenbroeck, Sébastien, *La proportionnalité dans le droit de la Convention européenne des Droits de l'homme: prendre l'idée simple au sérieux* (Brussels: Bruylant, 2001).

Van Duffel, Siegfried, 'Sovereignty as a Religious Concept', 90 *The Monist* 126 (2007), 126–42.

Dummet, Ann, 'The Transmigration of People seen from within a Natural Law Tradition', in Brian Barry and Robert E. Goodin (eds), *Free Movement. Ethical Issues in the Transnational Migration of People and Money* (London: Harvester Wheatsheaf, 1992), 169–80.

Dummett, Michael, *On Immigration and Refugees* (London: Routledge, 2001).

Dumont, Hugues, 'La politique Européenne d'immigration. Synthèse des travaux en atelier', in Jean-Yves Carlier (ed.) *L'étranger face au droit. XXes Journées d'etudes juridiques Jean Dabin* (Brussels: Bruylant, 2010), 365–87.

ECOTEC Research and Consulting Limited (on behalf of European Commission (DG Justice and Home Affairs)), *Admission of Third Country Nationals for Paid Employment or Self-employment Activity* (2001).

Eicke, Tim, 'Paradise Lost? Exclusion and Expulsion from the EU' in Kees Groenendijk, Elspeth Guild and Paul Minderhoud (eds), *In Search of Europe's Borders* (The Hague/London/New York: Kluwer Law International, 2003), 147–68.

Emiliou, Nicholas, *The Principle of Proportionality in European Law. A Comparative Study*, European Monographs (London: Kluwer Law International, 1996).

Feldman, David, 'Proportionality and the Human Rights Act 1988', in Evelyn Ellis (ed.), *The Principle of Proportionality in the Laws of Europe* (Oxford: Hart Publishing, 1999), 117–44.

Ferdinandusse, Ward, *Direct Application of International Criminal Law in National Courts*, PhD thesis (Amsterdam, 2005).

Finnis, John, *Natural Law and Natural Rights* (Oxford: Oxford University Press, 1980).

Fisher, David, Martin, Susan and Schoenholtz, Andrew, 'Migration and Security in International Law' in Alexander T. Aleinikoff and Vincent Chetail (eds), *Migration and International Legal Norms* (The Hague: TCM Asser Press, 2003), 87–120.

Foqué, R. and 't Hart, A.C., *Instrumentaliteit en Rechtsbescherming. Grondslagen van een Strafrechtelijke Waardendiscussie* (Arnhem: Gouda Quint, 1990).

Foucault, Michel, *Sécurité, Territoire, Population: Cours au Collège de France, 1977–1978* (Paris: Gallimard, 2004).

Gérard, Philippe, Ost, François and Van De Ker, Et (eds), *Droit et Intérêt* (Brussels: Facultés Universitaires Saint-Louis, 1990).

Van Gerven, Walter, *Beginselen van Belgisch Privaatrecht I. Algemeen Deel* (Antwerpen: Standaard Wetenschappelijke Uitgeverij, 1969).

——, *Hoe Blauw is het Bloed van de Prins* (Antwerpen: Kluwer Rechtswetenschappen, 1984).

——, 'The Effect of Proportionality on the Actions of Member States of the European Community: National Viewpoints from Continental Europe', in Evelyn Ellis (ed.), *The Principle of Proportionality in the Laws of Europe* (Oxford: Hart Publishing, 1999), 37–63.

Gilissen, John, 'Le statut des étrangers', in *L'Étranger, Recueils de la Société Jean Bodin pour l'Histoire Comparative des Institutions*, IX, Vol. 1, 2nd edn (Paris: Dessain et Tolra, 1984) [1958].

Gilissen, John and Gorlé, Frits, *Historische Inleiding tot het Recht. Ontstaan en evolutie van de belangrijkste rechtsstelsels*, I (Antwerpen: Kluwer rechtswetenschappen, 1991).

Goodin, Robert E., 'Commentary: The political realism of free movement' in Brian Barry and Robert E. Goodin (eds), *Free Movement. Ethical issues in the Transnational Migration of People and Money* (London: Harvester Wheatsheaf, 1992), 248–64.

Goodwin-Gill, Guy S., *International Law and the Movement of Persons* (Oxford: Clarendon Press, 1978).

Groenendijk, Kees, 'New Borders Behind Old Ones: Post-Schengen Controls Behind the Internal Borders and Inside the Netherlands and Germany', in Kees Groenendijk, Elspeth Guild and Paul Minderhoud (eds), *In Search of Europe's Borders* (The Hague/London/New York: Kluwer Law International, 2003), 131–46.

——, 'Citizens and Third Country Nationals: Differential Treatment or Discrimination' in Jean-Yves Carlier and Elspeth Guild (eds), *L'avenir de la libre circulation des personnes dans l'EU. Analyse de la directive 2004/38 du 29 avril 2004 relative au droit des citoyens de circuler et de séjourner librement* (Brussels: Bruylant, 2006), 79–101.

Grotius, H., *De Juri Belli ac Pacis Libri Tres*, [1646], Publications of the Carnegie Endowment for International Peace, Division of International Law, Washington (Oxford: Clarendon Press, 1913).

Guild, Elspeth, 'The Border Abroad – Visas and Border Controls' in Kees Groenendijk, Elspeth Guild and Paul Minderhoud (eds), *In Search of Europe's Borders* (The Hague/London/New York: Kluwer Law International, 2003), 87–104

Guild, Elspeth and Minderhoud, Paul (eds), *Immigration and Criminal Law in the European Union: The Legal Measures and Social Consequences of Criminal Law in Member States on Trafficking and Smuggling Human Beings* (Leyden/Boston: Martinus Nijhoff Publishers, 2006).

Guiraudon, Virginie, 'Before the EU Border: Remote Control of the "Huddled Masses" in Kees Groenendijk, Elspeth Guild and Paul Minderhoud (eds), *In Search of Europe's Borders* (The Hague/London/New York: Kluwer Law International, 2003), 191–214.

Gutwirth, Serge, 'De toepassing van het finaliteitsbeginsel van de Privacywet van 8 december 1992 tot bescherming van de persoonlijke levenssfeer ten opzichte van de verwerking van persoonsgegevens', *Tijdschrift voor Privaatrecht* (1993), 1409–77.

—— *Waarheidsaanspraken in recht en wetenschap. Een onderzoek naar de verhouding tussen recht en wetenschap met bijzondere illustratie uit het informaticarecht* (Brussels/Antwerp: VUBPress/MAKLU, 1993).

—— *Privacy and the Information Age* (Lanham/Oxford: Rowman & Littlefield, 2002).

Habermas, Juergen, 'Constitutional Democracy: A Paradoxical Union of Contradictory Principles' (trans. William Regh) *Political Theory* (2001), 766–81.

Hailbronner, K. *Asylum Law and Policy of the European Union* (The Hague/London/Boston: Kluwer Law International, 2000).

Harris, N., *Thinking the Unthinkable: The Immigration Myth Exposed* (London: I. B. Tauris, 2001).

't Hart, A.C., *Recht als schild van Perseus. Voordrachten over strafrechtstheorie* (Arnhem: Gouda Quint, 1991).

Held, D., McGrew, A., Goldblatt, D. and Perraton, J., *Global Transformation: Politics, Economics and Culture* (Cambridge: Polity Press, 1999).

Higgins, Imelda and Hailbronner, Kay (eds), *Migration and Asylum Law and Policy in the European Union* (Cambridge: Cambridge University Press, 2004).

Hildebrandt, Mireille, *Straf(begrip) en procesbeginsel. Een onderzoek naar de betekenis van straf en strafbegrip en de waarde van het procesbeginsel naar aanleiding van de consensuele afdoening van strafzaken* (Sanders Instituut/Kluwer, 2002).

Hirschberg, Lothar, *Der Grundsatz der Verhältnismäßigkeit* (Göttingen: Verlag Otto Schwartz & Co., 1981).

Hoffmann, Rt. Hon. Lord, 'The Influence of the European Principle of Proportionality upon UK law', in Evelyn Ellis (ed.), *The Principle of Proportionality in the Laws of Europe* (Oxford: Hart Publishing, 1999), 107–15.

Honig, Bonnie, 'Between Decision and Deliberation: Political Paradox in Democratic Theory', *Rechtsfilosofie en Rechtstheorie* (2008a), 2, 115–36.

——, 'An Agonist's Reply', *Rechtsfilosofie en Rechtstheorie* (2008b), 2, 186–99.

House of Lords Select Committee on Economic Affairs, *The Economic Impact of Immigration*, Volume I: Report, April 2008.

Hudson, James L., 'The Philosophy of Immigration', 3 *The Journal of Libertarian Studies* (1986), 51–62.

Huizinga, Johan, *Nederland's Beschaving in de Zeventiende Eeuw. Een Schets en Hugo de Groot en zijn Eeuw* (Groningen: Open Universiteit/Wolters-Noordhoff, 1984) [1941].

Huysmans, Jef, *The Politics of Insecurity. Fear, Migration and Asylum in the EU* (London/New York: Routledge, 2006).

Jacobs, Francis G., 'Recent Developments in the Principle of Proportionality in European Community Law', in Evelyn Ellis (ed.), *The Principle of Proportionality in the Laws of Europe* (Oxford: Hart Publishing, 1999), 1–21.

Jandl, M. (ed.), *Innovative Concepts for Alternative Migration Policies: Ten Innovative Approaches to the Challenges of Migration in the 21st Century* (Amsterdam: Amsterdam University Press, 2007).

Jans, J.H., 'Evenredigheid Revisited', *Sociaal-Economische Wetgeving. Tijdschrift voor Europees en Economisch Recht* (2000), 270–82.

Jenning, R.Y., *The Acquisition of Territory in International Law* (Manchester: Manchester University Press, 1963).

Jenning, Robert and Watts, Arthur, *Oppenheim's International Law* (Harlow: Longman Group UK, 1992).

Jones, Brian and Thompson, Katharine, 'Administrative Law in the United Kingdom', in René Seerden and Frits Stroink (eds), *Administrative Law of the European Union, its Member States and the United States* (Antwerpen: Intersentia, 2002), 199–258.

Kant, Immanuel, *Perpetual Peace* (New York: Columbia University Press, 1939).

Kapteyn, P.J.G. and VerLoren van Themaat, P., *Introduction to the Law of the European Communities. From Maastricht to Amsterdam* (London/The Hague/Boston: Kluwer Law International, 1998).

Kolb, Robert, 'La règle résiduelle de liberté en droit public ("Tout ce qui n'est pas interdit est permis"), aspects théoriques', 34 *Revue Belge de Droit International* (2001), 100–27.

——, *Réflexions de philosophie du droit international. Problèmes fondementaux du droit international public: Théorie et philosophie du droit international*, La Collection de droit international, (Brussels: Éditions Bruylant/Éditions de l'Université Libre de Bruxelles, 2003)

Kostakopoulou, Dora and Thomas, Robert, 'Unweaving the Threads: Territoriality, Asylum Policy and National Ownership of Land', 6 *European Journal of Migration and Law* (2004), 5–26.

——, 'The Area of Freedom, Security and Justice and the Ethics of Migration' (Paper Presented at Conference on the Normative Foundations of European Immigration Policy, Tilburgh University, 10–11 May).

——, 'The "Protective Union": Change and Continuity in Migration Law and Policy in post-Amsterdam Europe', 38 *Journal of Common Market Studies* (2007), 497–518.

Kukathas, Chandran, 'Immigration', in Hugh La Follette (ed.), *The Oxford Handbook of Practical Ethics* (Oxford: Oxford University Press, 2003), 567–90.

Kymlicka, Will and Banting, Keith, 'Immigration, Multiculturalism, and the Welfare State', *Ethics & International Affairs* (2006), vol 20(3), 281–304.

La Torre, Massimo, 'On Two Distinct and Opposing Versions of Natural Law: "Exclusive" versus "Inclusive" ', 19 *Ratio Juris* (2006), 197–216.

Ladeur, Karl-Heinz and Prelle, Rebecca, 'Judicial Control of Administrative Procedural Mistakes in Germany: A Comparative European View of Environmental Impact Assessments', in Karl-Heinz Ladeur (ed.), *The Europeanisation of Administrative Law. Transforming National Decision-making Procedures* (Aldershot: Dartmouth, 2002), 93–111.

Latour, Bruno, *La Fabrique du Droit: Une Ethnographie du Conseil d'État* (Paris: Découverte, 2002).

Lauwaars, R.H., 'De Institutionele Structuur', in P.J.G. Kapteyn and P. VerLoren van Themaat (eds), *Het Recht van de Europese Unie en van de Europese Gemeenschappen* (Deventer: Kluwer, 2003), 147–227.

Lindahl, Hans, 'Dialectic and Revolution: Confronting Kelsen and Gadamer on Legal Interpretation' 24 *Cardozo Law Review* (2003), 769–98.

——, 'Jus Includendi et Excludendi: Europe and the Borders of Freedom, Security and Justice. A review of Europe's Area of Freedom, Security and Justice edited by Neil Walker 2004', 16 *The King's College Law Journal* (2005), 234–47.

——, 'The Paradox of Constituent Power. The Ambiguous Self-Constitution of the European Union' 20 *Ratio Juris* (2007), 485–505.

——, 'Breaking Promises to Keep Them: Immigration and the Boundaries of Distributive Justice', in Hans Lindahl (ed.), *A Right to Inclusion and Exclusion? Normative Fault Lines of the EU's Area of Freedom, Security and Justice* (Oxford: Hart, 2009), 137–59.

Locke, John, *Two Treatises of Government*, [based on text of 1690] (London: Everyman's Library, 1984).

Van Maanen, G.E., *Eigendomsschijnbewegingen. Juridische, historische en politiek-filosofische opmerkingen over eigendom* (Nijmegen: Ars Aequi Libri, 1987).

Marchetti, Raffaele, 'Right to Universal Mobility: A Consequentialist Cosmopolitan Reading', 4 *Éthique et économique/Ethics and Economics* 1 (2006).

Martin, David A., 'The Authority and Responsibility of States' in Alexander T. Aleinikoff and Vincent Chetail (eds), *Migration and International Legal Norms* (The Hague: TCM Asser Press, 2003), 31–45.

McKinsey Company *et al.*, *21minuten.nl* (2005).

McCloskey, Mary A., 'Kant's Kingdom of Ends', *Philosophy* (1976) vol. 51, no. 198, at 331–9.

Meijers Committee (P. Boeles *et al.*), 'Draft directive on Minimum Guarantees for Individual Freedom, Security and Justice in Relation to Decisions Regarding Movement of Persons', *European Journal of Migration and Law*, 7 (2005), 301–19.

Meilaender, Peter C., *Towards a Theory of Immigration*, (Basingstoke: Palgrave, 2001).

Miller, David, 'Why Immigration Controls are not Coercive: A Reply to Arash Abizadeh', *Political Theory* (2010), 38, 111–20.

——, *On Nationality* (Oxford: Clarendon Press, 1995).

Mouffe, Chantal, 'Carl Schmitt and the Paradox of Liberal Democracy' in Chantal Mouffe (ed.) *The Challenge of Carl Schmitt* (New York: Verso, 1999).

Nafziger, J.A.R., 'The General Admission of Aliens under International Law' 77 *American Journal of International Law* (1983), 804–47.

——, 'A Commentary on American Legal Scholarship Concerning the Admission of Aliens', 17 *University of Michigan Journal of Law Reform* (1984), 165–81.

——, 'Review of Visa Denials by Consular Officers' 66 *Washington Law Review* (1991), 1–105.

Nagel, Thomas, 'The Problem of Global Justice', *Philosophy & Public Affairs* (2005) vol. 33(2), 113–47.

Noll, Gregor, 'The Exclusionary Construction of Human Rights in International and Political Theory' in Zenon Bankowski (ed.), *Epistomology and Ontology*. IVR Symposium Lund 2003 (Stuttgart: Franz Steiner Verlag, 2005), 103–17.

Oliver, Peter and Jarvis, Malcolm, *Free Movement of Goods in the European Community under Articles 28 to 30 of the EC Treaty* (London: Sweet and Maxwell, 2003).

Ost, François, *Entre droit et non-droit: l'intérêt. Essai sure les functions qu'exerce la notion d'intérêt en droit privé*, 2 (Brussels: Facultés Universitaires Saint-Louis, 1990)

Ouguergouz, Fatsah, *The African Charter on Human and People's Rights. A Comprehensive Agenda for Human Dignity and Sustainable Democracy in Africa* (The Hague/London/New York: Martinus Nijhoff Publishers, 2003).

Pastore, F., 'Visas, Borders, Immigration: Formation, Structure, and Current Evolution of the EU Entry Control System', in Neil Walker (ed.), *Europe's Area of Freedom, Security and Justice* (Oxford: Oxford University Press, 2004), 89–142.

Pécoud, Antoine, and de Guchteneire, Paul, *Migration without Borders: An Investigation into the Free Movement of People*, Global Migration Perspectives, 27 (Geneva: Global Commission on International Migration, 2005).

Peers, Steve and Rogers, Nicolas (eds), *EU Immigration an Asylum Law. Text and Commentary* (Leyden/Boston: Martinus Nijhoff Publishers, 2006).

Perez-Vera, E., *Citoyenneté de l'Union européenne, nationalité et conditions des étrangers*, in Académie de Droit International, Recueil des Cours (The Hague/Boston/London: Martinus Nijhoff Publishers, 1996).

Plender, Richard, *International Migration Law* (Dordrecht/Boston/The Hague: Martinus Nijhoff Publishers, 1988).

—— (ed.), *Basic Documents on Migration Law*, 2nd edn (The Hague: Kluwer Law International, 1997).

Pufendorf, Samuel, *De Jure Naturae et Gentium Libri Octo*, II, [1688], Publications of the Carnegie Endowment for International Peace, Division of International Law, Washington (Oxford: Clarendon Press, 1934).

Rasch, Wilhelm, 'The Limit of Modernity: Luhmann and Lyotard on Exclusion', in W. Rasch and C. Wolfe (eds), *Observing Complexity, Systems Theory and Postmodernity* (Minneapolis: University of Minnesota Press, 2000), 199–214.

Raz, Joseph, *The Authority of Law. Essays on Law and Morality* (Oxford: Clarendon Press, 1979).

——, *The Concept of a Legal System. An Introduction to the Theory of a Legal System* (Oxford: Clarendon Press, 1980).

——, *The Morality of Freedom* (Oxford: Clarendon Press, 1988).

——, 'Authority, Law and Morality' in Joseph Raz (ed.), *Ethics in the Public Domain: Essays in the Morality of Law and Politics* (Oxford: Clarendon Press, 1994), 194–221.

——, *Practical Reason and Norms* (Oxford: Oxford University Press, 1999).

——, 'The Amoralist' in Joseph Raz (ed.), *Engaging Reason. On the Theory of Value and Action* (Oxford: Oxford University Press, 1999), 273–302.

Redor, M.-J. (ed.), *L'ordre public: Ordre public ou ordres publics? Ordre public et droits fondamentaux*, Actes du colloque de Caen des jeudi 11 et 12 mai 2000 (Brussels: Bruylant, 2001).

Rigaux, François, 'L'immigration: droit international et droits fondamentaux' in *Les Droits de l'homme au Seuil du Troisième Millénair. Mélanges en Hommage à Pierre Lambert* (Brussels: Bruylant, 2000), 693–722.

Van Roermund, Bert, 'Sovereignty: Unpopular and Popular' in Neil Walker (ed.), *Sovereignty in Transition* (Oxford/Portland: Hart Publishing, 2003), 33–54.

Rousseau, Charles, *Droit International Public. Les sujets de droit*, vol. 2 (Paris: Editions Sirey, 1974).

Saroléa, Sylvie, 'La souveraineté en droit belge: mythe *et* réalite', in Jean-Yves Carlier (ed.) *L'étranger face au droit. XXes Journées d'etudes juridiques Jean Dabin*, (Brussels: Bruylant, 2010), 75–111.

Schmitt, Carl, *Gesetz und Urteil. Eine Untersuchung zum Problem der Rechtspraxis* (Berlin: Verlag von Otto Liebmann Buchhandlung fuer Rechts- und Staatswissenschaften. Verlag der Deutschen Juristen Zeitung, 1912).

——, *Verfassungslehre* (Munich/Leipzig: Duncker & Humblot, 1928).

——, *Der Begriff des Politischen*, [1932] (Berlin: Duncker & Humbolt, 1963).

——, 'Die Rheinlande als Objekt internationaler Politik' [1925], in *Positionen und Begriffe. Im Kampf mit Weimar-Genf-Versailles1923–1939* (Hamburg: Hanseatische Verlagsanstalt, 1940).

——, 'Voelkerrechtlichen Formen des modernen Imperialismus', [1932], in *Positionen und Begriffe. Im Kampf mit Weimar-Genf-Versailles 1923–1939* (Hamburg: Hanseatische Verlagsanstalt, 1940).

——, *Politische Theologie. Vier Kapitel zur Lehre von der Souveraenitaet* (Munich/ Leipzig: Duncker & Humblot, 1934).

——, *Ueber die drei Arten des rechtswissenschaftlichen Denkens* (Hamburg: Hanseatische Verlagsanstalt, 1934).

——, *Der Nomos der Erde im Voelkerrecht des Jus Publicum Europeanum* (Koeln: Greven Verlag, 1950).

——, *The Theory of the Partisan: A Commentary/Remark on the Concept of the Political*, [1963] (trans. A.C. Goodson) (Michigan: Michigan State University Press, 2004).

Schoenborn, W., 'La Nature Juridique du Territoir', in *Académie de Droit International. Recueil des Cours*, vol. 30 (Paris: Librairie Hachette, 1929).

Scholten, Paul, *Algemeen Deel – Mr. C. Asser's Handleiding tot de Beoefening van het Nederlands Burgerlijk Recht* (Zwolle: W.E.J. Tjeenk Willink, 1974).

Schotel, Bas, *Protecting the Alien's Interest in Immigration. Arguments from Law and Political Theory for Changing our Admission Laws and Practices* (2008), Vrije Universiteit Brussel, PhD dissertation.

——, 'Defending our Legal Practices: A Legal Critique of Giorgio Agamben's State of Exception', *Amsterdam Law Forum* (2009) vol. 1(2), 113–25.

——, 'EU's Management of Migration Flows and the Rule of Law. From legal norm subject to migration flow', *Journal of Ethnic and Migration Studies* (forthcoming 2011).

Schröder, Meinhard, 'Administrative Law in Germany', in René Seerden and Frits Stroink (eds), *Administrative Law of the European Union, its Member States and the United States* (Antwerpen: Intersentia, 2002), 91–143.

Schuck, Peter, 'Immigration at the Turn of the New Century', 33 *Case Western Journal of International Law* (2001), 1–11.

Schwarze, Jürgen, *European Administrative Law* (London/Luxemburg: Office for Official Publications of the European Communities/Sweet and Maxwell, 2006).

Seerden, René and Stroink, Frits, 'Administrative Law in the Netherlands', in René Seerden and Frits Stroink (eds), *Administrative Law of the European Union, its Member States and the United States* (Antwerpen: Intersentia, 2002), 145–97.

Seglow, Jonathan, 'The Ethics of Migration', 3 *Political Studies Review* (2005), 317–34.

Shanks, Cheryl, *Immigration and the Policy of American Sovereignty 1890–1990* (Ann Arbor: Michigan University Press, 2001).

Shapiro, Scott, 'Authority' in Jules Coleman and Scott Shapiro (eds), *The Oxford Handbook of Jurisprudence and Philosophy of Law* (Oxford: Oxford University Press, 2002), 382–439.

Shaw, Malcom N., *Title to Territory in Africa. International Legal Issues* (Oxford: Clarendon Press, 1986).

Shue, Henry, *Basic Rights: Subsistence, Affluence and U.S. Foreign Policy* (Princeton: Princeton University Press, 1980).

Spijkerboer, Thomas, 'The Human Costs of Border Control', *European Journal of Migration and Law* 9 (2007), 127–39.

Staples, Helen, 'Adjudicating the External Schengen Border' in Kees Groenendijk, Elspeth Guild and Paul Minderhoud (eds), *In Search of Europe's Borders* (The Hague/London/New York: Kluwer Law International, 2003), 215–50.

Steiner, Hillel, 'Libertarianism and the transnational migration of people', in Brian Barry and Robert E. Goodin (eds), *Free Movement. Ethical Issues in the Transnational Migration of People and Money* (London: Harvester Wheatsheaf, 1992), 87–94.

De Sutter, Laurent, 'How to Get Rid of Legal Theory' in Zenon Bankowski (ed.), *Epistomology and Ontology* (2005), 39–48.

De Sutter, Laurent and Gutwirth, Serge, 'Droit et cosmopolitique. Notes sur la contribution de Bruno Latour à la pensée du droit', *Droit et société* (2004), 259–89.

Teubner, G. (ed.), *Global Law without a State* (Ashgate/Dartmouth: Hants/Burlington, 1997).

Tholen, Berry, 'The Europeanisation of Migration Policy – The Normative Issues', 6 *European Journal of Migration and Law* (2004), 323–51.

Tiburcio, C., *The Human Rights of Aliens under International and Comparative Law*, International Studies in Human Rights (The Hague: Kluwer Law International, 2001).

Torpey, John, *The Invention of the Passport. Surveillance, Citizenship and the State* (Cambridge: Cambridge University Press, 2000).

Ugur, Mehmet, 'A Reinterpretation of the "Insider"–"Outsider" Divide in the European Union', xxix *International Migration Review* (1995), 964–99.

UK Home Office/UK Border Agency, *Final Impact Assessment of Draft Immigration Bill*, 12 November 2009, available at www.ukba.homeoffice.gov.uk/managingborders/simplifying, last accessed June 2010.

De Vattel, E., *The Law of Nations or the Principles of Natural Law Applied to the Conduct and to the Affairs of Nations and of Sovereigns*, III, [1758] (Washington: Carnegie Institution of Washington, 1916).

Vaughan, Lowe, 'Jurisdiction' in Malcom D. Evans (ed.), *International Law* (Oxford: Oxford University Press, 2003), 329–55.

Veenkamp, Theo, Bentley, Tom and Buofino, Alessandra, *People Flow. Managing Migration in a New European Commonwealth* (London: Demos, 2003).

Waldron, Jeremy, 'Theoretical Foundations of Liberalism', 37 *The Philosophical Quarterly* (1987), 127–50.

Walzer, Michael, *Spheres of Justice: A Defence of Pluralism and Equality* (New York: Basic Books, 1983).

Whelan, Frederick G., 'Citizenship and Freedom of Movement: An Open Admission Policy?' in Mark Gibney (ed.), *Open Borders? Closed Societies? The Ethical and Political Issues* (Westport (CT)/London: Greenwood Press, 1988), 3–39.

Wieacker, Franz, 'Geschichtlige Wurzeln des Prinzips de verhältnismäßigen Rechtsanwendung', in Marcus Lutter, Walter Stimpel and Herbert Wiedemann (eds), *Festschrift für Robert Fischer* (Berlin/New York: Walter de Gruyter, 1979), 867–81.

de Wilde, Marc, *Verwantschap in Extremen. Politieke Theory bij Walter Benjamin en Carl Schmitt*, PhD dissertation (Amsterdam: Amsterdam University Press, 2008).

Wolff, Christian, *Jus Gentium Methodo Scientifica Pertractatum*, II, [1764], Publications of the Carnegie Endowment for International Peace, Division of International Law, Washington (Oxford: Clarendon Press, 1934).

Woodward, James, 'Commentary: Liberalism and migration', in Brian Barry and Robert E. Goodin (eds), *Free Movement. Ethical Issues in the Transnational Migration of People and Money* (London: Harvester Wheatsheaf, 1992), 59–84.

Author index